FELLOWSHIP WITH THE HOLY SPIRIT

*Understanding The Communion With
The Consuming Fire Power Of God*

DR. ABRAHAM PETERS

DR. ABRAHAM PETERS

Copyright © 2020 Dr. Abraham Peters – All rights reserved.

ISBN: 9781716412073

No part of this book may be reproduced, stored in a retrieval system, or transmitted by any means—electronic, mechanical, photocopy, record, or otherwise—without written permission from the author.

All correspondence to: abrahampeters@rocketmail.com

Table of Contents

Dedication 11
Acknowledgement 12
Introduction 13
Part One 34
Chapter One *Intimacy With The Holy Spirit*Error! Bookmark not defined.

   God, The Holy Spirit 37
   Nature Of The Holy Spirit 38
      Omnipresent: 39
      Omnipotent: 39
      Eternal: 39
   The Personality Of The Holy Spirit 40
      Has A Mind: 40
      Searches Out The Human Mind: 40
      Has A Will: 40
   Speaks: 41
      He Spoke To Philip: 41
      He Spoke To Peter: 41
      He Spoke To The Elders In The City Of Antioch: 41
      The Specific Messages To Seven Churches Of Revelation .. 41
      Loves: 44
      Intercedes: 44
   Sensitivity Of The Holy Spirit 45
      Lie To The Holy Spirit: 45
      Resist The Spirit: 45

    Quench The Spirit: 45
    Grieve The Spirit: 46
    The Bible Warns: 46
    Insult The Spirit: 46
    Blaspheme The Spirit: 47
    Vex The Holy Spirit: 48
  The Characteristics Of The Holy Spirit 64

Chapter Two *The Bible Symbols Of The Holy Spirit* 75
  The Holy Spirit Comes As Wind: 81
  The Holy Spirit Comes As Fire: 82
  The Holy Spirit Comes As Rivers: 85
  The Holy Spirit Comes As Rain: 86
  The Holy Spirit Comes As Wine: 87
  The Holy Spirit Comes As Oil: 87
  The Holy Spirit Comes As Light: 92
  Still Small Voice: 92

Chapter Three *The Work Of The Holy In The Old Testament* . 99
Chapter Four *The Work Of The Holy Spirit In Christ And The Church* 113
  How The Holy Spirit Work In The Church 122

Chapter Five *The Work Of The Holy Spirit In The Believer* ... 130
Chapter Six *The Offenses Against The Holy Spirit* 143
Chapter Seven *The Baptism Of The Holy Spirit* 156
Chapter Eight *Speaking With Other Tongues* 173
  Speaking With Tongues 178
  The Evidence, The Gift And The Ministry 178

Chapter Nine *The Fruit Of The Spirit* 184
Chapter Ten *The Gifts Of The Holy Spirit* 205

Chapter Eleven *The Word Of Wisdom And The Word Of Knowledge* **238**
   Fallen Man's Supernatural Knowledge 240

Chapter Twelve *The Gift Of Prophecy* **254**
   Judging Prophecy 266

Chapter Thirteen *The Power Gifts: Faith, Healing And Miracle* **280**

Chapter Fourteen *The Discerning Of Spirits, Tongues And Interpretation Of Tongues* **303**

Part Two **321**

Chapter Fifteen *Knowing The Will Of God* **322**
   Knowing The Voice Of God 324
   Many Voices 327
      The Voice Of Satan: 327
   Hearing The Voice Of God 329
   The Voice And The Will 330
   When God Speaks 331
   Types Of Listeners 332
   Seed By The Wayside: 334
   Seed In Stony Places: 334
   Seed Among The Thorns: 334
   Seed On Good Ground: 334
   How Can You Know God's Voice? 335

Chapter Sixteen *"If Any Man Will Do. . .* **336**
He Shall Know" **336**
   Born-Again Experience 337
   Indwelling Of The Holy Spirit 341
      The Bible Says: 341

    Philip: 342
    Peter: 342
    Paul: 343
Spiritual Maturity 343
Transformation 345
Renewing Your Mind 347

Chapter Seventeen *The Will Of God* 353

The Meaning Of "Will" 354
Self-Will: 354
Satan's Will: 355
God's Will: 356
The Meaning Of God's Will 356
Jesus And God's Will 357
The Importance Of God's Will 359

    It Determines Your Eternal Destiny: 359

The Proper Motivation 365
Three Meanings Of "The Will Of God" 366

Chapter Eighteen *Heading The Wrong Direction* 368

The Occult 369
Methods Of Chance 371
Fleeces 372
False Prophets 373
Wrong Counsel 377
Emulations 378
The Pattern Of God's Will 380
Facts About God's Will 380
God's Will Is Planned: 382
Two Divisions Of God's Will 386
Two Divisions Of God's Will 392

The Pattern Of God's Will 393
An Example From Scripture 395
Walking In The Will 396
A Biblical Example 397

Chapter Nineteen *How God Speaks To Man* 398

The Written Word 399
Prayer 399
Counselors 400
Circumstances 401
Open And Closed Doors 402
Angels 403
Miracles 404
Dreams 405
Visions 406
An Audible Voice 407
The Inner Voice Of The Holy Spirit 407
Gifts Of The Holy Spirit 410
Miscellaneous Methods 411
God Is Not Limited 412

Chapter Twenty *The Bush Still Burns* 417

Times Past: The Burning Bush 418
The Present Time: The Bush Still Burns 419
What If There Is No Bush? 420
Assurance Of The Will Of God 427
A Step At A Time 428
The Bush Still Burns 430

Chapter Twenty One *Avoiding Questionable Practices* 433

What Are Some Questionable Practices 434
When Believers Differ 441

Cultivate Your Own Convictions: 442
Summary: When Believers Differ 445
Decision Making On Questionable Practices 445

Chapter Twenty Two *A Biblical Model For Decision Making* 447

The Model 448
The Umpire Of Peace 450
Tried And Failed? 451
Failures Who Were Successes 452
Failures Who Were Failures 453
What Made The Difference? 453
Tried And Failed? 456

Chapter Twenty Three *God's Will And Suffering* 461

The Reasons For Suffering 462
The Proper Attitude Towards Suffering 467
Positive Benefits Of Suffering 469
The Storms Of Life 478
Suffering Is To Be Expected 481
When The Brook Runs Dry 483

Chapter Twenty Four *The Stages Of Revelation* 487

Revelation Knowledge 488
Stage One: Direction 489
Stage Two: Revelation 489
Stage Three: Hesitation 490
Stage Four: Resignation 491
Stage Five: Verification 491
Stage Six: Exaltation 491
A Final Word--Listen For His Voice 492

Appendix **505**
Biblical References To The Holy Spirit **514**

Genesis	515
Exodus	515
Numbers	515
Judges	515
1 Samuel	515
1 Kings	515
2 Kings	516
2 Chronicles	516
Psalm	516
Isaiah	516
Ezekiel	516
Daniel	517
Joel	517
Micah	517
Haggai	517
Matthew	517
Mark	518
Luke	518
John	519
Acts	519
Romans	521
1 Corinthians	522
2 Corinthians	523
Galatians	523
Ephesians	524
Philippians	524
1 Thessalonians	524
2 Thessalonians	524
1 Timothy	524
2 Timothy	525
Titus	525

Hebrews 525
1 Peter 525
1 John 525
Jude 525
Revelation 526
About The Book 527
About The Author Dr.Abraham Peters 531

DEDICATION

This book is dedicated

In Honor of the Holy Spirit,

To the glory of God the Father and to

Our lord and savior Jesus Christ

DR. ABRAHAM PETERS

ACKNOWLEDGEMENT

A very special gratitude I give to my beloved wife, wonderful woman of God and covenant partner in the ministry Reverend, Teresa Y H Peters, who has always been a constant encourager, prophetess, inspiration and strong supports. I am also very grateful to all other family members. Many thanks to our friends, to mention a few, Lady Gloria Gooden and Mrs. Kathleen Earl, for being a blessing to our ministry.

A million thanks to the family of Engr. Enrique, Pastora Nancy, Henry and Japheth Moran, your demonstration of love to God and faithfully walking in obedience of faith is exemplary. I am ever grateful for your family for all your love, devotion and dedication to our Lord God. Praying that our Father God continually bless you all immensely!

To all who have helped in the technical process of publishing this Book, I am ever grateful for your labor of love and excellence. To everyone who's searching for answers in their walk of faith and who will come in contact with this book, I can assure you that this is one book inspired by the Holy Spirit and definitely will be worth reading, studying and keeping in your reference library for training and equipping of every Christian minister.

Above all, I would like to express my deepest profound appreciation to my ABBA Father Jehovah GOD Almighty for our redemption through His only begotten Son, our Lord Jesus Christ and the inspiration of His Holy Spirit for the success of this book. To GOD be all the glory. Amen.

INTRODUCTION

FELLOWSHIP OF THE HOLY SPIRIT

DR. ABRAHAM PETERS

What it does mean that God is a consuming fire!

God is first identified as a "consuming fire" in Deuteronomy 4:24 and 9:3. The writer to the Hebrews reiterates, warning the Hebrews to worship God with reverence and awe "for our God is a consuming fire." There is nothing mysterious about the Hebrew and Greek words translated "consuming fire." They mean exactly that—a fire that utterly consumes or destroys. How, then, can a loving and merciful God also be a consuming fire that utterly destroys? In both Deuteronomy passages in which God is called a consuming fire, Moses is speaking first to warn the Israelites against idolatry (Deuteronomy 4:23-25) because God is a "jealous God" and will not share His glory with worthless idols. Idolatry provokes Him to a righteous anger which is justified when His holiness is disrespected. In Deuteronomy 9:3, Moses again refers to God as a consuming (or devouring) fire who would go ahead of the Israelites into the Promised Land, destroying and subduing their enemies before them. Here again we see God's wrath against those who oppose Him depicted as fire that utterly consumes and destroys anything in His path.

There are several incidents in which God's wrath, judgment, holiness or power are displayed by fire from heaven. Aaron's sons Abihu and Nadab were destroyed by fire when they offered a profane sacrifice, "strange fire," in the tabernacle, a sign of their disregard for the utter holiness of God and the need to honor Him in solemn and holy fear. The confrontation between Elijah and the prophets of Baal on Mount Carmel is another example of consuming fire from God. The prophets of Baal called upon their god all day long to rain fire from heaven to no avail. Then Elijah built an altar of stones, dug a ditch around it, put the sacrifice on the top of wood and called for water to be poured over his sacrifice three times. Elijah called upon God, and God sent fire down from heaven, completely consuming the sacrifice, the wood, and the stones and licked up the water in the ditch. Then His anger turned against the false prophets, and they were all killed. When prophesying the destruction of the Assyrians, who resisted the true and living God and warred against His people, Isaiah refers to the tongue of the Lord as a consuming fire and His "arm coming down with raging anger and consuming fire" (Isaiah 30:27-30).

God's holiness is the reason for His being a consuming fire, and it burns up anything unholy. The holiness of God is that part of His nature that most separates Him from sinful man. The godless, Isaiah writes, tremble before Him: "Who of us can dwell with the consuming fire? Who of us can dwell with everlasting burning?" Isaiah answers this by saying that only the righteous can withstand the consuming fire of God's wrath against sin, because sin is an offense to God's holiness. But Isaiah also assures us that no amount of our own righteousness is sufficient (Isaiah 64:6). Fortunately, God has provided the righteousness we need by sending Jesus Christ to die on the cross for the sins of all who would ever believe in Him. In that one act, Christ mitigates God's wrath, exchanging His perfect righteousness for our sin. "God made him who had no sin to be sin for us, so that in him we might become the righteousness of God" (2 Corinthians 5:21). All the wrath of God was poured out on Jesus, so that those who belong to Him would not have to suffer the same fate as the Assyrians. "It is a fearful thing to fall into the hands of the living God" (Hebrews 10:31), but we need not fear the consuming fire of God's wrath if we are covered by the purifying blood of Christ.

DR. ABRAHAM PETERS

The times God has sent fire from heaven

Fire has come down from heaven several times in history. The Bible records at least six of these instances:

Fire fell from heaven and destroyed Job's flocks (Job 1:16). This was a direct attack from Satan, but, as the earlier part of Job 1 explains, Satan was acting with the permission of God (verse 12). It was a tragedy allowed by God and, in the end, bringing glory to God. On the other side of his trials, Job was blessed with even larger flocks (Job 42:12).

Fire coming down from heaven was also a means of God's judgment. Fire in the form of burning sulfur rained from the heavens and destroyed Sodom and Gomorrah (Genesis 19:24; Luke 17:29). God also used fire from heaven to judge the soldiers sent by the wicked king Ahaziah to arrest Elijah—twice, fire descended from heaven to consume a group of fifty soldiers sent on the king's business (2 Kings 1:10, 12). But fire from heaven is not exclusively a means of judgment. On at least three occasions, God sent fire from above in order to consume a sacrifice: fire came down from heaven to consume the sacrifice that David offered on the threshing floor of Araunah the Jebusite (1 Chronicles 21:26); to consume the sacrifice at the dedication of the temple, in the presence of King Solomon and the people of Israel (2 Chronicles 7:1); and to consume Elijah's sacrifice on Mt. Carmel, in response to the prophet's simple prayer (1 Kings 18:38).

In each sacrifice consumed by fire from heaven, God was making an important point. In David's case, God was forgiving David's sin in conducting a census and halting a plague in Israel. He was also choosing the place where the future temple would be built. In Solomon's case, God was consecrating that location as the place where His name would dwell forever (2 Chronicles 7:16). The people's reaction was to worship the Lord and say, "He is good; his love endures forever" (2 Chronicles 7:3). In Elijah's case, God was shaming the prophets of Baal, whose god sent no fire, and claiming His rightful title as Lord God of Israel. The people on Mt. Carmel "fell prostrate and cried, 'The LORD—he is God! The LORD—he is God!'" (1 Kings 18:39).

Interestingly, during Jesus' earthly ministry, two of His disciples, James and John, wanted to call down fire from heaven in judgment of a Samaritan village that did not welcome the Lord. Jesus, however, "turned and rebuked them" (Luke 9:55). He had not come "to condemn the world, but to save the world" (John 3:17). James and John, rightly called the "sons of thunder" (Mark 3:17), wanted what they thought was justice, but their idea went against God's plan of mercy. God's justice will come, but on His terms, not ours. In the end-times tribulation, the false prophet will cause fire to come down from heaven as a means of deceiving people into worshiping the Antichrist (Revelation 13:13). And, at the end of the millenium, God promises that He will destroy the armies of Gog and Magog with fire from heaven (Revelation 20:9).

According to the Bible, Enoch and Elijah are the only two people God took to heaven without them dying. Genesis 5:24 tells us, "Enoch walked with God; then he was no more, because God took him away." Second Kings 2:11 tells us, "Suddenly a chariot of fire and horses of fire appeared and separated the two of them, and Elijah went up to heaven in a whirlwind." Enoch is described as a man who "walked with God for 300 years" (Genesis 5:23). Elijah was one of the most powerful of God's prophets in the Old Testament. There are also prophecies of Elijah's return (Malachi 4:5-6). Why did God take Enoch and Elijah? The Bible does not specifically give us the answer. Some commentaries speculate that they were taken in preparation for a role in the end times, possibly as the two witnesses in Revelation 11:3-12. This is possible, but not explicitly taught in the Bible. It may be that God desired to save Enoch and Elijah from experiencing death due to their great faithfulness in serving and obeying Him. Whatever the case, God has His purpose, and while we don't always understand God's plans and purposes, we know that "His way is perfect" (Psalm 18:30).

Firepower is the military capability to direct force at an enemy. It is not to be confused with the concept of rate of fire, which describes the cycling of the firing mechanism in a weapon system. Firepower involves the whole range of potential weapons. The concept is generally taught as one of the three key principles of modern warfare wherein the enemy forces are destroyed or have their will to fight negated by sufficient and preferably overwhelming use of force as a result of combat operations. Through the ages firepower has come to mean offensive power applied from a distance, thus involving ranged weapons as opposed to one-on-one close quarters combat. Firepower is thus something employed to keep enemy forces at a range where they can be defeated in detail or sapped of the will to continue. In the field of naval artillery, the weight of a broadside was long used as a figure of merit of a warship's firepower.

What fellowship with God is.

The Greek word translated "fellowship" in the New Testament is koinonia, meaning "partnership, sharing in common, or communion," and the essence of partnership is agreement or unity of purpose. Fellowship with God is, at its most basic, agreement with Him in all things. The New Testament assures believers of this partnership. Not only do we have fellowship with God the Father, but we also have fellowship with His Son and the Holy Spirit (1 Corinthians 1:9; 2 Corinthians 13:14; 1 John 1:3).

To have fellowship with others, there must be a oneness of the heart, something that links two people together: "Can two walk together unless they are agreed?" (Amos 3:3). At the very heart of fellowship, there must be like-mindedness. Two in fellowship must have like wishes and like desires, which is why Paul exhorts believers to not be "unequally yoked with unbelievers. For what partnership has righteousness with lawlessness? Or what fellowship has light with darkness?" (2 Corinthians 6:14). Believers have true fellowship with one another because of the Holy Spirit who indwells all believers (John 14:17). Through the Spirit we have true fellowship, unlike any relationship we can have with those who do not know Christ.

Fellowship with God is only possible through the blood of Christ. Before we are saved, we are at enmity with God (Colossians 1:21). But Jesus reconciled us to God through His death on the cross (Romans 5:10). When we repent of our sin and trust in Christ, the result is that "now we live in fellowship with the true God because we live in fellowship with his Son, Jesus Christ. He is the only true God, and he is eternal life" (1 John 5:20). It is important to know that fellowship with God comes exclusively through Jesus Christ. Jesus is the only way to the Father (John 14:6), yet throughout the ages man has attempted to devise other paths to God through false religions or to live in such a way as to merit His approval. We cannot have fellowship with God if we reject His Son (1 John 5:10–11), dispute His foreordained plan of salvation, or attempt to find another path to His presence.

Scripture identifies some things that are at odds with true fellowship with God: the "mind governed by the flesh" that does "not submit to God's law" (Romans 8:7) and "friendship with the world" (James 4:4). God is light, and light cannot have fellowship with darkness: "If we claim to have fellowship with him and yet walk in the darkness, we lie and do not live out the truth. But if we walk in the light, as he is in the light, we have fellowship with one another, and the blood of Jesus, his Son, purifies us from all sin" (1 John 1:6–7). Those in fellowship with God are trusting in Christ. Their sins are forgiven. They are filled with the Spirit. They believe that in all things God deserves to be glorified. They spend time in Bible reading and prayer in a pursuit of "spiritual wisdom and insight so that [they] might grow in [their] knowledge of God" (Ephesians 1:17, NLT).

For us to be in fellowship with His Holy Spirit, we glorify Him by submitting to His will and obeying the commands contained in His Word. "But from everlasting to everlasting the LORD's love is with those who fear him" (Psalm 103:17). May we enjoy the harmony, contentment, and joy of the fellowship God has provided us with. May we follow the example of Enoch, a man who, throughout his long life, was known for "walking in close fellowship with God" (Genesis 5:24, NLT).

The Apostle Paul closed his letter to the Corinthians by writing "the fellowship of Holy Spirit be with you all." We can have fellowship with the Spirit because of the grace of Jesus Christ and love of God. Fellowship of the Spirit is more than a simple friendly relationship.

In order to fully understand what Paul meant by the fellowship of the Spirit, we should look at other passages with the same word. The Greek word for "fellowship" is koinonia, which can also mean communion, and the same Greek word is used in the epistle to the Philippians: Therefore if there is any consolation in Christ, if any comfort of love, if any fellowship of the Spirit, if any affection and mercy, fulfill my joy by being like-minded, having the same love, being of one accord, of one mind. (Philippians 2:1–2)

The Spirit dwelling within believers is a part of this concept, as all believers have the same Spirit dwelling within them. Paul wrote in Ephesians 4:4–6 that "there is one body and one Spirit, just as you were called in one hope of your calling; one Lord, one faith, one baptism." Believers are "baptized into one body" (i.e., the church of which Christ is the head) by the one Spirit (1 Corinthians 12:13). Just as believers have one Spirit, we should also have one mind working toward the one goal—"striving together for the faith of the Gospel" (Philippians 1:27). The fellowship of the Holy Spirit unifies believers, since we all have the one Spirit dwelling within us. Paul concluded his epistle with an exhortation of unity through the Holy Spirit.

Furthermore, just as Christ loved us, we should also walk in love (Ephesians 5:2) not only love for Christ but for others as well. Loving others just as Christ loved us will help us be of one mind (2 Corinthians 13:11). Love and fellowship of the Spirit go hand in hand, and participating in the fellowship of the Holy Spirit with fellow believers is a reason to rejoice.

The Hebrew Ruach means "wind," "breath," or "spirit." The corresponding Greek word is pneuma. Both words are commonly used in passages referring to the Holy Spirit. The word's first use in the Bible appears in the second verse: "The Spirit of God [Ruach Elohim] was hovering over the waters" (Genesis 1:2). In Genesis 6:17 ruach is translated "breath of life." Genesis 8:1 uses ruach to describe the "wind" God sent over the earth to recede the Flood waters. Altogether, the word ruach is found almost 400 times in the Old Testament. Often, when the Old Testament talks about the "Spirit of the Lord" or the "Spirit of God," the word for "Spirit" is Ruach. Use of ruach as "spirit" when not linked with God usually is in reference to the human spirit. This can mean the actual spirit of a human (the immaterial part of humans akin to the soul) or one's mood, emotional state, or general disposition. Ruach as "breath" or "wind" can be a reference to literal breath or wind, or it can take on a figurative meaning such as in the idiom "a mere breath."

God's Ruach is the source of life. The Ruach of God is the One who gives life to all creation. We could say that God's Ruach has created every other (non-divine) ruach that exists. All living creatures owe the breath of life to the Creative Spirit of God. Moses states this truth explicitly: "God . . . gives breath [ruach] to all living things" (Numbers 27:16). Job understood this truth as well: "As long as I have life within me, the breath [ruach] of God in my nostrils" (Job 27:3). Later, Elihu tells Job, "The Spirit of God has made me; the breath of the Almighty gives me life" (Job 33:4). God used the phrase Ruach Yahweh in His promise that the Messiah would be empowered by the Holy Spirit: "The Spirit of the LORD will rest on him—the Spirit of wisdom and of understanding, the Spirit of counsel and of might, the Spirit of the knowledge and fear of the LORD" (Isaiah 11:2; see also Isaiah 42:1). This prophecy was fulfilled in Jesus; at His baptism in the Jordan River, John saw "the

Spirit of God descending like a dove and alighting on him" (Matthew 3:16).

Have ye received the Holy Spirit since ye believed? – Acts 19:2

Scripture clearly separates being born again, the baptism of the Holy Spirit, and being filled with the Holy Spirit. These three are not lumped together as one in Scripture. Instead, they are presented as separate experiences for the Lord's people. Today, however, few people know exactly what the Scriptures say regarding the Holy Spirit, and the consequence is men trying to do things in their own strength. Sadder still is how one group denies the power of the Holy Spirit, while another group pursues the things of the Spirit more than they pursue Christ Himself. Somewhere in the middle is the truth. This book takes a close look at Scripture to see what the Lord Himself tells us regarding His Holy Spirit and how it relates to us today.

Many people find the Holy Spirit mysterious and confounding. Why is the third person in the Godhead, the one Jesus said would be the believer's ultimate source of truth and comfort, he source of such confusion? This book clearly explains that the Holy Spirit's chief desire is for relationship, fellowship, to offer us the encouragement and guidance of a trusted friend. This insightful and biblically-based book moves beyond theological jargon, religious tradition, and cultural misconceptions to clarify what the Holy Spirit promises to do in your life:

· Dwell within you
· Be your helper
· Guide you into all truth

- Comfort you
- Pray for you
- Show you things to come
- Never leave you

It's time to experience the Holy Spirit in a fresh, new way to meet the God you may have never known. Tap into God's Power source by welcoming the Holy Spirit into your life. Have you ever felt dissatisfied in your Christian walk? Have you felt that your love relationship with Christ hit a plateau and there is no power in your prayers anymore? You can experience a deeper level in the Lord, and see life-changing results by learning how to welcome the Holy Spirit's abiding presence and power into your daily life! Through the person and power of the Holy Spirit. This book is a catalyst for those desiring a more power-filled Christian walk. Enjoy this new walk with the Holy Spirit, the person who wants to be your Counselor, Advocate, Strengthener and Forever-Stand-By Friend.

God Wants to Talk to You!

Many people go through life wishing they could hear from God. They long to know His plans and purposes for their lives, and they long to benefit from His direction in their daily decisions. The truth is, you were made to hear God's voice! God created you for intimacy with Him, and He longs to speak with you, moment by moment!

"My sheep listen to my voice; I know them, and they follow me."
John 10:27, NLT

In this book, You will learn how to hear God's Voice, biblical principles in this book helps you develop your ability to hear God's words every day.

Learn to recognize God's voice apart from other voices.
Encounter new clarity in knowing God's will.
Access your many rights and privileges as a believer.
Walk in increased discernment through Holy Spirit power.
Experience transformation by renewing your mind.
As you walk and talk with God, you will find yourself living the abundant life of blessing that you were meant to live!

Do you feel that the ability to hear God's voice is for other people and not for you? Is it only for people who lived in Biblical times? Not at all! The God who loved you enough to die for you loves you enough to talk to you. And wherever you are in your spiritual walk, God will find a way to speak to you in a way you will understand. Become acquainted with the Voice that has spoken from a fire and a cloud, with visible signs and an invisible Spirit, through a burning bush and burning hearts. This book helps you discover for yourself how you can discern the voice of God. Divided in to two parts, the first lays biblical in-depth introduction to be acquainted with the person of the Holy Spirit while the section two contains insights that will aid you in your desire to hear Him speak. Discover the treasure of recognizing how God keeps in touch with his beloved people. Stop merely going through the motions of life by learning how to recognize and respond to the Lord's divine appointments for you. This book helps to un-complicate the idea of listening to God as you use the key questions to help you determine if what you're discerning is from Him or not.

Discover the joy of truly walking with the Lord as you learn how to live in expectation of hearing from Him. With the commotion from our fast-paced world, it's difficult enough to hear our own thoughts, let alone try to listen for the voice of God. But in order to fulfill the great plans He has for us, we need to be able to recognize His voice. Through this book, I've provided helps for you to…

Develop the sensitivity and receptiveness to hearing God's voice
Block out negative influences that distract you from hearing Him
Learn that God's willingness to speak to you has no limits
Discover what will open the doors of communication with God
God reaches out to us every day, offering guidance for everything from major life issues to small, ordinary problems.

What the difference is between the Holy Spirit and Holy Ghost

Of the modern English translations of the Bible, it is only the King James Version of the Bible which uses the term "Holy Ghost." It occurs 90 times in the KJV. The term "Holy Spirit" occurs 7 times in the KJV. There is no clear reason as to why the KJV translators used Ghost in most places and then Spirit in a few. The exact same Greek and Hebrew words are translated "ghost" and "spirit" in the KJV in different occurrences of the words. By "ghost," the KJV translators did not intend to communicate the idea of "the spirit of a deceased person." In 1611, when the KJV was originally translated, the word "ghost" primarily referred to "an immaterial being."

With recent Scripture translations, "Spirit" has replaced "Ghost" in most instances. Some of this came about because words don't always hold their meanings. In the days of Shakespeare or King

James, ghost meant the living essence of a person. Looking back, we see that "breath" or "soul" were often used as synonyms of "ghost." During these times, spirit normally meant the essence of a departed person or a demonic or paranormal apparition. As language evolved, people started saying "ghost" when speaking of the vision of a dead person while "spirit" became the standard term for life or living essence, often also for "soul." With slight exceptions, "ghost" and "spirit" changed places over some 300 years.

The real issue is that both "Holy Ghost" and "Holy Spirit" refer to the Third Person of the Trinity, coequal and consubstantial with the Father and the Son (Matthew 28:19; Acts 5:3,4; 28:25,26; 1 Corinthians 12:4-6). He is the gift of the Father to His people on earth to initiate and complete the building of the body of Christ (1 Corinthians 12:13). He is also the agency by which the world is convicted of sin, the Lord Jesus is glorified, and believers are transformed into His image (John 16:7-9; Acts 1:5, 2:4; Romans 8:29; 2 Corinthians 3:18; Ephesians 2:22). Whichever term we use, we remember that this Holy Ghost is God's active breath, blowing where He wishes, creating faith through water and Word.

Have you surrendered yet to the Holy Spirit Control? Acknowledge your weakness and recognize His power, omniscience, and wisdom. The Lord doesn't call you to live the Christian life, which is human impossibility. Rather, He wants you to yield control and let Him live His life through you.

What follows are 50 things the Holy Spirit does according to the New Testament.

1. The Spirit convicts the world of sin, righteousness, and judgment (John 16:8).
2. The Spirit guides us into all truth (John 16:13).
3. The Spirit regenerates us (John 3:5-8; Titus 3:5).
4. The Spirit glorifies and testifies of Christ (John 15:26; 16:14).
5. The Spirit reveals Christ to us and in us (John 16:14-15).
6. The Spirit leads us (Romans 8:14; Galatians 5:18; Matthew 4:1; Luke 4:1).
7. The Spirit sanctifies us (2 Thessalonians 2:13; 1 Peter 1:2; Romans 5:16).
8. The Spirit empowers us (Luke 4:14; 24:49; Romans 15:19; Acts 1:8).
9. The Spirit fills us (Ephesians 5:18; Acts 2:4; 4:8, 31; 9:17).
10. The Spirit teaches us to pray (Romans 8:26-27; Jude 1:20).
11. The Spirit bears witness in us that we are children of God (Romans 8:16).
12. The Spirit produces in us the fruit or evidence of His work and presence (Galatians 5:22-23).
13. The Spirit distributes spiritual gifts and manifestations (the outshining) of His presence to and through the body (1 Corinthians 12:4, 8-10; Hebrews 2:4).
14. The Spirit anoints us for ministry (Luke 4:18; Acts 10:38).
15. The Spirit washes and renews us (Titus 3:5).
16. The Spirit brings unity and oneness to the body (Ephesians 4:3; 2:14-18). Here the Spirit plays the same role that He plays in the Godhead. The Spirit is the life that unites Father and Son. The Spirit plays the same role in the church. When the Spirit is operating in a group of people, He unites them in love. Therefore, a sure evidence of the Holy Spirit

working in a group is Love and Unity, Miracles, Signs and Wonders.
17. The Spirit is our guarantee and deposit of the future resurrection (2 Corinthians 1:22; 2 Corinthians 5:5).
18. The Spirit seals us unto the day of redemption (Ephesians 1:13; 4:30).
19. The Spirit sets us free from the law of sin and death (Romans 8:2).
20. The Spirit quickens our mortal bodies (Romans 8:11).
21. The Spirit reveals the deep things of God to us (1 Corinthians 2:10).
22. The Spirit reveals what has been given to us from God (1 Corinthians 2:12).
23. The Spirit dwells in us (Romans 8:9; 1 Corinthians 3:16; 2 Timothy 1:14; John 14:17).
24. The Spirit speaks to, in, and through us (1 Corinthians 12:3; 1 Timothy 4:1; Revelation 2:11; Heb 3:7; Matthew 10:20; Acts 2:4; 8:29; 10:19; 11:12, 28; 13:2; 16:6,7; 21:4,11).
25. The Spirit is the agent by which we are baptized into the body of Christ (1 Corinthians 12:13).
26. The Spirit brings liberty (2 Corinthians 3:17).
27. The Spirit transforms us into the image of Christ (2 Corinthians 3:18).
28. The Spirit cries in our hearts, "Abba, Father" (Galatians 4:6).
29. The Spirit enables us to wait (Galatians 5:5).
30. The Spirit supplies us with Christ (Philippians 1:19, KJV).
31. The Spirit grants everlasting life (Galatians 6:8).
32. The Spirit gives us access to God the Father (Ephesians 2:18).
33. The Spirit makes us (corporately) God's habitation (Ephesians 2:22).

34. The Spirit reveals the mystery of God to us (Ephesians 3:5).
35. The Spirit strengthens our spirits (Ephesians 3:16).
36. The Spirit enables us to obey the truth (1 Peter 1:22).
37. The Spirit enables us to know that Jesus abides in us (1 John 3:24; 4:13).
38. The Spirit confesses that Jesus came in the flesh (1 John 4:2).
39. The Spirit says "Come, Lord Jesus" along with the bride (Revelation 22:17).
40. The Spirit dispenses God's love into our hearts (Romans 5:5).
41. The Spirit bears witness to the truth in our conscience (Romans 9:1).
42. The Spirit teaches us (1 Corinthians 2:13; John 14:26).
43. The Spirit gives us joy (1 Thessalonians 1:6).
44. The Spirit enables some to preach the gospel (1 Peter 1:12).
45. The Spirit moves us (2 Peter 1:21).
46. The Spirit knows the things of God (1 Corinthians 2:11).
47. The Spirit casts out demons (Matthew 12:28).
48. The Spirit brings things to our remembrance (John 14:26).
49. The Spirit comforts us (Acts 9:31).
50. The Spirit makes some overseers in the church and sends some out to the work of church planting [through the body] (Acts 20:28; 13:2).

The Holy Spirit unites us to Jesus Christ and to His body. The Spirit reveals Christ to us, gives us His life, and makes Christ alive in us. The Spirit takes the experiences of Jesus: His incarnation, ministry, crucifixion, resurrection, and ascension and brings them into our own experience. Because of the Holy Spirit, the history of Jesus Christ becomes our story and experience. Unfortunately, some movements have become known for their disregard to the Holy Spirit's work and denial of the supernatural moves of God.

The outpouring of the Holy Spirit—the pouring out of God's Spirit to fill and indwell people—was prophesied in the Old Testament and fulfilled at Pentecost (Acts 2). This event was predicted in the Old Testament: in Isaiah 44:3 God said to Israel, "I will pour water on the thirsty land, and streams on the dry ground; I will pour out my Spirit on your offspring, and my blessing on your descendants." The Holy Spirit is pictured as the "water of life" that saves and blesses a dying people. On the day of Pentecost, Peter quoted another prophecy as being fulfilled: "I will pour out my Spirit on all people. Your sons and daughters will prophesy, your old men will dream dreams, your young men will see visions. Even on my servants, both men and women, I will pour out my Spirit in those days. . . . And everyone who calls on the name of the Lord will be saved" (Joel 2:28–29, 32).

The outpouring of the Holy Spirit ushered in a new era, the church age. In the Old Testament, the Holy Spirit was a rare gift that was only given to a few people, and usually for only short periods of time. When Saul was anointed king of Israel, the Holy Spirit came upon him (1 Samuel 10:10), but when God removed His blessing on Saul, the Holy Spirit left him (1 Samuel 16:14). The Holy Spirit came for specific moments or seasons in the lives of Othniel (Judges 3:10), Gideon (Judges 6:34), and Samson (Judges 13:25; 14:6) as well, to enable them to do His will and serve Israel. At Pentecost, the Holy Spirit was poured out on all believers in Christ, and He came to stay. This marked a major change in the Holy Spirit's work.

Before His arrest, Jesus had promised to send His disciples the Holy Spirit (John 14:15–17). The Spirit "lives with you and will be in you," Jesus said (John 14:17). This was a prophecy of the indwelling of the Spirit, another distinctive of the church age. The outpouring of the Holy Spirit in Acts 2 marked the fulfillment of Jesus' words, too, as the Holy Spirit came upon all believers in a powerful, visible (and audible) way. Luke records the event: "Suddenly a sound like the blowing of a violent wind came from heaven and filled the whole house where they were sitting. They saw what seemed to be tongues of fire that separated and came to rest on each of them. All of them were filled with the Holy Spirit and began to speak in other tongues as the Spirit enabled them" (Acts 2:2–4). Immediately, the Spirit-filled believers went into the streets of Jerusalem and preached Christ. Three thousand people were saved and baptized that day; the church had begun (verse 41).

The outpouring of the Holy Spirit upon humanity was the inauguration of the New Covenant, which had been ratified by Jesus' blood (Luke 22:20). According to the terms of the New Covenant, every believer is given the Holy Spirit (Ephesians 1:13). Ever since Pentecost, the Holy Spirit has baptized every believer into Christ at the moment of salvation (1 Corinthians 12:13), as He comes to permanently indwell God's children.

In the book of Acts, there are three "outpourings" of the Holy Spirit, to three different people groups at three different times. The first was to Jews and proselytes in Jerusalem (Acts 2). The second was to a group of believing Samaritans (Acts 8:14 -17. The third was to a group of believing Gentiles (Acts 10). Significantly, Peter was present at all three outpourings. Three times, God sent the Holy Spirit with demonstrable signs, as the Great Commission was being fulfilled. The same Holy Spirit coming upon Jews, Samaritans, and Gentiles in the same manner in the presence of the same apostle kept the early church unified. There was not a "Jewish" church, a

"Samaritan" church, and a "Roman" church—there was one church, "one Lord, one faith, one baptism" (Ephesians 4:5).

The outpouring of the Spirit is different from the filling of the Spirit. The outpouring was a unique coming of the Holy Spirit to earth; the filling happens whenever we are surrendered to God's control of our lives. We are commanded to be filled with the Spirit (Ephesians 5:18). In this regard it is possible for the believer either to be "filled with the Spirit" or to "quench" the Spirit (1 Thessalonians 5:19). In either case, the Holy Spirit remains with the believer, as opposed to the Old Testament era, when the Holy Spirit would come and go. The filling of the Spirit comes as a direct result of submission to God's will, and the quenching is a direct result of rebelling against God's will.

The church has already begun; the apostles have already laid that foundation (Ephesians 2:20). Sometimes we sing songs that ask the Holy Spirit to "come"; the reality is that He has already come to us—at the moment of salvation—and, once He comes, He doesn't leave. The outpouring of the Spirit is a completed prophecy that ushered in the church age and the New Covenant in which all believers are given the Holy Spirit.

DR. ABRAHAM PETERS

PART ONE

KNOWING

THE

HOLY

SPIRIT

CHAPTER ONE

INTIMACY WITH THE HOLY SPIRIT

And Jesus, when He was baptized, went up straightway out of the water; and, lo, the heavens were opened unto Him, and He saw the Spirit of God descending like a dove, and lighting upon Him; And lo a voice from heaven, saying, This is my beloved Son, in whom I am well pleased.(Matthew 3:16-17)

This chapter introduces the Holy Spirit. It explains His position in the Trinity of God, discusses His personality traits, and warns about His sensitive nature. The title "Holy Ghost" is used to identify the Holy Spirit. The personal pronoun "He" is also used, as the Holy Spirit is one of three persons of the Trinity of God. Jesus spoke of the Holy Spirit as "He." Jesus said:

-He shall speak of me.	John 15:26
-I will send Him unto you.	John 16:7
-He shall glorify me.	John 16:14
-He shall not speak of Himself.	John 16:13

THE TRIUNE NATURE OF GOD

There are many gods worshiped throughout the world, but there is only one true God. The Holy Bible contains the story of this true God. The Bible is the Word of God which reveals His special plan for all mankind. One of the things the Bible reveals is that God has a triune nature. This means His personality is revealed in three different forms. He is three persons, yet one God. The Holy Spirit is part of the triune nature of God which consists of the Father, the Son Jesus Christ, and the Holy Spirit. The three personalities are united as one in the Godhead.

Each part of the Trinity...the Father, the Son Jesus Christ, and the Holy Spirit...have special functions on behalf of mankind. This book concerns the ministry and purpose of the Holy Spirit.

GOD, THE HOLY SPIRIT

The Holy Spirit is called God:

But Peter said, Ananias, why hath Satan filled thine heart to lie to the Holy Ghost...thou hast not lied unto men, but unto God. (Acts 5:3-4)

Since He is called God, the Holy Spirit is equal with God the Father and Jesus Christ the Son. The Key Verses for this chapter reveal clearly the triune nature of God. Jesus is being baptized, the Holy Spirit descends on Him, and God speaks:

And Jesus, when He was baptized, went up straightway out of the water: and, lo, the heavens were opened unto Him, and He saw the Spirit of God descending like a dove, and lighting upon Him:

And lo a voice from heaven saying, This is my beloved Son, in whom I am well pleased. (Matthew 3:16-17)

Prior to returning to Heaven after His ministry on earth, Jesus spoke of the Holy Spirit:

But when the Comforter is come, whom I will send unto you from the Father, even the Spirit of truth, which proceedeth from the Father, He shall testify of me. (John 15:26)

The Apostle Paul spoke of the triune nature of the Holy Spirit:

> *For the law of the Spirit of life in Christ Jesus hath made me free from the law of sin and death.*
>
> *For what the law could not do, in that it was weak through the flesh, God sending His own Son, in the likeness of sinful flesh, and for sin, condemned sin in the flesh. (Romans 8:2-3)*
>
> *The grace of the Lord Jesus Christ, and the love of God, and the communion of the Holy Ghost, be with you all. (2 Corinthians 13:14)*
>
> *For through Him [the Son] we both have access by one Spirit unto the Father. (Ephesians 2:18)*

The Apostle Peter also spoke of the triune nature of God:

> *If ye be reproached for the name of Christ, happy are ye; for the Spirit of glory and of God resteth upon you: on their part He is evil spoken of, but on your part He is glorified. (1 Peter 4:14)*

The book of Acts also verifies the triune nature of God:

> *Therefore being by the right hand of God exalted, and having received of the Father the promise of the Holy Ghost, He hath shed forth this, which ye now see and hear. (Acts 2:33)*

NATURE OF THE HOLY SPIRIT

As part of the Trinity of God, the Holy Spirit has a special nature. When we speak of His nature we mean the basic qualities which describe Him. The Bible teaches that the Holy Spirit is:

OMNIPRESENT:

This means He is present everywhere:

> *Whither shall I go from thy Spirit? or whither shall I flee from thy presence? (Psalms 139:7)*

OMNISCIENT:

This means He knows all things:

> *But God hath revealed them unto us by His Spirit; for the Spirit searcheth all things, yea the deep things of God.*

> *For what man knoweth the things of a man, save the spirit of man which is in him? even so the things of God knoweth no man, but the Spirit of God. (1 Corinthians 2:10-11)*

OMNIPOTENT:

This means the Holy Spirit is all powerful:

> *God hath spoken once; twice have I heard this; that power belongeth unto God. (Psalms 62:11)*

> *But ye shall receive power after that the Holy Ghost is come upon you... (Acts 1:8)*

ETERNAL:

This means He is everlasting. He had no beginning and will have no ending:

How much more shall the blood of Christ, who through the eternal Spirit offered Himself without spot to God, purge your conscience from dead works to serve the living God? (Hebrews 9:14)

THE PERSONALITY OF THE HOLY SPIRIT

The Holy Spirit is part of the triune nature of God, but the Holy Spirit also has an individual personality. The Bible reveals that the Holy Spirit...

HAS A MIND:

And He that searcheth the hearts knoweth what is the mind of the Spirit... (Romans 8:27)

SEARCHES OUT THE HUMAN MIND:

But God hath revealed them unto us by His Spirit; for the Spirit searcheth all things, yea, the deep things of God. (1 Corinthians 2:10)

HAS A WILL:

But all these worketh that one and the selfsame Spirit, dividing to every man severally as He will. (1 Corinthians 12:11)

The will of the Holy Spirit guides believers by denying permission for certain actions:

Now when they had gone throughout Phrygia and the region of Galatia, and were forbidden of the Holy Ghost to preach the word in Asia,

After they were come to Mysia, they assayed to go into Bithynia; but the Spirit suffered them not. (Acts 16:6-7)

The will of the Holy Spirit also guides believers by granting permission:

And after he had seen the vision, immediately we endeavored to go into Macedonia, assuredly gathering that the Lord had called us for to preach the Gospel unto them. (Acts 16:10)

SPEAKS:

He spoke to Philip:

Then the Spirit said unto Philip, Go near, and join thyself to this chariot.
(Acts 8:29)

He spoke to Peter:

While Peter thought on the vision, the Spirit said unto him, Behold, three men seek thee. (Acts 10:19)

He spoke to the elders in the city of Antioch:

As they ministered to the Lord, and fasted, the Holy Ghost said, Separate me Barnabas and Saul for the work whereunto I have called them. (Acts 13:2)

Revelation chapters 2 and 3 records several messages spoken by the Holy Spirit to seven churches in Asia.

The Specific Messages to Seven Churches of Revelation

Some of these seven churches kept closer to the gospel than others. The Holy Spirit gave each one a short "report card." The seven churches described in Revelation 2-3 are seven literal churches at the time that John the apostle was writing Revelation. Though they were literal churches in that time, there is also spiritual significance for churches and believers today.

The first purpose of the letters was to communicate with the literal churches and meet their needs at that time.
The second purpose is to reveal seven different types of individuals/churches throughout history and instruct them in God's truth.
A possible third purpose is to use the seven churches to foreshadow seven different periods in the history of the Church.

This view points to the fact that each of the seven churches describes issues that could fit the Church in any time in its history. So, although there may be some truth to the seven churches representing seven eras, there is far too much speculation in this regard. Our focus should be on what message God is giving us through the seven churches. The seven churches are

(1) Ephesus (Revelation 2:1-7) - the church that had forsaken its first love (2:4). They abandoned the love it had at first, lost their first love for Christ, which in turn affected the love they had for others.

(2) Smyrna (Revelation 2:8-11) - the church that would suffer persecution (2:10). The Holy Spirit encouraged them to be faithful unto death and he would give them the crown of life—eternal life.

(3) Pergamum (Revelation 2:12-17) - the church that needed to repent (2:16). It had fallen prey to a cult called the Nicolaitans, heretics who taught that since their bodies were evil, only what they

did with their spirit counted. This led to sexual immorality and eating food sacrificed to idols. The Holy Spirit said those who conquered such temptations would receive "hidden manna" and a "white stone," symbols of special blessings.

(4) Thyatira (Revelation 2:18-29) - the church whose false prophetess was leading people astray (2:20). Jesus promised to give himself, the morning star to those who resisted her evil ways.

(5) Sardis (Revelation 3:1-6) - the church that had fallen asleep, had the reputation of being dead, and this sleeping church is called to wake up (3:2). Jesus told them to wake up and repent. Those who did would receive white garments, have their name listed in the book of life, and would be proclaimed before God the Father.

(6) Philadelphia (Revelation 3:7-13) - the church that had endured patiently persevered (3:10). The Holy Spirit pledged to stand with them in future trials, granting special honors in heaven, the New Jerusalem.

(7) Laodicea (Revelation 3:14-22) - the church with the lukewarm faith (3:16). Its members had grown complacent because of the riches of the city. To those who returned to their former zeal, Jesus vowed to share his ruling authority.

Even though John wrote these warnings over 2,000 years ago, they still apply to Christian churches today. Christ remains the head of the worldwide Church, lovingly overseeing it. Many modern Christian churches have wandered from biblical truth, such as those that teach doctrines of devil and do not believe in the Trinity. Others have grown lukewarm, their members just going through the motions with no passion for God. Many churches in Asia and the Middle East face persecution. Increasingly popular are "progressive" churches that base their theology more on current culture than solid doctrine found in the Bible.

The huge number of denominations proves thousands of churches have been founded on little more than the stubbornness of their leaders. While these Revelation letters are strongly warning today's drifting churches that discipline will come to those who do not repent. Just as the Old Testament trials of the nation of Israel are a metaphor for the individual's relationship with God, the warnings in the book of Revelation speak to every Christ-follower today. These letters act as a gauge to reveal each believer's faithfulness.

The Nicolaitans are gone, but millions of Christians are being tempted by filthiness on the Internet. The false prophetess of Thyatira has been replaced by motivational preachers who avoid talking about Christ's atoning death for sin. Countless believers have turned from their love for Jesus to idolizing material possessions.

As in ancient times, backsliding continues to be a danger for people who believe in Jesus Christ, but reading these short letters to the seven churches of Revelation serves as a stern reminder. In a society flooded with temptation, they bring the Christian back to the First Commandment. Only the True God is worthy of our worship.

LOVES:

Now I beseech you, brethren, for the Lord Jesus Christ's sake, and for the love of the Spirit, that ye strive together with me in your prayers to God for me. (Romans 15:30)

INTERCEDES:

One of the personality traits of the Holy Spirit is that He is an intercessor. This means He prays to God on behalf of others:

Likewise the Spirit also helpeth our infirmities; for we know not what we should pray for as we ought; but the Spirit itself maketh intercession for us with groanings which cannot be uttered [spoken]. (Romans 8:26)

SENSITIVITY OF THE HOLY SPIRIT

The Holy Spirit has a sensitive nature. This means He has feelings that can be affected by the actions of man. Because of the sensitive nature of the Holy Spirit, the Bible warns that you should not:

LIE TO THE HOLY SPIRIT:

But Peter said, Ananias, why hath Satan filled thine heart to lie to the Holy Ghost, and to keep back part of the price of the land?

...Thou has not lied unto me, but unto God. (Acts 5:3-4)

RESIST THE SPIRIT:

The Holy Spirit has specific ministries on behalf of the believer which will be discussed in the Chapter Three of this book. Resisting the Holy Spirit is not yielding to Him when He tries to minister in your life:

Ye stiffnecked and uncircumcised in heart and ears, ye do always resist the Holy Ghost: as your fathers did, so do ye. (Acts 7:51)

QUENCH THE SPIRIT:

You quench the Holy Spirit when you refuse to do what the Holy Spirit would have you to do. The word "quench" is used elsewhere in the Bible in reference to putting out a fire. When you quench the Holy Spirit it stops the flow of His power within you. It is like throwing water on a fire. The Bible warns:

Quench not the Spirit. (I Thessalonians 5:19)

GRIEVE THE SPIRIT:

Quenching the Holy Spirit is not doing what the Holy Spirit would have us do. Grieving the Holy Spirit is doing something that the Holy Spirit does NOT want us to do. The nation of Israel grieved the Holy Spirit:

How oft did they provoke Him in the wilderness, and grieve Him in the desert! (Psalms 78:40)

The Bible warns:

And grieve not the Holy Spirit of God, whereby ye are sealed unto the day of redemption. (Ephesians 4:30)

INSULT THE SPIRIT:

You insult the Holy Spirit by going back into sin after you have experienced forgiveness through the blood of Jesus Christ:

Of how much sorer punishment, suppose ye, shall he be thought worthy, who hath trodden under foot the Son of God, and hath counted the blood of the covenant, wherewith he was sanctified, an unholy thing, and hath done despite unto the Spirit of grace? (Hebrews 10:29)

For it is impossible for those who were once enlightened, and have tasted of the heavenly gift, and were made partakers of the Holy Ghost, And have tasted the good word of God, and the powers of the world to come. If they shall fall away, to renew them again unto repentance; seeing they crucify to themselves the Son of God afresh, and put Him to an open shame. (Hebrews 6:4-6)

BLASPHEME THE SPIRIT:

Wherefore I say unto you, All manner of sin and blasphemy shall be forgiven unto men: but the blasphemy against the Holy Ghost shall not be forgiven unto men.

And whosoever speaketh a word against the Son of man, it shall be forgiven him; but whosoever speaketh against the Holy Ghost, it shall not be forgiven him, neither in this world neither in the world to come. (Matthew 12:31-32)

The sin of blasphemy against the Holy Spirit has been called the "unpardonable sin" because according to this passage it is the one sin for which there is no forgiveness. To blaspheme means to speak abusive words which reject the power of the Holy Spirit as being of God and claim it is of Satan. If a person totally rejects the power of the Holy Spirit then he can never be saved because it is the Holy Spirit which draws sinful men to Jesus Christ.

The Holy Spirit produces many visible confirming signs of God's power. Jesus was saying that if a person could not accept these miraculous signs as proof of the truth of the Gospel, then what could ever possibly convince them to believe?

DR. ABRAHAM PETERS

VEX THE HOLY SPIRIT:

To vex the Holy Spirit means to irritate, annoy, provoke, or make angry. The Holy Spirit is vexed by the disobedience and unbelief of mankind. The Prophet Isaiah records what happened to God's people, Israel, when they vexed the Holy Spirit:

But they rebelled, and vexed His Holy Spirit: therefore He was turned to be their enemy, and He fought against them. (Isaiah 63:10)

Why We Should Study the Holy Spirit: The ways we see the Scripture affirming the deity of the Holy Spirit. There are several lines of proof for the deity of the Holy Spirit in the Scripture. The very name of the Holy Spirit suggests that He is a supernatural being. The third person of the Godhead is "spirit." A spirit is an invisible being that is not restricted by a physical body (Luke 24:39). We know that God is spirit (John 4:24) and is supernatural in being. The third person of the Godhead is "Holy." There are many kinds of beings in the spirit world that are not holy. There are evil spirits, unclean spirits, seducing spirits and lying spirits (Judges 9:23; 1 Kings. 22:22; Matthew 10:1; Mark 9:25; I Timothy 4:1). But the Spirit of God is characterized by the qualities of God seen by Isaiah when he declared "Holy, Holy, Holy is the Lord of hosts" (Isaiah 6:3).

The Holy Spirit is described as having the essential attributes of God. The Holy Spirit is eternal (Hebrews 9:14; Compare Genesis 21:33). If He is eternal then He is not created. If He is not created then He is God.

For if the blood of bulls and goats and the ashes of a heifer, sprinkling the unclean, sanctifies for the purifying of the flesh, how much more shall the blood of Christ, who through the eternal Spirit offered Himself without spot to God, cleanse your conscience from dead works to serve the living God? Hebrews 9:13-14

The Holy Spirit is omnipresent or everywhere present (Psalms 139:7-10; Compare 2 Chronicles 6:18).

Where can I go from Your Spirit? Or where can I flee from Your presence? If I ascend into heaven, You are there; if I make my bed in hell, behold, You are there. If I take the wings of the morning, and dwell in the uttermost parts of the sea, even there Your hand shall lead me, and Your right hand shall hold me. Psalm 139:7-10

The Holy Spirit is omnipotent or all powerful (Zechariah 4:6; Micah 3:8; Luke 1:35; Romans 15:13; Job 26:13; Compare Isaiah 40:28).

And the angel answered and said to her, "The Holy Spirit will come upon you, and the power of the Highest will overshadow you; therefore, also, that Holy One who is to be born will be called the Son of God." Luke 1:35

The Holy Spirit is omniscient or all knowing (1 Corinthians 2:10-11; John 14:26; 16:12-13; Isaiah 40:13; Compare 1 John 3:20; Psalm 147:5).

But God has revealed them to us through His Spirit. For the Spirit searches all things, yes, the deep things of God. For what man knows the things of a man except the spirit of the man which is in him? Even so no one knows the things of God except the Spirit of God. 1 Corinthians 2:10-11

The Holy Spirit is described as having the moral attributes of God. The Holy Spirit is the Spirit of Love (Romans 15:30; Compare 1 John 4:16).

Now I beg you, brethren, through the Lord Jesus Christ, and through the love of the Spirit, that you strive together with me in prayers to God for me... Romans 15:30

The Holy Spirit is the Spirit of Holiness (Romans 1:4; Compare Exodus 15:11).

...concerning His Son Jesus Christ our Lord, who was born of the seed of David according to the flesh, and declared to be the Son of God with power according to the Spirit of holiness, by the resurrection from the dead. Romans 1:3-4

The Holy Spirit is the Spirit of Truth (1 John 5:6; Compare John 14:6).

This is He who came by water and blood--Jesus Christ; not only by water, but by water and blood. And it is the Spirit who bears witness, because the Spirit is truth. 1 John 5:6

The Holy Spirit is seen doing the works of God. The Holy Spirit was involved in creation (Genesis 1:2; Job 33:4; Psalm 104:30). Actually, all three persons of the Godhead were involved in creation. Genesis 1:1 tells us that God or "Elohim" created the heavens and the earth. The name "Elohim" is actually a plural noun form that is always used with singular verb forms. So the Father had His part, the Word (Jesus) had His part and the Holy Spirit had His part.

In the beginning God created the heavens and the earth. The earth was without form, and void; and darkness was on the face of the deep. And the Spirit of God was hovering over the face of the waters. Genesis 1:1-2

The Spirit of God has made me, and the breath of the Almighty gives me life. Job 33:4

You send forth Your Spirit, they are created; and You renew the face of the earth. Psalm 104:30

The Holy Spirit imparts life and resurrection power (John 6:63; Romans 8:11).

It is the Spirit who gives life; the flesh profits nothing. The words that I speak to you are spirit, and they are life. John 6:63

But if the Spirit of Him who raised Jesus from the dead dwells in you, He who raised Christ from the dead will also give life to your mortal bodies through His Spirit who dwells in you. Romans 8:11

The Holy Spirit inspired prophecy and the Scriptures (2 Peter 1:21; 2 Samuel 23:2; 2 Timothy 3:16).

...no prophecy of Scripture is of any private interpretation, for prophecy never came by the will of man, but holy men of God spoke as they were moved by the Holy Spirit. 2 Peter 1:20-21]

DR. ABRAHAM PETERS

The Spirit of the LORD spoke by me, and His word was on my tongue. 2 Samuel 23:2

The Holy Spirit regenerates the spirit of man (John 3:2-5).

This man came to Jesus by night and said to Him, "Rabbi, we know that You are a teacher come from God; for no one can do these signs that You do unless God is with him." 3 Jesus answered and said to him, "Most assuredly, I say to you, unless one is born again, he cannot see the kingdom of God." 4 Nicodemus said to Him, "How can a man be born when he is old? Can he enter a second time into his mother's womb and be born?" 5 Jesus answered, "Most assuredly, I say to you, unless one is born of water and the Spirit, he cannot enter the kingdom of God."

The Holy Spirit exercises sovereignty as God (1 Corinthians 12:11; John 3:8; Acts 13:2-3; 20:28).

But one and the same Spirit works all these things, distributing to each one individually as He wills. 1 Corinthians 12:11

The wind blows where it wishes, and you hear the sound of it, but cannot tell where it comes from and where it goes. So is everyone who is born of the Spirit. John 3:8

As they ministered to the Lord and fasted, the Holy Spirit said, "Now separate to Me Barnabas and Saul for the work to which I have called them." Acts 13:2

The Holy Spirit was responsible for the begetting of Christ (Luke 1:35).

And the angel answered and said to her, "The Holy Spirit will come upon you, and the power of the Highest will overshadow you; therefore, also, that Holy One who is to be born will be called the Son of God.

The Holy Spirit anointed and empowered Christ (Isaiah 61:1, Luke 4:14-21; John 3:34; Matthew 12:28; Acts 10:38).

Then Jesus returned in the power of the Spirit to Galilee, and news of Him went out through all the surrounding region. 15 And He taught in their synagogues, being glorified by all. 16 So He came to Nazareth, where He had been brought up. And as His custom was, He went into the synagogue on the Sabbath day, and stood up to read. 17 And He was handed the book of the prophet Isaiah. And when He had opened the book, He found the place where it was written: 18 "The Spirit of the LORD is upon Me, because He has anointed Me to preach the gospel to the poor; He has sent Me to heal the brokenhearted, to proclaim liberty to the captives and recovery of sight to the blind, to set at liberty those who are oppressed; 19 To proclaim the acceptable year of the LORD." 20 Then He closed the book, and gave it back to the attendant and sat down. And the eyes of all who were in the synagogue were fixed on Him. 21 And He began to say to them, "Today this Scripture is fulfilled in your hearing." Luke 4:14-21

The Holy Spirit gives divine gifts (1 Corinthians 12:4-11).

There are diversities of gifts, but the same Spirit. There are differences of ministries, but the same Lord. ⁶ And there are diversities of activities, but it is the same God who works all in all.

> *⁷ But the manifestation of the Spirit is given to each one for the profit of all: ⁸ for to one is given the word of wisdom through the Spirit, to another the word of knowledge through the same Spirit, ⁹ to another faith by the same Spirit, to another gifts of healings by the same Spirit, ¹⁰ to another the working of miracles, to another prophecy, to another discerning of spirits, to another different kinds of tongues, to another the interpretation of tongues. ¹¹ But one and the same Spirit works all these things, distributing to each one individually as He wills.*

The Statements, which at times refer to the Lord God, are equally applied to the Holy Spirit.

Compare the following: Isaiah 6:8-10 with Acts 28:25-27

> *Also I heard the voice of the Lord, saying: "Whom shall I send, and who will go for Us?" Then I said, "Here am I! Send me." 9 And He said, "Go, and tell this people: "Keep on hearing, but do not understand; keep on seeing, but do not perceive. 10 Make the heart of this people dull, and their ears heavy, and shut their eyes; lest they see with their eyes, and hear with their ears, and understand with their heart, and return and be healed." Isaiah 6:8-10*

In Isaiah it is the voice of the Lord. When this passage is quoted in the New Testament it is attributed to the Holy Spirit.

> *So when they did not agree among themselves, they departed after Paul had said one word: "The Holy Spirit spoke rightly through Isaiah the prophet to our fathers, saying, "Go to this people and*

say: "Hearing you will hear, and shall not understand; and seeing you will see, and not perceive..." Acts 28:25-26

Luke 1:68-70 with 2 Peter 1:20-21

Blessed is the Lord God of Israel, for He has visited and redeemed His people, and has raised up a horn of salvation for us in the house of His servant David, as He spoke by the mouth of His holy prophets, who have been since the world began... Luke 1:68-70

...knowing this first, that no prophecy of Scripture is of any private interpretation, for prophecy never came by the will of man, but holy men of God spoke as they were moved by the Holy Spirit. 2 Peter 1:20-21

Psalm 78:17-19 with Isaiah 63:10

But they sinned even more against Him by rebelling against the Most High in the wilderness. And they tested God in their heart by asking for the food of their fancy. Yes, they spoke against God: They said, "Can God prepare a table in the wilderness?" Psalm 78:17-19

But they rebelled and grieved His Holy Spirit; so He turned Himself against them as an enemy, and He fought against them. Isaiah 63:10

The name of the Holy Spirit is coupled with that of the Father and the Son (Matthew 28:19; Acts 2:38-39; 8:16; 10:48; 2 Corinthians 13:14; 1 Corinthians 12:4-6; Ephesians 2:18; Hebrews 9:14; 1 John 5:7-8).

Go therefore and make disciples of all the nations, baptizing them in the name of the Father and of the Son and of the Holy Spirit...
Matthew 28:19

Then Peter said to them, "Repent, and let every one of you be baptized in the name of Jesus Christ for the remission of sins; and you shall receive the gift of the Holy Spirit. ^{39} For the promise is to you and to your children, and to all who are afar off, as many as the Lord our God will call." Acts 2:38-39

The grace of the Lord Jesus Christ, and the love of God, and the communion of the Holy Spirit be with you all. Amen. 2 Corinthians 13:14

For there are three that bear witness in heaven: the Father, the Word, and the Holy Spirit; and these three are one. 1 John 5:7

For through Him we both have access by one Spirit to the Father. Ephesians 2:18

The Holy Spirit is called "God" (Acts 5:3-4; 2 Corinthians 3:18, NIV).

But Peter said, "Ananias, why has Satan filled your heart to lie to the Holy Spirit and keep back part of the price of the land for yourself? ^{4} While it remained, was it not your own? And after it was sold, was it not in your own control? Why have you conceived this thing in your heart? You have not lied to men but to God." Acts 5:3-4

And we, who with unveiled faces all reflect the Lord's glory, are being transformed into his likeness with ever-increasing glory, which comes from the Lord, who is the Spirit. 2 Corinthians 3:18, NIV

Divine names are ascribed to the Holy Spirit.

1. The Spirit of God (1 Peter 4:14; Genesis 1:2; 1 Corinthians 2:10-14)
2. The Spirit of Jesus (Acts 16:7, NIV)
3. The Spirit of the Living God (2 Corinthians 3:3)
4. The Spirit of the Father (Matthew 10:20).

The terms "Spirit of God" or "Spirit of the Lord" are used nearly seventy times in the Scripture in reference to the Holy Spirit.

How the Holy Spirit is distinguished from the Father and the Son

God has revealed Himself as three persons in one God. The persons of the Godhead are distinguishable, yet indivisible.

There are certain characteristics of the divine persons that are consistent throughout the Scripture as illustrated by the following chart:

Triune God		
Father	Son	Holy Spirit

Source	Central	Fruitfulness
Beginning	Begotten	Proceeding
Foundation	Sacrifice	Quickening
Covenants	Word	Gifts
Promises	Blood	Seal
First	Second	Third

The relationship is also seen in the following order of headship:

Sending

1. The Father sent the Son (John 3:16).
2. The Son sent the Spirit (John 16:7; 1 John 3:22-23).
3. The Spirit gave gifts to men (1 Corinthians 12:4-11).

Witness/Exaltation

1. The Spirit bears witness to and glorifies the Son (John 16:13-15).
2. The Son bears witness to and glorifies the Father (John 17:4).

Some of the demonstration representations of the Trinity in the Scripture

In creation (Genesis 1:1-3, 26; John 1:1-3; 1 John 5:7-8)

1. The Father spoke.
2. The Word went forth.
3. The Spirit moved.

In God's revealed name (Exodus 3:15).

1. The God of Abraham
2. The God of Isaac
3. The God of Jacob

In the typology of Aaron's rod (Number 17:1-10)

1. The Bud
2. The Flower
3. The Almond Fruit

At the immaculate birth of Christ (Matthew 1:20-21; Luke 1:31-35)

1. The Father sent.
2. The Son was incarnated.
3. The Holy Spirit overshadowed Mary.

At the water baptism of Christ (Luke 3:21-22)

When all the people were baptized, it came to pass that Jesus also was baptized; and while He prayed, the heaven was opened. [22] And the Holy Spirit descended in bodily form like a dove upon Him, and a voice came from heaven which said, "You are My beloved Son; in You I am well pleased." Luke 3:21-22

1. The Father spoke from heaven.
2. The Son was baptized in the Jordan.
3. The Spirit descended upon Jesus.

In Christ's ministry (Acts 10:38)

> *God anointed Jesus of Nazareth with the Holy Spirit and with power, who went about doing good and healing all who were oppressed by the devil, for God was with Him. Acts 10:38*

1. God anointed Jesus.
2. Jesus was anointed.
3. The Holy Spirit was the anointing.

In the commissioning of the disciples (Matthew 28:19)

> *Therefore go and make disciples of all nations, baptizing them in the name of the Father and of the Son and of the Holy Spirit...*

The disciples were to baptize in the name of the Father, the Son and the Holy Spirit.

At the exaltation of Christ (Acts 2:33)

> *This Jesus God has raised up, of which we are all witnesses. Therefore being exalted to the right hand of God, and having received from the Father the promise of the Holy Spirit, He poured out this which you now see and hear. Acts 2:32-33*

1. The Father fulfilled His promise to the exalted Son.
2. Jesus, at the right hand of the Father, received the promise.
3. The Holy Spirit is given by Jesus to the waiting disciples.

At the receiving of the Gentiles (Ephesians 2:18)

For through him we both have access to the Father by one Spirit.

At the martyrdom of Stephen (Acts 7:55-56)

But Stephen, full of the Holy Spirit, looked up to heaven and saw the glory of God, and Jesus standing at the right hand of God. "Look," he said, "I see heaven open and the Son of Man standing at the right hand of God."

1. The Father is seen as the "glory of God."
2. The Son is the Son of Man standing at the right hand of God.
3. Stephen is full of the Holy Spirit.

In His role in relation to the Church (1 Corinthians 12:4-6).

There are diversities of gifts, but the same Spirit. There are differences of ministries, but the same Lord. And there are diversities of activities, but it is the same God who works all in all.

1. The Holy Spirit gives gifts.
2. The Lord Jesus dispenses ministries (Ephesians 4:7-11).
3. God the Father provides the spiritual motivation and energy to activate the gifts and ministries.

DR. ABRAHAM PETERS

Other references in John:

1. John 14:16

And I will ask the Father, and he will give you another Counselor to be with you forever—

The Son prays to the Father.
The Father gives Holy Spirit (another Comforter/Counselor).

2. John 14:26

But the Counselor, the Holy Spirit, whom the Father will send in my name, will teach you all things and will remind you of everything I have said to you.

The Father sends the Comforter.
The Comforter is sent in the name of the Son.
The Holy Spirit teaches.

3. John 15:26

When the Counselor comes, whom I will send to you from the Father, the Spirit of truth who goes out from the Father, he will testify about me.

The Father is the source from which the Comforter comes.
The Son goes away and sends the Comforter.

Fellowship With The Holy Spirit

The Holy Spirit is the Comforter who testifies of the Son.

4. John 16:7, 10

But I tell you the truth: It is for your good that I am going away. Unless I go away, the Counselor will not come to you; but if I go, I will send him to you... 10 in regard to righteousness, because I am going to the Father, where you can see me no longer...

The Father is the One to whom the Son returns.
The Son goes away and sends the Comforter.

5. John 16:13-15

But when he, the Spirit of truth, comes, he will guide you into all truth. He will not speak on his own; he will speak only what he hears, and he will tell you what is yet to come. He will bring glory to me by taking from what is mine and making it known to you. All that belongs to the Father is mine. That is why I said the Spirit will take from what is mine and make it known to you.

The Father possesses all things and gives to the Son.
The Son is glorified by the Spirit.

You can study the following passages also: Ephesians 3:14-16; Philippians 3:3; Hebrews 9:14; 1 Peter 1:2; 3:18; 1 John 3:22-23; Jude 20-21; Revelation 1:4-5

For this reason I bow my knees to the Father of our Lord Jesus Christ, from whom the whole family in heaven and earth is named,

that He would grant you, according to the riches of His glory, to be strengthened with might through His Spirit in the inner man...
Ephesians 3:14-16

How much more shall the blood of Christ, who through the eternal Spirit offered Himself without spot to God, cleanse your conscience from dead works to serve the living God? Hebrews 9:14

...who have been chosen according to the foreknowledge of God the Father, through the sanctifying work of the Spirit, for obedience to Jesus Christ and sprinkling by his blood: Grace and peace be yours in abundance. 1 Peter 1:2

*But you, beloved, building yourselves up on your most holy faith, praying in the
Holy Spirit, keep yourselves in the love of God, looking for the mercy of our Lord
Jesus Christ unto eternal life.* Jude 20-21

The grace of the Lord Jesus Christ, and the love of God, and the communion of the Holy Spirit be with you all. Amen. 2 Corinthians 13:14

THE CHARACTERISTICS OF THE HOLY SPIRIT

The Holy Spirit is not only true God, but the Holy Spirit must be regarded as a person. There are those who relate to the Holy Spirit as a cosmic influence. To some the Holy Spirit is referred to as "it" rather than with the personal pronoun "He." Even though the word for spirit is neuter in its gender assignment, it is usually used with masculine pronouns (violating the rules of grammar).

The word "spirit" or "pneuma" in both the Hebrew and the Greek can be translated "wind, breath or spirit."

Why it is important to acknowledge the Holy Spirit as a person: It is important from the standpoint of worship and recognition. If we think of the Holy Spirit as an abstract or impersonal influence or power, we are robbing a Divine Person of the worship, love and recognition which are His due. It is important from the practical standpoint. If He is thought of as merely an influence or power, we will say, "How can I get a hold of it and use it?" But if we recognize Him as a Divine Person, our thoughts will be, "How can the Holy Spirit get a hold of me and use me?" This brings humility instead of self-exaltation.

It is important from the standpoint of experience. When we see the Holy Spirit as a person, we realize that a Divine Person actually dwells within us, not just a power or an influence over us. This will lead us to a richer experience of the "communion of the Holy Spirit" to which Paul refers (2 Corinthians 13:14).Every believer is called to a personal relationship with the Holy Spirit.

What are some of the lines of proof relative to the personality of the Holy Spirit?

The Holy Spirit is a person because Jesus referred to the Holy Spirit as a person (John 14:15:26; 16:7-8, 13-15). The personal pronouns are always associated with a person (masculine) not an "it" (neuter).

DR. ABRAHAM PETERS

But when the Helper comes, whom I shall send to you from the Father, the Spirit of truth who proceeds from the Father, He will testify of Me. John 15:26

However, when He, the Spirit of truth, has come, He will guide you into all truth; for He will not speak on His own authority, but whatever He hears He will speak; and He will tell you things to come. [14] He will glorify Me, for He will take of what is Mine and declare it to you. [15] All things that the Father has are Mine. Therefore I said that He will take of Mine and declare it to you.
John 16:13-15

The Holy Spirit is a person because His work is to carry on the ministry of a person, the Lord Jesus Christ (John 14:16-17). The "Another Helper" refers to "another of the same kind." If the Holy Spirit is to be able to do the work of and fulfill the ministry of Jesus in and through the church, He must be a person.

And I will pray the Father, and He will give you another Helper, that He may abide with you forever--the Spirit of truth, whom the world cannot receive, because it neither sees Him nor knows Him; but you know Him, for He dwells with you and will be in you. John 14:16-17

The Holy Spirit is a person because He has the three elements of personality.

1. The Holy Spirit has a mind (Romans 8:27).

Now He who searches the hearts knows what the mind of the Spirit is...

2. The Holy Spirit has a will (1 Corinthians 12:11).

But one and the same Spirit works all these things, distributing to each one individually as He wills.

3. The Holy Spirit has emotions (Romans 8:26-27; 15:30; Ephesians 4:30).

And do not grieve the Holy Spirit of God, by whom you were sealed for the day of redemption. Ephesians 4:30

Now I beg you, brethren, through the Lord Jesus Christ, and through the love of the Spirit, that you strive together with me in prayers to God for me... Romans 15:30

The Holy Spirit is a person because He performs actions that only a person can perform.

4. He speaks (2 Samuel 23:2; Acts 13:2; 1 Timothy 4:1; Revelation 2:7, 11, 17, 29).

As they ministered to the Lord and fasted, the Holy Spirit said, "Now separate to Me Barnabas and Saul for the work to which I have called them." Acts 13:2

5. He searches all things (1 Corinthians 2:10b).

For the Spirit searches all things, yes, the deep things of God.

1. He reveals or inspires (2 Peter 1:21).
2. He teaches (John 14:26).
3. He cries (Galatians 4:6).
4. He intercedes (Romans 8:26).
5. He calls and places men in service (Acts 13:2; 20:28).
6. He leads (Romans 8:14).
7. He rules (Acts 16:6-7).
8. He creates (Job 33:4).
9. He sanctifies (Romans 15:16; 2 Thessalonians 2:13).
10. He helps (Romans 8:26).
11. He gives gifts (1 Corinthians 12:7-11).
12. He works miracles (Acts 2:4; 8:39).
13. He bears witness (1 John 5:6).
14. He reproves (John 16:8-11).
15. He regenerates (John 3:5-6).
16. He guides into truth (John 16:13).
17. He glorifies Christ (John 16:14).
18. He strives with men (Genesis 6:3).
19. He guides into truth (John 16:13).
20. He sends (Isaiah 48:16).
21. He directs men in service (Acts 8:29; 10:19; 16:6-7).
22. He issues commands (Acts 16:6-7).
23. He has fellowship or communion (2 Corinthians 13:14).
24. He speaks to the churches (Revelation 2:7, 11, 17, 29; 3:6, 13, 22).
25. He comforts (John 14:26).

The Holy Spirit is a person because He has personal feelings ascribed to Him.

He can be:

1. Grieved (Ephesians 4:30).
2. Vexed or Rebelled Against (Isaiah 63:10).
3. Insulted (Hebrews 10:29).
4. Lied to (Acts 5:3).
5. Blasphemed (Matthew 12:31-32).
6. Resisted (Acts 7:51).
7. Put to the Test (Acts 5:9).
8. Quenched (1 Thessalonians 5:19).
9. Provoked (Psalm 106:33).
10. Pleased (Acts 15:28).

The Holy Spirit is a person because of the fact of His association with the Father and the Son who are persons (Matthew 28:19; 2 Corinthians 13:14; John 16:14; 1 John 5:7).

The Holy Spirit is a person because moral goodness is ascribed to Him (Nehemiah 9:20; Psalm 143:10; Compare Matthew 19:17).

You also gave Your good Spirit to instruct them, and did not withhold Your manna from their mouth, and gave them water for their thirst. Nehemiah 9:20

Teach me to do Your will, for You are my God; Your Spirit is good. Lead me in the land of uprightness. Psalm 143:10

So He said to him, "Why do you call Me good? No one is good but One, that is, God." Matthew 19:17

DR. ABRAHAM PETERS

The Holy Spirit is a person because various names are ascribed to Him that suggest personality. Further in the next chapter we will be looking at the various names and titles of the Holy Spirit. To avoid repetition, suffice it to say that many of the names and titles of the Holy Spirit link the Holy Spirit to the Father and the Son who are also persons. For the sake of this discussion of the quality characteristics personality of the Holy Spirit there is perhaps no stronger evidence than that of Jesus own reference to the Holy Spirit as "the Comforter."

What Jesus tell us about the Holy Spirit when He referred to Him as "the Comforter"

One of the most endearing names or titles of the Holy Spirit is that of "Comforter." The Greek word *parakletos* (Paraclete) is also rendered "counselor, helper or advocate." Jesus used this term four times in reference to the Holy Spirit (John 14:16; 26; 15:26; 16:7). This word is also used in reference to Jesus as our advocate with the Father (I John 2:1).

Comfort, aid and help are part of the nature of God toward His creation.

1. God the Father is described as the source of and the "God of all comfort" (2 Corinthians 1:3-4; See also Romans 15:5; 2 Thessalonians 2:16-17; Isaiah 51:12; 66:13).

   Blessed be the God and Father of our Lord Jesus Christ, the Father of mercies and God of all comfort, who comforts us in all

Fellowship With The Holy Spirit

our tribulation, that we may be able to comfort those who are in any trouble, with the comfort with which we ourselves are comforted by God. 2 Corinthians 1:3-4

2. Jesus is seen as our helper and our advocate (same word) with the Father (Luke 2:25; John 14:16; Philippians 2:1; I John 2:1).

Jesus was anticipated as the "Consolation of Israel."

And behold, there was a man in Jerusalem whose name was Simeon, and this man was just and devout, waiting for the Consolation of Israel, and the Holy Spirit was upon him. And it had been revealed to him by the Holy Spirit that he would not see death before he had seen the Lord's Christ. Luke 2:25-26

3. The Holy Spirit is called "the Comforter" by Jesus (John 14:16; 26; 15:26; 16:7; See also Acts 9:31).

4. The Word of God or the Scripture is also to be a "comforter" to God's people (Romans 15:4).

For whatever things were written before were written for our learning, that we through the patience and comfort of the Scriptures might have hope.

5. As believers, we are to share in this ministry one to another (2 Corinthians 1:4).

There are several characteristics of a comforter that are drawn from the meaning of the word itself. Think of these things in the context of Jesus' personal ministry to His disciples.

The job description of "comforters" looks like this:

6. They come to the side of and encourage people in times of tribulation, affliction, sorrow and bereavement (Matthew 2:18, 5:4; 1 Thessalonians 3:2-3).

7. They intercede or "stand in the gap" for those that are sick (Matthew 8:5).

8. They encourage and exhort people regarding their future in relation to God's purposes (1 Thessalonians 5:16-18; Luke 3:18).

9. They admonish people when they are not entering into the full privileges of their inheritance (Luke 15:28).

10. They warn the careless and apathetic of impending danger and encourage watchfulness (Romans 16:17).

11. They exhort and encourage people to follow the ways of God (Acts 2:40; 11:23; Ephesians 4:1; Jude 3).

12. They warn others of dangers they sense in the course they have set for themselves (Acts 21:12; 1Thessalonians 5:14; 2 Thessalonians 3:11-12).

13. They come to the side of those who have fallen, but have demonstrated repentance (2 Corinthians 2:7-8).

The Holy Spirit ministers as a comforter to us in the same way that Jesus ministered comfort to His disciples.

14. Jesus said that He would send another comforter to be with them.

There are two words that are used in the Greek language for "another."

    a. One word means "another of a different kind."

    b. The other word means "another of the same kind."

The word that Jesus used in reference to the Holy Spirit is this second usage. The Holy Spirit was to be another comforter "of the same kind" as Jesus. It is important for us to note that Jesus was assuring His disciples that the Holy Spirit would minister to them in exactly the same way that He had ministered to them.

15. Jesus said that it would be to our advantage that He go away and ascend to the Father (John 16:7).

Nevertheless I tell you the truth. It is to your advantage that I go away; for if I do not go away, the Helper will not come to you; but if I depart, I will send Him to you.

Prior to His ascension, Jesus was limited by His physical body. He was only able to minister to one set of circumstances or one group of people at a time. By sending the Holy Spirit, He would be able

DR. ABRAHAM PETERS

to minister to everyone, everywhere in the world at the same time. That is a huge advantage!

CHAPTER TWO

THE BIBLE SYMBOLS OF THE HOLY SPIRIT

DR. ABRAHAM PETERS

The Symbols and metaphors are where natural elements with which we are familiar are used to help us to understand things with which we are less familiar. They are like word parables. Every symbol can be taken beyond its intended function, however in the right setting, they can be very useful in explaining spiritual things by using natural things

For since the creation of the world His invisible attributes are clearly seen, being understood by the things that are made, even His eternal power and Godhead, so that they are without excuse...
(Romans 1:20).

When looking at symbols, it is important not to take a particular symbol beyond its biblical application. The Bible uses a number of symbols to describe the person and work of the Holy Spirit. These symbols show the nature, character and work of the Holy Spirit. They includes:

The Holy Spirit Comes as a Dove: When the Bible says that the Holy Spirit is like a dove, it does not mean that the Holy Spirit has two legs, two wings and eats seeds. The Bible itself will highlight the qualities that make the Holy Spirit like a dove. If we take the analogy beyond that of the biblical revelation we will open ourselves up to all kinds of misunderstandings and even false teaching. A Dove (Matthew 3:16; Luke 3:21-22; John 1:32)

When all the people were baptized, it came to pass that Jesus also was baptized; and while He prayed, the heaven was opened. And the Holy Spirit descended in bodily form like a dove upon Him, and a voice came from heaven which said, "You are My beloved Son; in You I am well pleased." Luke 3:21-22

This is one of the more common symbols of the Holy Spirit even in the church culture of our day. When someone wants people to know that their church is "Spirit-filled" they will often use a dove in the logo for that church or organization.

The first reference to the Holy Spirit in the Bible implies this symbol of a dove (or at least a bird) in connection with the Holy Spirit (Genesis 1:2).

The earth was without form, and void; and darkness was on the face of the deep. And the Spirit of God was hovering over the face of the waters.

The earth was without form and an empty waste, and darkness was upon the face of the very great deep. The Spirit of God was moving (hovering, brooding) over the face of the waters. –AMP

The Hebrew word for "hovered" or "brooded" over is depictive of a bird sitting on a nest of eggs to warm them to life.

The Latin Vulgate uses the word "*incubabat*" from which we get the English word "incubate." Figuratively used of the Spirit of God, who brooded over the shapeless mass of the earth cherishing and vivifying.

In this verse the moving of the Holy Spirit precedes the coming forth of light at the command of God (Genesis 1:3). The Holy Spirit is the one who prepares our hearts for the coming of the light of the Gospel.

DR. ABRAHAM PETERS

This Hebrew word only appears twice in the Old Testament:

As an eagle stirs up its nest, hovers over its young, spreading out its wings, taking them up, carrying them on its wings, so the LORD alone led him, and there was no foreign god with him.
(Deuteronomy 32:11-12).

When you put these two verses together they speak of the ministry of the Holy Spirit to both bring life and sustain life. Even though the second reference is specifically that of an eagle, the thought of God being our sustainer is the same.

The first specific mention of a dove in the Old Testament also gives us a picture of the ministry and work of the Holy Spirit :

So it came to pass, at the end of forty days, that Noah opened the window of the ark which he had made. 7 Then he sent out a raven, which kept going to and fro until the waters had dried up from the earth. 8 He also sent out from himself a dove, to see if the waters had receded from the face of the ground. 9 But the dove found no resting place for the sole of her foot, and she returned into the ark to him, for the waters were on the face of the whole earth. So he put out his hand and took her, and drew her into the ark to himself. 10 And he waited yet another seven days, and again he sent the dove out from the ark. 11 Then the dove came to him in the evening, and behold, a freshly plucked olive leaf was in her mouth; and Noah knew that the waters had receded from the earth. 12 So he waited yet another seven days and sent out the dove, which did not return again to him anymore. (Genesis 8:6-12).

The purpose of the sending out of the dove from the ark of Noah was to find a resting place on the earth. Had it found a resting place, Noah and his family would have known that it was safe to leave the ark themselves. The purpose of God in sending the Holy Spirit was for the Spirit to find a resting place in the hearts of men.

The dove (a clean bird) went out as well as a raven (an unclean bird). The Spirit of God has been sent out into a world where the devil also roams as a roaring lion seeking whom he may devour (Job 1:7; 2:2; 1 Peter 5:8).

And the LORD said to Satan, "From where do you come?" So Satan answered the LORD and said, "From going to and fro on the earth, and from walking back and forth on it." Job 1:7

Be sober, be vigilant; because your adversary the devil walks about like a roaring lion, seeking whom he may devour. 1 Peter 5:8

The three sendings forth of the dove give us a picture of the work and ministry of the Holy Spirit in the three dispensations of redemptive history.

FATHER	SON	HOLY SPIRIT
Dove & Raven Sent	*Dove Sent*	*Dove Sent*
♦ Dove Returns	♦ Dove Returns Olive Branch	♦ Remains
♦ No Rest	♦ No Rest	♦ Rest

The natural attributes of a dove make it a fitting symbol for the Holy Spirit.

DR. ABRAHAM PETERS

The dove is associated with gentleness (Matthew 10:16). *Behold, I send you out as sheep in the midst of wolves. Therefore be wise as serpents and harmless as doves.*

One reason that is given for the gentleness of the dove is that the bird has no gall, the gall being considered by the naturalists of old as the source and fountain of contention, the bitterness of gall being supposed to infuse itself into the spirit.

The dove is absolutely faithful in love (Song 1:15; 2:14; 5:12).

Doves have only one mate for life. The black dove will not reconnect with another dove even when its mate dies. It will remain a widow or a widower.

The dove (especially the white dove) is a symbol of purity. The dove was a clean bird that fed on seeds (the Word).

The dove was one of two birds that were used in the sacrifices of the Old Testament (Gen. 15:9; Lev. 12:6; Luke 2:24).

The dove is a universal symbol of peace. Of course the Holy Spirit is the agent of reconciliation or peace between God and man.

"And immediately, coming up from the water, He saw the heavens parting and the Spirit descending upon Him like a dove. (Mark 1:10). The Holy Spirit, coming as a dove, is gentle and a symbol of peace. What the dove did is important as well, the dove came and rested on Jesus (Matthew 3:16). The Holy Spirit wants to come and rest upon you and me. Not sweeping throughout the world as a tidal wave of revival, but to come to each of us personally. Today, I want to ask you to invite Him by saying, "Holy Spirit, come upon me." In fact, for the next week, take one symbol of the Holy Spirit each day and invite Him to do that freshly in your life. Let Jesus minister the richness of the Holy Spirit to you. The dove represents the gentleness and peace which the Holy Spirit provides the believer "And the Holy Spirit descended in bodily form like a dove upon Him, and a voice came from heaven which said, "You are My beloved Son; in You I am well pleased" (Luke 3:22). The Bible says it is Jesus who baptizes with the Holy Spirit (Mark 1:8), and He will:

> *Pour rain on you*
> *Open rivers in you*
> *Breathe wind into your life*
> *Anoint you with oil*
> *Fill you with holy wine*
> *Refine and temper you with fire*
> *Send the Holy Spirit to come to you*

The Holy Spirit Comes as Wind:

The Bible has several symbols for the Holy Spirit. The Greek and Hebrew words translated "spirit" (pneuma and ruach) are also translated either "wind" or "breath. One is wind, which in the original Greek in the New Testament is the same word as breath. Wind helps us to visualize the invisible and mysterious movement of the Spirit. The Holy Spirit, coming as wind, depicts His power and His guidance. When Jesus tells Nicodemus about the new birth experience (John 3:8), He tells him that it is not like a tangible birth where you can see the baby is born and check the clock for its time of arrival. The work of the Spirit breathes into a life, and something transpires that people cannot recognize. There is a dynamism but also a gentleness, like the wisp of a breeze. You can't necessarily see where it came from or where it goes, but all of us can attest to times when God has come and dealt with us, and no human being knew how it happened.

Wind Or Breath, the wind symbolizes the invisible yet powerful work of the Holy Spirit. And suddenly there came a sound from heaven, as of a rushing mighty wind, and it filled the whole house where they were sitting (Acts 2:2). At Pentecost (Acts 2:3), it wasn't a wind that blew in; it was the sound of a rushing wind just like a hurricane. That sound, not the sound of the people speaking in tongues, is what drew the crowd in. The Holy Spirit as sovereign God is dynamic, irresistible, and unstoppable. A dove symbolized the Spirit during Jesus' baptism. "Just as Jesus was coming up out of the water, he saw heaven being torn open and the Spirit descending on him like a dove" (Mark 1:10). The Holy Spirit is all-powerful yet strangely gentle and sensitive in His dealings with us. We can all too easily grieve Him.

The Holy Spirit Comes as Fire:

At Pentecost, the Bible says that tongues as of fire appeared over the heads of each of those who gathered together (Acts 2:3). The Holy Spirit comes as fire to work something deep into the substance of our lives that will shape things around us, rather than us taking on the shape of the world. As fire, He works in a dual way: to probe the inner recesses of our life and to refine us as gold or silver is refined in the fire; and to temper our personalities by causing there to be the penetration of fire into our system.

The purifying fire burns out the Adversary. When the three Hebrew children were thrown into the furnace, not only were their lives spared, but also their clothes didn't burn. But the ropes holding them in bondage burned. The Bible speaks of the Holy Spirit being "a spirit of judgment and burning" (Isaiah 4:4). Judgment has to do with deliverance, in the way the judges of Israel led people out of bondage. The Holy Spirit, coming like fire, burns away any binding grip that the Enemy has imposed on us.

Fire speaks of the holiness of God and the judging of sin in the life of the believer. "When the Lord has washed away the filth of the daughters of Zion, and purged the blood of Jerusalem from her midst, by the spirit of judgment and by the spirit of burning (Isaiah 4:4). Fire is one of my favorite symbols for the Holy Spirit. It is used to represent the power and presence of God. When John the Baptist came on the scene before Jesus appeared, he said, "I baptize you with water. But one who is more powerful than I will come . . . He will baptize you with the Holy Spirit and fire" (Luke 3:16, emphasis added).

Holy Spirit Fire (Matthew 3:11) It is not uncommon for one symbol to be used to represent more than one thing in the Bible. For instance a lion is sometimes applied to Christ as the Lion of the Tribe of Judah (Revelation 5:5) and sometimes a lion is applied to Satan like, as a roaring lion (1 Pet. 5:8). Fire is used as a symbol for several things in the Bible; The Presence of the Lord (Exodus 3:2; 8:21; Zechariah 2:5) The Lord's Approval, when fire came down from heaven (Leviticus 9:24; 2 Chronicles 7:1; 1 Kings. 18:38) God's Nature (Hebrews 12:29) The Word of God (Jeremiah 5:14; 20:9) Discipline and Testing (Malachi 3:3; 1 Peter 1:7; Revelation 1:14) Judgment (Leviticus 10:2; 2 Kings. 1:10-12)

Fire consumes wood, hay and stubble (Isaiah 4:4; 1 Corinthians 3:12-15). The Holy Spirit consumes the chaff in our lives.

When the Lord has washed away the filth of the daughters of Zion, and purged the blood of Jerusalem from her midst, by the spirit of judgment and by the spirit of burning, then the LORD will create above every dwelling place of Mount Zion, and above her assemblies, a cloud and smoke by day and the shining of a flaming fire by night. For over all the glory there will be a covering. Isaiah 4:4-5

Now if anyone builds on this foundation with gold, silver, precious stones, wood, hay, straw, each one's work will become clear; for the Day will declare it, because it will be revealed by fire; and the fire will test each one's work, of what sort it is. If anyone's work which he has built on it endures, he will receive a reward. If anyone's work is burned, he will suffer loss; but he himself will be saved, yet so as through fire. 1Corinthians 3:12-15

Fire purifies gold, silver and precious stones (Isaiah 6:7; 1 Cor. 3:12-15). The Holy Spirit takes us through testings that bring out the best in us (1 Peter 1:7; Job 23:10).

In this you greatly rejoice, though now for a little while, if need be, you have been grieved by various trials, that the genuineness of your faith, being much more precious than gold that perishes, though it is tested by fire, may be found to praise, honor, and glory at the revelation of Jesus Christ... 1Peter 1:6-7

But He knows the way that I take; when He has tested me, I shall come forth as gold. Job 23:10

Fires causes things to heat up (Isaiah 64:1-2). The Holy Spirit inspires a holy zealousness in the people of God and warms our spiritual temperature (Isaiah 44:16).

Oh, that You would rend the heavens! That You would come down! That the mountains might shake at Your presence as fire burns brushwood, as fire causes water to boil--to make Your name known to Your adversaries, that the nations may tremble at Your presence! Isaiah 64:1-2

Fire illuminates the obscure and gives light to our path (Psalm 78:14; 1 Cor. 2:9-10; Ephesians 1:17-18).The Holy Spirit is the revealer who shows us the deep things of God and illuminates the Word of God to our hearts.

In the daytime also He led them with the cloud, and all the night with a light of fire. Psalm 78:14

But as it is written: "Eye has not seen, nor ear heard, nor have entered into the heart of man the things which God has prepared for those who love Him." But God has revealed them to us through His Spirit. For the Spirit searches all things, yes, the deep things of God. 1 Corinthians 2:9-10

The Holy Spirit Comes as Rivers:

Rivers are channels or conduits to places where the refreshing of water is needed. John pinpoints that the work of the Spirit as "rivers of living water" was to become available after Jesus' ascension (John 7:37-39). The Holy Spirit is manifest in rivers in order that the rain not only be a refreshing upon you, but also that the Lord would make you an overflowing tributary of His Holy Spirit fullness, life, and love to others. The Lord wants people to get in touch with who He is, and that takes people who will let the rivers of living water be awakened in them and then gush out of their lives. So the Holy Spirit is manifest in rivers. The Holy Spirit is symbolized by water. This speaks of refreshing, cleansing and washing the believer of his sins. Jesus said: If anyone thirsts, let him come to Me and drink. He who believes in Me, as the Scripture has said, out of his heart will flow rivers of living water. But this He spoke concerning the Spirit, whom those believing in Him would receive; for the Holy Spirit was not yet given, because Jesus was not yet glorified (John 7:37-39).

The Holy Spirit Comes as Rain:

Rain has a dual implication. First as refreshing where there has been dryness and barrenness (Joel 2:23-29). Second, as restoration where there has been loss (Isaiah 28:11-12). The "pouring out" Peter refers to at Pentecost (Acts 2:17) is not an abstract use of the word; it has to do with "latter rain" that brought about the hastening of the harvest and fruitful crops. The Lord is saying that He will send rain to fields [people] that are totally barren as a promise of hope. Needing to be refreshed doesn't mean that I've backslid or sinned. When the lawn endures a hot day, it dries up and needs the refreshing of rain. The Holy Spirit, coming as rain, comes to bring refreshing and restoration.

The Holy Spirit Comes as Wine:

Ephesians 5:18 draws an analogy for the symbolism of the Holy Spirit as wine. In the Gospels, Jesus describes the new work of God, conveyed by the ministry of the Spirit, as new wine coming into old vessels. So it's a perfectly appropriate symbol in light of the Word. Still, let me ask you, what does it take to excite your life? The issue isn't just alcohol; the issue is, how much of what the world offers does it take to get you going? The Bible doesn't say we are disallowed from enjoying a number of the things that come with life, but you can find out how much a person is living the Jesus life by how much they need the stimulants of the world. The separated, holy Christian life is not a call to isolation but to insulation. You live in the world, but His Spirit in you keeps out the world's pollution.

The Holy Spirit Comes as Oil:

The anointing, the oil of Scripture is directly related to the Holy Spirit's work in our life (2 Corinthians 1:21-22). The Holy Spirit's anointing makes us sensitive (1 John 2:20). How many times have you sensed something was wrong, or something was right, but you didn't know why or how you knew? The Holy Spirit, by His anointing and presence, confirms what He is the Spirit of Truth, of Holiness, of Wisdom. Obeying the Holy Spirit means that He will give us wisdom when we need it in the practicals of our everyday life.

Oil was involved in the anointing of the prophets, priests and kings for ministry to their offices. Oil symbolizes the soothing and healing presence of the Holy Spirit. God anointed Jesus of Nazareth with the Holy Spirit and with power, who went about doing good and healing all who were oppressed by the devil, for God was with Him (Acts

10:38). Oil is a symbol often used for the Holy Spirit in the Old Testament. The anointing of the Holy Spirit is likened to the oil that was put on almost everything in the tabernacle. When it was built as a place of worship, not only were the temple objects anointed with oil, but so also were the priests. Later the elders of the early church were instructed to pray for the sick and to anoint the ailing believers with oil as a symbol of the Holy Spirit (James 5:14).

"And Moses took the anointing oil and anointed the tabernacle and all that was therein, and sanctified them. . . . And he poured of the anointing oil upon Aaron's head, and anointed him to sanctify him." Leviticus 8:10,12

"The Spirit of the Lord GOD is upon me; because the LORD hath anointed me to preach good tidings unto the meek . . . " Isaiah 61:1

These two texts show a close connection between the holy anointing oil and the work of the holy spirit. The olive tree was a staple of ancient Israel's agricultural economy. Olive oil was one of the main commodities used in the services of ancient Israel's tabernacle in the wilderness. It was used for anointing and as fuel for the golden candlesticks. It was baked into certain wafers used in sacrifice and poured upon other sacrifices. In fact the word oil appears some ninety times in the books of Exodus and Leviticus alone.

Here are some of the places where there's a parallel in the operation of the holy spirit: Anointing. The act of anointing indicated the bestowal of authorization through the spirit to act in certain capacities.

Kings were anointed. Not only were kings of Israel anointed (1 Samuel 10:1; 16:13) but even the wicked king Hazael of Syria was spoken of as being anointed (1 Kings 19:16). Cyrus of Persia is spoken of as anointed (Isaiah 45:1). The custom of anointing kings was not unique to Israel; the el-Amarna letters of Egypt record some 37 instances of the practice.

Priests were anointed. In establishing a priesthood for Israel, not only was Aaron anointed (Leviticus 8:12), his sons were too (Numbers 3:3). The unity of the priesthood's anointing with the high priest is nicely expressed in Psalm 133:1,2.

A Prophet was anointed. The only biblical example was when Elijah was told to anoint Elisha as his successor (1 Kings 19:16).

Jesus was anointed. The anointing of Isaiah 61:1 is applied by Jesus to himself in Luke 4:18,19. The same anointing authorizes the church as his body to spread the good tidings in his name.

This was the formula for the oil used for anointing: "Take unto thee principal spices, of pure myrrh five hundred shekels, and of sweet cinnamon half so much, even two hundred and fifty shekels, and of sweet calamus two hundred and fifty shekels, and of cassia five hundred shekels, after the shekel of the sanctuary, and of olive oil an hin: and thou shalt make it a holy ointment, an ointment compound after the art of the apothecary: it shall be an holy anointing oil" (Exodus 30:23-25). These four spices might correspond to the four attributes of the holy spirit given in Isaiah 11:2, "The spirit of the LORD shall rest upon him, (1) the spirit of wisdom and understanding, (2) the spirit of counsel and might, (3) the spirit of knowledge and (4) of the fear of the LORD." (Exodus 31:3.)

Medicinal properties. "Is any sick among you? let him call for the elders of the church, and let them pray over him, anointing him with oil in the name of the Lord" (James 5:14). The word here translated sickness in the next verse is astheneo, and literally means "without strength" and may refer to spiritual depression as well as physical sickness. In verse 15 the word sick is the Greek kamnos and is translated "be wearied" in Hebrews 12:3.

The prophet wrote of medical treatment using oil: "From the sole of the foot even to the head there is no soundness in it, but wounds, and bruises, and putrefying sores: they have not been closed, neither bound up, neither mollified with ointment" (Isaiah 1:6). The Good Samaritan "bound his wounds, pouring in oil and wine, and set him on his own beast, and brought him to an inn, and took care of him." When the Master sent out the twelve two by two, among other acts they "cast out many devils, and anointed with oil many that were sick, and healed them" (Mark 6:13).

It was for a similar purpose that the familiar twenty-third psalm says, "Thou anointest my head with oil." Here is a detailed description of this act - At the sheepfold there is a large bowl of olive oil mingled with spices, and a large jar of water. As the sheep pass through the gate, the shepherd examines each head and body for wounds. These are carefully cleaned as the shepherd dips his hand into the oil to anoint the injury. A cup is dipped into the water and comes out overflowing and the sheep drinks until refreshed.

Soap and toiletries. Processed oil has the texture of lotion and is used as a moisturizer. It was with this balm that a woman ministered unto Jesus in the Pharisee's house. Jesus said, "My head with oil thou didst not anoint; but this woman hath anointed my feet with ointment" (Luke 7:46). Likewise the prophet writes, "Then washed I thee with water; yea, I thoroughly washed away thy blood from thee, and I anointed thee with oil" (Ezekiel 16:9).

All the primary offices of Scripture, prophets, priests, and kings, involve anointing. And all of these are offices to which all of us are called. As prophets, we are called to speak the Word of the Lord. There are times when the Holy Spirit will give you words of comfort, exhortation, or sensitive counsel to say to other people. As priests, the Lord wants to anoint us for worship to renew us, so that our worship doesn't become stale, habitual, or formal. And as kings, we don't just get anointed once for all. It takes fresh anointing from the Holy Spirit for the dominion of His Kingdom and the authority of His life to happen through us. When it does, we can move in confidence about how to rule our homes and our businesses, and how to deal with our kids and our relationships. God's not going to anoint us with the ability to rule when we try to manage things our own way.

The Lord also wants to anoint those who have been overcome by the spirit of mourning with the oil of rejoicing. That anointing brings the lifting of our heads with the refreshing of seeing beyond today, not with superficial optimism, but with a deep abiding of hope that has been begotten in us by God.

The Holy Spirit Comes as Light:

The most noted use of olive oil is as fuel for the golden lampstand in the holy of the tabernacle (Exodus 35:14). The operation of these lampstands can be seen by comparing Zechariah 4:1-14 with Revelation 11:1,2. In Zechariah the oil for the lampstand's seven lamps comes from two olive trees, which are identified in Revelation as God's "two witnesses" (the Old and New Testaments). The seven pipes carrying the oil represent the means of conveying this oil to the lamps, i.e., the seven messengers of Revelation 2 and 3. The concept of the oil of the holy spirit being used for light is also shown in the parable of the wise and foolish virgins (Matthew 25:1-13). There the supply of oil distinguishes the one group from the other. This illustrates how some Christians with a sufficiency of the holy spirit become a part of the wedding party, while those having little or none do not. Number Seven: Seven speaks of completion. When used of the Holy Spirit it symbolizes the Spirits fullness and perfection. John, to the seven churches which are in Asia: Grace to you and peace from Him who is and who was and who is to come, and from the seven Spirits who are before His throne (Revelation 1:4).

Still Small Voice:

The Spirit is the voice of God that speaks to our innermost being. "Then He said, "Go out and stand on the mountain of the Lord." And behold, the Lord passed by, and a great and strong wind tore into the mountains and broke the rocks in pieces before the Lord, but the Lord was not in the wind; and after the wind an earthquake, but the Lord was not in the earthquake; and after the earthquake a fire, but the Lord was not in the fire; and after the fire a still small voice. So it was, when Elijah heard it, that he wrapped his face in his mantle and went out and stood in the entrance of the cave. And suddenly a voice came to him, and said, "What are you doing here, Elijah?" (1 Kings 19:11-13).

The Holy Spirit is referred to as the "deposit," "seal," and "earnest" in the hearts of Christians (2 Corinthians 1:22; 5:5; Ephesians 1:13-14; 4:30).

The Holy Spirit is God's seal on His people, His claim on us as His very own. The Greek word translated "earnest" in these passages is arrhabōn which means "a pledge," that is, part of the purchase money or property given in advance as security for the rest. The gift of the Spirit to believers is a down payment on our heavenly inheritance, which Christ has promised us and secured for us at the cross. It is because the Spirit has sealed us that we are assured of our salvation. No one can break the seal of God.

The Holy Spirit is given to believers as a "first installment" to assure us that our full inheritance as children of God will be delivered. The Holy Spirit is given to us to confirm to us that we belong to God who grants to us His Spirit as a gift, just as grace and faith are gifts (Ephesians 2:8-9). Through the gift of the Spirit, God renews and sanctifies us. He produces in our hearts those feelings, hopes, and desires which are evidence that we are accepted by God, that we are regarded as His adopted children, that our hope is genuine, and that our redemption and salvation are sure in the same way that a seal guarantees a will or an agreement. God grants to us His Holy Spirit as the certain pledge that we are His forever and shall be saved in the last day. The proof of the Spirit's presence is His operations on the heart which produce repentance, the fruit of the Spirit (Galatians 5:22-23), conformity to God's commands and will, a passion for prayer and praise, and love for His people. These things are the evidences that the Holy Spirit has renewed the heart and that the Christian is sealed for the day of redemption. So it is through the Holy Spirit and His teachings and guiding power that we are sealed and confirmed until the day of redemption, complete and free from the corruption of sin and the grave. Because we have the seal of the Spirit in our hearts, we can live joyfully, confident of our sure place in a future that holds unimaginable glories. Earnest: The earnest was the down payment, a pledge of more to come. The Spirit pledges that our salvation will be completed when we are glorified with Christ. Who is the guarantee of our inheritance until the redemption of the purchase possession, to the praise of His glory

> *In Him you also trusted, after you heard the word of truth, the gospel of your salvation; in whom also, having believed, you were sealed with the Holy Spirit of promise, who is the guarantee of our inheritance until the redemption of the purchased possession, to the praise of His glory.* (Ephesians 1:13-14)

This symbol emphasizes the work of the Holy Spirit in confirming our place in the family of God and that the Holy Spirit is God's stamp of authenticity upon us that we are indeed His property. The concept of a seal was common in ancient cultures. The seal was used to give proof of authenticity to letters or royal commands (1 Kings. 21:8; Esther. 8:8, 10; 3:12).

The seal was used to give formal ratification to a transaction or covenant (Jeremiah 32:10-14, 44). The seal was used in relation to the preservation and security of important of books. In order for someone to open the book they had to have the authorization to break the seal (Jeremiah 32:14; Revelation 5:1-9; 6:1-3).

The seal was an object representing authority and power that was at times given to a king's official representative so that he could act in behalf of the king (Genesis 41:42; Esther 3:10; 8:2).

Then Pharaoh took his signet ring off his hand and put it on Joseph's hand; and he clothed him in garments of fine linen and put a gold chain around his neck. Genesis 41:42

The seal was even used to stamp possessions as a sign of ownership much like a potter or an artist would sign his work (Job 38:14). This concept is applied to God's relationship with us.

The Holy Spirit is God's way of authenticating us as a genuine part of His family. God's indication or signature on the covenant that has been given to us *Now He who establishes us with you in Christ and has anointed us is God, who also has sealed us and given us the Spirit in our hearts as a guarantee.* (2 Corinthians 1:21-22).

God's assurance that even as a book is sealed and cannot be opened until the proper time by the proper person, so we are sealed by the Holy Spirit unto the day of redemption *And do not grieve the Holy Spirit of God, by whom you were sealed for the day of redemption.* Ephesians 4:30. God's sign that we are His official representatives on earth with the power and authority to use His name *And these signs will follow those who believe: In My name they will cast out demons; they will speak with new tongues; they will take up serpents; and if they drink anything deadly, it will by no means hurt them; they will lay hands on the sick, and they will recover.* (Mark 16:17-18).

God's mark of ownership upon our lives. He is the potter we are the clay (Isaiah 64:8). We are the work of his hands (Psalm 8:3-5). *But now, O LORD, You are our Father; we are the clay, and You our potter; and all we are the work of Your hand.* Isaiah 64:8

Firstfruits: The firstfruits were a symbol of the coming harvest. The initial work of the Holy Spirit symbolizes the final salvation and glorification of each believer. "And not only they, but we also who have the firstfruits of the Spirit, even we ourselves groan within ourselves, eagerly waiting for the adoption, the redemption of our body (Romans 8:23)

CLOUD/GLORY – Presence: This symbol could easily be argued as representing God Himself rather than the Holy Spirit. But because the presence of God is often displayed through workings of the Holy Spirit, and the common references to fire and cloud together in the Old Testament, I believe the presence of the Holy Spirit is also represented. The New Testament uses the word "glory" more to describe a tangible presence of God, explaining why I've combined the two here. Exodus 13:21-22, Exodus 16:10, Numbers 9:15, 1 Kings 8:10-11,Ezekiel 10:4, Mark 13:26, John 1:14, 2 Corinthians 3:7-8, 1 Peter 4:14, Revelation 15:8. He comes as a CLOUD! Exodus 33:9 - And it came to pass, as Moses entered into the tabernacle, the cloudy pillar descended, and stood at the door of the tabernacle, and the Lord talked with Moses. He will supply our needs as He did for Israel in the wilderness - Isaiah 44:3 For I will pour water upon him that is thirsty, and floods upon the dry ground: I will pour my spirit upon thy seed, and my blessing upon thine offspring:

CLOTHING/Enduement: Enduement speaks of the divine clothing of the believer with the Holy Spirit. Jesus said to His disciples: Behold, I send the Promise of My Father upon you; but tarry in the city of Jerusalem until you are endued with power from on high (Luke 24:49). There is an interesting correlation between Genesis and Galatians referring to clothing, which is clearly symbolic of Jesus Christ, but also indirectly the Holy Spirit. Genesis 2:25, Genesis 3:8-11, Genesis 3:21, Galatians 3:27, Romans 13:13. These different symbols that the Bible uses to describe the person and work of the Holy Spirit will begin to give us an idea of how He works in our life. Acts 19:11-12 Miracles Glorify Christ 11 Now God worked unusual miracles by the hands of Paul, 12 so that even handkerchiefs or aprons were brought from his body to the sick, and the diseases left them and the evil spirits went out of them.

The Holy Spirit doesn't seek to be mysterious, but He is the most mysterious of the Godhead. We can read in the Word about the Father, and we can read about the Son who came and walked among us. But Jesus tells us that when the Spirit comes, He will not speak of Himself; that "whatsoever he shall hear, that shall he speak: and he will shew you things to come" (John 16:13).

The workings of the Holy Spirit are invisible, glorious, and gentle, and within them, He never tells us about Himself. He comes to glorify Jesus helping us to see Jesus more, to understand Jesus better, to respond to Jesus more obediently, and to love Jesus with a deeper heart of commitment. So the symbols of the Holy Spirit become essential to our gaining an understanding of what He's like, not only in an objective way of analyzing truth, but also in the subjective way that He comes to penetrate our lives ways in which the reality of the invisible penetrate the visible. When we talk about the Holy Spirit as rain, for example, the purpose isn't to think, "Oh, the Holy Spirit is like rain." The purpose is to get wet. In each of these ways, the Lord desires to move into our realm. Just as the Holy Spirit manifested for a moment in a dove and lighted upon Jesus, He wants to penetrate you and me with the glory of the invisible God that becomes visible in us to flood His life into ours that we might then overflow it to others.

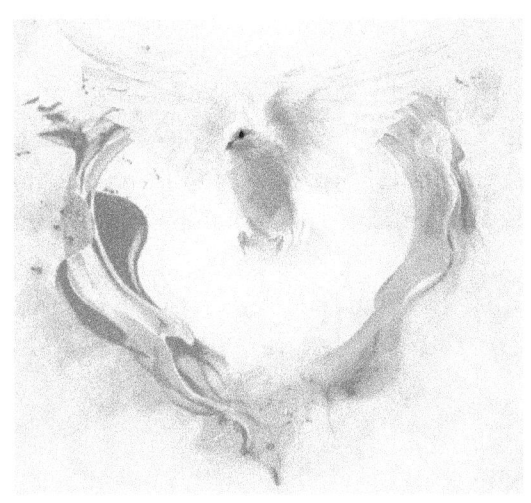

CHAPTER THREE

THE WORK OF THE HOLY IN THE OLD TESTAMENT

DR. ABRAHAM PETERS

While we often see the Holy Spirit in connection with the dispensation of the Holy Spirit under the New Covenant, as with all members of the Godhead, He has had His part to play even in the Old Testament.

How the Holy Spirit was involved in the Old Testament:

The Holy Spirit worked in creation. We have already noted that all of the members of the Godhead were actively involved in creation, just as they are all actively involved in our redemption. However, there are verses that indicate the particular role of the Holy Spirit.

The Heaven of Heavens and the Angelic Orders Psalm 33:6 *By the word of the LORD the heavens were made, and all the host of them by the breath of His mouth.*

The Atmospheric Heavens (Job 26:13a)

> *By His Spirit He adorned the heavens...*

The Earth (Genesis 1:1-2; Psalm 104:30; Isaiah 40:12-14)

The Holy Spirit is definitely connected with the planning and management of all that we see.

> *Who has measured the water in the hollow of His hand, measured heaven with a span and calculated the dust of the earth in a measure? Weighed the mountains in scales and the hills in a balance? 13 Who has directed the Spirit of the LORD, or as His counselor has taught Him? 14 With whom did He take counsel, and who instructed Him, and taught Him in the path of justice?*

Who taught Him knowledge, and showed Him the way of understanding? Isaiah 40:12-14

Animal Life (Psalm 104:24-30)

O LORD, how manifold are Your works! In wisdom You have made them all. The earth is full of Your possessions-- 25 This great and wide sea, in which are innumerable teeming things, living things both small and great. 26 There the ships sail about; there is that Leviathan which You have made to play there...30 You send forth Your Spirit, they are created; and You renew the face of the earth.
Psalm 104:24-26, 30

Human Life (Job 33:4)

The Spirit of God has made me, and the breath of the Almighty gives me life.

The Holy Spirit worked in the writing of Scripture (2 Timothy 3:16a).

All Scripture is God-breathed...

The Holy Spirit inspired holy men of God in the Old Testament (1 Peter 1:1012; 2 Peter 1:21).

Of this salvation the prophets have inquired and searched carefully, who prophesied of the grace that would come to you, searching what, or what manner of time, the Spirit of Christ who was in them was indicating when He testified beforehand the sufferings of Christ and the glories that would follow. To them it

> *was revealed that, not to themselves, but to us they were ministering the things which now have been reported to you through those who have preached the gospel to you by the Holy Spirit sent from heaven--things which angels desire to look into.* 1 Peter 1:10-12

> *...knowing this first, that no prophecy of Scripture is of any private interpretation, for prophecy never came by the will of man, but holy men of God spoke as they were moved by the Holy Spirit.* 2 Peter 1:20-21

The Old Testament writers recognized that they were inspired by God, the Holy Spirit (2 Samuel 23:1-2; Ezekiel 2:2; Micah 3:8).

> *Now these are the last words of David. Thus says David the son of Jesse; thus says the man raised up on high, the anointed of the God of Jacob, and the sweet psalmist of Israel: "The Spirit of the LORD spoke by me, and His word was on my tongue."* 2 Samuel 23:1-2

> *But truly I am full of power by the Spirit of the LORD, and of justice and might, to declare to Jacob his transgression and to Israel his sin.* Micah 3:8

The New Testament attributes many Old Testament verses specifically to inspiration of the Holy Spirit (Matthew 22:43; Mark 12:36; Acts 1:16; 4:25 [NIV]; 28:25 [Compare Isaiah 6:9-10]; Hebrews 3:7; 10:15-16).

> *While the Pharisees were gathered together, Jesus asked them, saying,*

"What do you think about the Christ? Whose Son is He? They said to Him, "The Son of David." He said to them, "How then does David in the Spirit call Him 'Lord,' saying: 'The LORD said to my Lord, sit at My right hand, till I make Your enemies Your footstool'? If David then calls Him 'Lord,' how is He his Son?" And no one was able to answer Him a word, nor from that day on did anyone dare question Him anymore. Matthew 22:41-46

And in those days Peter stood up in the midst of the disciples (altogether the number of names was about a hundred and twenty), and said, "Men and brethren, this Scripture had to be fulfilled, which the Holy Spirit spoke before by the mouth of David concerning Judas, who became a guide to those who arrested Jesus; for he was numbered with us and obtained a part in this ministry." Acts 1:15-17

You spoke by the Holy Spirit through the mouth of your servant, our father David... Acts 4:25a, NIV

The Holy Spirit worked with men of the New Testament to ensure our having God's word.

The New Testament writers recognized that they were inspired by God (1 Corinthians 11:23; 15:3; Galatians 1:11-12; Ephesians 3:3-5).

For I received from the Lord what I also passed on to you... 1 Corinthians 11:23a

I want you to know, brothers, that the gospel I preached is not something that man made up. I did not receive it from any man, nor was I taught it; rather, I received it by revelation from Jesus Christ. Galatians 1:11-12, NIV

For this reason I, Paul, the prisoner of Christ Jesus for you Gentiles--2 if indeed you have heard of the dispensation of the grace of God which was given to me for you, 3 how that by revelation He made known to me the mystery (as I have briefly written already 4 by which, when you read, you may understand my knowledge in the mystery of Christ 5 which in other ages was not made known to the sons of men, as it has now been revealed by the Spirit to His holy apostles and prophets: 6 that the Gentiles should be fellow heirs, of the same body, and partakers of His promise in Christ through the gospel, 7 of which I became a minister according to the gift of the grace of God given to me by the effective working of His power. Ephesians 3:1-7

Christ promised His disciples that the Holy Spirit would help them to provide an accurate recounting of His teaching and the events of His life (John 14:25-26).

These things I have spoken to you while being present with you. But the Helper, the Holy Spirit, whom the Father will send in My name, He will teach you all things, and bring to your remembrance all things that I said to you.

The Holy Spirit worked in bringing men to God. The Holy Spirit was striving with man (Genesis 6:1-3). The word "strive" also means to "contend or plead with."

Now it came to pass, when men began to multiply on the face of the earth, and daughters were born to them, that the sons of God saw

> *the daughters of men, that they were beautiful; and they took wives for themselves of all whom they chose. And the LORD said, "My Spirit shall not strive with man forever, for he is indeed flesh; yet his days shall be one hundred and twenty years."*

The Holy Spirit was often resisted in this work by the people of God themselves (Acts 7:51-53).

> *You stiff-necked and uncircumcised in heart and ears! You always resist the Holy Spirit; as your fathers did, so do you. Which of the prophets did your fathers not persecute? And they killed those who foretold the coming of the Just One, of whom you now have become the betrayers and murderers, who have received the law by the direction of angels and have not kept it.*

The Holy Spirit worked enabling men to do special tasks. Building the House of God

The Tabernacle of Moses (Exodus 31:1-6; 35:30-35)

> *Then the LORD spoke to Moses, saying: "See, I have called by name Bezalel the son of Uri, the son of Hur, of the tribe of Judah. And I have filled him with the Spirit of God, in wisdom, in understanding, in knowledge, and in all manner of workmanship, to design artistic works, to work in gold, in silver, in bronze, in cutting jewels for setting, in carving wood, and to work in all manner of workmanship. And I, indeed I, have appointed with him Aholiab the son of Ahisamach, of the tribe of Dan; and I have put wisdom in the hearts of all the gifted artisans, that they may make all that I have commanded you."* Exodus 31:1-6

DR. ABRAHAM PETERS

The Temple of Solomon (1 Chronicles 28:11-12, 19)

Then David gave his son Solomon the plans for the vestibule, its houses, its treasuries, its upper chambers, its inner chambers, and the place of the mercy seat; and the plans for all that he had by the Spirit, of the courts of the house of the LORD, of all the chambers all around, of the treasuries of the house of God, and of the treasuries for the dedicated things..."All this," said David, "the LORD made me understand in writing, by His hand upon me, all the works of these plans."

Delivering God's People from Bondage

The Holy Spirit enabled the judges in super-human ways (Judges 6:34; 11:29; 14:6, 19; 15:14).

Gideon Judges 6:34 When the Spirit of the Lord came upon Gideon, a timid man became a bold man and a mighty warrior, blowing a trumpet and assembling the people of God.

Jephthah Judges 11:29 When the Spirit of the Lord came upon Jephthah he was able to defeat a much superior enemy with ease.

Samson Judges 14:6, 19; 15:14 When the Spirit of the Lord was on Samson he was able to tear a lion apart with his bare hands; he was able to break ropes from his body as if they were nothing and he was able to kill 1000 men with the jawbone of a donkey. Without the Spirit of the Lord and the supernatural power of God, Samson was like any other man (Judges 16:19).

Leading the People of God

Moses and the elders of Israel were anointed with the Spirit (Numbers 11:2425). Imagine the task of leading 3,000,000 murmuring people through the wilderness.

So Moses went out and told the people the words of the LORD, and he gathered the seventy men of the elders of the people and placed them around the tabernacle. Then the LORD came down in the cloud, and spoke to him, and took of the Spirit that was upon him, and placed the same upon the seventy elders; and it happened, when the Spirit rested upon them, that they prophesied, although they never did so again.

Prophets were enabled by the Spirit (1 Kings 19:16; 2 Chronicles 15:1; 20:14; Ezekiel 3:12).

Now the Spirit of God came upon Azariah the son of Oded. And he went out to meet Asa, and said to him: "Hear me, Asa, and all Judah and Benjamin. The LORD is with you while you are with Him. If you seek Him, He will be found by you; but if you forsake Him, He will forsake you. 2 Chronicles 15:1-2

Priests were enabled by the Spirit (Leviticus 8:1-13, 20; 21:12).

And he [Moses] poured some of the anointing oil on Aaron's head and anointed him, to consecrate him. Leviticus 8:13

Kings were enabled by the Spirit (1 Samuel 11:6; 16:13-14; 1 Kings. 1:34-39).

DR. ABRAHAM PETERS

So he sent and brought him in. Now he was ruddy, with bright eyes, and good-looking. And the LORD said, "Arise, anoint him; for this is the one!" Then Samuel took the horn of oil and anointed him in the midst of his brothers; and the Spirit of the LORD came upon David from that day forward. So Samuel arose and went to Ramah.
1 Samuel 16:12-13

Making Wise Decisions:

The individuals who had the Spirit of God upon them were able to distinguish themselves in all realms of society from those without the Spirit of God.

Joseph (Genesis 41:38-40)

So the advice was good in the eyes of Pharaoh and in the eyes of all his servants. And Pharaoh said to his servants, "Can we find such a one as this, a man in whom is the Spirit of God?" Then Pharaoh said to Joseph, "Inasmuch as God has shown you all this, there is no one as discerning and wise as you. You shall be over my house, and all my people shall be ruled according to your word; only in regard to the throne will I be greater than you."

Daniel (Dan. 4:8-9, 18; 5:11-17; 6:3)

This dream I, King Nebuchadnezzar, have seen. Now you, Belteshazzar, declare its interpretation, since all the wise men of my kingdom are not able to make known to me the interpretation; but you are able, for the Spirit of the Holy God is in you. Daniel 4:18

> *"There is a man in your kingdom in whom is the Spirit of the Holy God. And in the days of your father, light and understanding and wisdom, like the wisdom of the gods, were found in him; and King Nebuchadnezzar your father--your father the king--made him chief of the magicians, astrologers, Chaldeans, and soothsayers. 12 Inasmuch as an excellent spirit, knowledge, understanding, interpreting dreams, solving riddles, and explaining enigmas were found in this Daniel, whom the king named Belteshazzar, now let Daniel be called, and he will give the interpretation." 13 Then Daniel was brought in before the king. The king spoke, and said to Daniel, "Are you that Daniel who is one of the captives from Judah, whom my father the king brought from Judah? 14 I have heard of you, that the Spirit of God is in you, and that light and understanding and excellent wisdom are found in you. 15 Now the wise men, the astrologers, have been brought in before me, that they should read this writing and make known to me its interpretation, but they could not give the interpretation of the thing. 16 And I have heard of you, that you can give interpretations and explain enigmas. Now if you can read the writing and make known to me its interpretation, you shall be clothed with purple and have a chain of gold around your neck, and shall be the third ruler in the kingdom." 17 Then Daniel answered, and said before the king, "Let your gifts be for yourself, and give your rewards to another; yet I will read the writing to the king, and make known to him the interpretation."* Daniel 5:11-17

Other Special Tasks: Facilitating the translation of Elijah (2 Kings. 2:16)

Inspiring certain dramatic prophecies by Saul's servants (1 Samuel 19:20)

Teaching the people of God (Nehemiah 9:20)

Helping God's people to make godly plans (Isaiah 30:1)

The Holy Spirit is the subject of prophecies regarding the New Covenant (Isaiah 28:11-12; 32:15; 44:3; Ezekiel 39:29; Joel 2:28-29).

> *For I will pour water on him who is thirsty, and floods on the dry ground; I will pour My Spirit on your descendants, and My blessing on your offspring...* Isaiah 44:3

What is the distinction between how the Holy Spirit operated in the Old Testament and how the Holy Spirit operates in the New Testament in relation to God's people?

There is different terminology connected with the Spirit's activity in relation to man in the Old Testament.

In the Old Testament the Spirit of the Lord...

Rested upon men (Numbers 11:25; Isaiah 11:2)

> *...and it happened, when the Spirit rested upon them, that they prophesied, although they never did so again.* Numbers 11:25b

Came upon men (Judges 6:34; 11:29; 14:6, 19; 15:14; 1 Samuel 10:6, 10)

When they came there to the hill, there was a group of prophets to meet him; then the Spirit of God came upon him, and he prophesied among them. 1 Samuel 10:10

Moved upon men (Judges 13:25)

And the Spirit of the LORD began to move upon him at Mahaneh Dan between Zorah and Eshtaol.

Fell upon men (Numbers 11:29; Ezekiel 11:5)

Then the Spirit of the LORD fell upon me, and said to me, "Speak!" Ezekiel 11:5

Poured out upon men (Proverbs 1:23)

Turn at my rebuke; surely I will pour out my spirit on you; I will make my words known to you.

Old Testament believers were not "born of" or "indwelt" by the Spirit.

This new age of the Spirit was revealed by Jesus (John 14:16-17).

And I will pray the Father, and He will give you another Helper, that He may abide with you forever--the Spirit of truth, whom the world cannot receive, because it neither sees Him nor knows Him; but you know Him, for He dwells with you and will be in you.

This new age of the Spirit was revealed to John the Baptist (John 1:29-34).

> *The next day John saw Jesus coming toward him, and said, "Behold! The Lamb of God who takes away the sin of the world! 30 This is He of whom I said, 'After me comes a Man who is preferred before me, for He was before me.' 31 I did not know Him; but that He should be revealed to Israel, therefore I came baptizing with water." 32 And John bore witness, saying, "I saw the Spirit descending from heaven like a dove, and He remained upon Him. 33 I did not know Him, but He who sent me to baptize with water said to me, 'Upon whom you see the Spirit descending, and remaining on Him, this is He who baptizes with the Holy Spirit.' 34 And I have seen and testified that this is the Son of God."*

This new age of the Spirit was foretold by the Old Testament prophets (Ezekiel 36:26-27; 37:14).

> *I will give you a new heart and put a new spirit within you; I will take the heart of stone out of your flesh and give you a heart of flesh. I will put My Spirit within you and cause you to walk in My statutes, and you will keep My judgments and do them.   Ezekiel 36:26-27*

CHAPTER FOUR

THE WORK OF THE HOLY SPIRIT IN CHRIST AND THE CHURCH

As we know when Christ became a man He fully functioned on earth as a man. He laid aside His prerogatives to act as God and functioned the same way that you and I must function (Philippians 2:5-8). In this way Christ is an example of the believer in His relationship to the Holy Spirit. Because just like you and I must depend upon the Holy Spirit to fulfill our call and destiny, even so Jesus had to rely on the Holy Spirit. This is why the Bible indicates that we are not only saved by Jesus death in atoning for our sins, we are also saved by His life in that He provided an example for us to follow (Romans 5:10).

How we see the Holy Spirit operating in the life of Jesus in His earthly walk

In the life of Christ we see an intimate relationship to the Holy Spirit. This is meant to be a model for all believers. When Jesus came He ushered in the new age of the Spirit (Matthew 11:13).

The Holy Spirit was a big factor in Christ's personal experience. Christ was foretold by the Spirit though prophecy (Luke 24:26-27; 1 Peter 1:11; 2 Peter 1:21).

"Ought not the Christ to have suffered these things and to enter into His glory?" And beginning at Moses and all the Prophets, He expounded to them in all the Scriptures the things concerning Himself. Luke 24:26-27

Of this salvation the prophets have inquired and searched carefully, who prophesied of the grace that would come to you, searching what, or what manner of time, the Spirit of Christ who was in them was indicating when He testified beforehand the sufferings of Christ

and the glories that would follow. To them it was revealed that, not to themselves, but to us they were ministering the things which now have been reported to you through those who have preached the gospel to you by the Holy Spirit sent from heaven--things which angels desire to look into. 1 Peter 1:10-12

...for prophecy never came by the will of man, but holy men of God spoke as they were moved by the Holy Spirit. 2 Peter 1:21

Christ was born of the Spirit (Matthew 1:18-20; Luke 1:35).

Now the birth of Jesus Christ was as follows: After His mother Mary was betrothed to Joseph, before they came together, she was found with child of the Holy Spirit. Then Joseph her husband, being a just man, and not wanting to make her a public example, was minded to put her away secretly. But while he thought about these things, behold, an angel of the Lord appeared to him in a dream, saying, "Joseph, son of David, do not be afraid to take to you Mary your wife, for that which is conceived in her is of the Holy Spirit." Matthew 1:18-20

And the angel answered and said to her, "The Holy Spirit will come upon you, and the power of the Highest will overshadow you; therefore, also, that Holy One who is to be born will be called the Son of God." Luke 1:35

Christ was baptized in or with the Holy Spirit (Matthew 3:16-17; Luke 3:21-22; John 1:32-34).

When He had been baptized, Jesus came up immediately from the water; and behold, the heavens were opened to Him, and He saw the

DR. ABRAHAM PETERS

Spirit of God descending like a dove and alighting upon Him .Matthew 3:16

Christ was filled with the fullness of the Spirit (John 3:34; Ephesians 4:7; Colossians 2:9).

For He whom God has sent speaks the words of God, for God does not give the Spirit by measure .John 3:34

Christ was led by the Spirit (Matthew 4:1; Luke 4:1; John 8:29).

Then Jesus, being filled with the Holy Spirit, returned from the Jordan and was led by the Spirit into the wilderness... Luke 4:1

Christ was empowered by the Spirit (Luke 4:14-15; Acts 10:38).

Then Jesus returned in the power of the Spirit to Galilee, and news of Him went out through all the surrounding region. And He taught in their synagogues, being glorified by all. Luke 4:14-15

Christ was anointed by the Spirit (Luke 4:18; Acts 4:27; 10:38; Hebrews 1:9).

The word which God sent to the children of Israel, preaching peace through Jesus Christ--He is Lord of all--that word you know, which was proclaimed throughout all Judea, and began from Galilee after the baptism which John preached: how God anointed Jesus of Nazareth with the Holy Spirit and with power, who went about doing good and healing all who were oppressed by the devil, for God was with Him. Acts 10:36-38

Christ was sealed with the Holy Spirit (John 6:27).

Do not labor for the food which perishes, but for the food which endures to everlasting life, which the Son of Man will give you, because God the Father has set His seal on Him.

Even though the Holy Spirit is not directly referred to in this passage, we know from other verses that the Holy Spirit is associated with the seal of God (Ephesians 1:13).

Christ was crucified or offered up by the Spirit (Hebrews 9:13-14).

For if the blood of bulls and goats and the ashes of a heifer, sprinkling the unclean, sanctifies for the purifying of the flesh, how much more shall the blood of Christ, who through the eternal Spirit offered Himself without spot to God, cleanse your conscience from dead works to serve the living God?

Christ was resurrected by the Spirit (Romans1:4; 8:11; 1 Peter 3:18).

But if the Spirit of Him who raised Jesus from the dead dwells in you, He who raised Christ from the dead will also give life to your mortal bodies through His Spirit who dwells in you. Romans 8:11

For Christ also suffered once for sins, the just for the unjust, that He might bring us to God, being put to death in the flesh but made alive by the Spirit... 1 Peter 3:18

Christ was justified by the Spirit (1 Timothy 3:16).

And without controversy great is the mystery of godliness: God was manifested in the flesh, justified in the Spirit, seen by angels, preached among the Gentiles, believed on in the world, received up in glory. 1 Timothy 3:16

Christ was gladdened or rejoiced in the Spirit (Psalm 45:7; Luke 10:21; Hebrews 1:9).

In that hour Jesus rejoiced in the Spirit... Luke 10:21a

At that time Jesus, full of joy through the Holy Spirit... --NIV

At that, Jesus rejoiced, exuberant in the Holy Spirit... --MSG

You love righteousness and hate wickedness; therefore God, Your God, has anointed You with the oil of gladness more than Your companions. Psalm 45:7

You love what is right and hate what is wrong. Therefore God, your God, has anointed you, pouring out the oil of joy on you more than on anyone else. Psalm 45:7, NLT

The Holy Spirit was a big factor in Christ's earthly ministry. Christ taught and preached by the Spirit (Luke 4:18; John 3:34).

The Spirit of the LORD is upon Me, because He has anointed Me to preach the gospel... Luke 4:18a

Perhaps this is why Jesus' teaching was so distinct to that of the religious leaders of the day. He spoke with authority because of the anointing of the Holy Spirit on His words (Matthew 7:29; Mark 1:22).

Then they went into Capernaum, and immediately on the Sabbath He entered the synagogue and taught. And they were astonished at His teaching, for He taught them as one having authority, and not as the scribes. Mark 1:21-22

Christ healed the sick by the Spirit (Luke 4:18; Acts 10:38).

The Spirit of the LORD is upon Me, because He has anointed Me to preach the gospel to the poor; He has sent Me to heal the brokenhearted, to proclaim
liberty to the captives and recovery of sight to the blind, to set at liberty those who are oppressed... Luke 4:18

Christ cast out devils by the Spirit (Matthew 12:28; Luke 4:18, 36; 11:20; Acts 10:38).

But if I cast out demons by the Spirit of God, surely the kingdom of God has come upon you. Matthew 12:28

Then they were all amazed and spoke among themselves, saying, "What a word this is! For with authority and power He commands the unclean spirits, and they come out." Luke 4:36

...how God anointed Jesus of Nazareth with the Holy Spirit and with power, who went about doing good and healing all who were oppressed by the devil, for God was with Him. Acts 10:38

Christ breathed the Holy Spirit upon His disciples after His resurrection (John 20:21-22).

So Jesus said to them again, "Peace to you! As the Father has sent Me, I also send you." And when He had said this, He breathed on them, and said to them, "Receive the Holy Spirit."

Christ gave commandments by the Spirit (Acts 1:1-2).

The former account I made, O Theophilus, of all that Jesus began both to do and teach, until the day in which He was taken up, after He through the Holy Spirit had given commandments to the apostles whom He had chosen...

The Holy Spirit is a big factor in Christ's heavenly ministry. Christ baptized and empowered the Church with the Spirit (Acts 1:5, 8; 2:1-4).

And being assembled together with them, He commanded them not to depart from Jerusalem, but to wait for the Promise of the Father, "which," He said, "you have heard from Me; for John truly baptized with water, but you shall be baptized with the Holy Spirit not many days from now...But you shall receive power when the Holy Spirit has come upon you; and you shall be witnesses to Me in Jerusalem, and in all Judea and Samaria, and to the end of the earth." Acts 1:4-5, 8

Christ still baptizes with the Holy Spirit (Matthew 3:11).

I indeed baptize you with water unto repentance, but He who is coming after me is mightier than I, whose sandals I am not worthy to carry. He will baptize you with the Holy Spirit and fire.

Christ directs and governs the Church by the Spirit (Revelation 1-3).

Jesus is seen in Revelation chapter one as the exalted High Priest. He appeals to John to write to the seven churches of Asia and give His message to them as the Lord of the Church. Yet when the message is delivered, seven times the statement is made, *"He who has an ear, let him hear what the Spirit says to the churches."*

Christ is glorified by the Spirit (John 16:13-14).

However, when He, the Spirit of truth, has come, He will guide you into all truth; for He will not speak on His own authority, but whatever He hears He will speak; and He will tell you things to come. He will glorify Me, for He will take of what is Mine and declare it to you.

The Holy Spirit is seen in relationship to Jesus in divine titles that connect the Spirit and the Son.

1. The Spirit of Jesus (Acts 16:6-7)
2. The Spirit of Christ (Rom. 8:9; I Pet. 1:11)
3. The Spirit of Jesus Christ (Phil. 1:19)
4. The Spirit of His Son (Gal. 4:6)
5. His Witness (Acts 5:30-32).
6. Another Comforter (John 14:16)

DR. ABRAHAM PETERS

HOW THE HOLY SPIRIT WORK IN THE CHURCH

When Christ was here on earth the world was confronted with a ministry that fully operated in the power of the Holy Spirit. Christ is now ascended into heaven, but it is His desire to continue to minister on earth the same way that He did while He was here on earth. Now, however, He wants to minister in and through His people by the Holy Spirit. In this way His ministry can be carried out in the entire world at the same time. We see the Holy Spirit working in the Church in various ways:

The Holy Spirit gave life to the Church on the day of Christ's resurrection when Jesus breathed on His disciples (John 20:22). The Holy Spirit empowered the Church on the Day of Pentecost (Acts 2:1-4).

When the Day of Pentecost had fully come, they were all with one accord in one place. And suddenly there came a sound from heaven, as of a rushing mighty wind, and it filled the whole house where they were sitting. Then there appeared to them divided tongues, as of fire, and one sat upon each of them. And they were all filled with the Holy Spirit and began to speak with other tongues, as the Spirit gave them utterance.

The Holy Spirit distributes and sets His gifts in the Church (1 Corinthians 12:4, 11).

There are diversities of gifts, but the same Spirit...But one and the same Spirit works all these things, distributing to each one individually as He wills.

The Holy Spirit sets leadership in the churches (Acts 20:17, 28). Paul was speaking to the elders of the church at Ephesus and he challenged them to…

…take heed to yourselves and to all the flock, among which the Holy Spirit has made you overseers, to shepherd the church of God which He purchased with His own blood.

The Holy Spirit calls and sends forth workers from the churches (Acts 13:2-4).

As they ministered to the Lord and fasted, the Holy Spirit said, "Now separate to Me Barnabas and Saul for the work to which I have called them. "Then, having fasted and prayed, and laid hands on them, they sent them away. So, being sent out by the Holy Spirit, they went down to Seleucia, and from there they sailed to Cyprus.

The Holy Spirit speaks to each local church just as we discussed in the chapter one of the seven churches in Asia (Revelation 2:7, 11, 17, 29; 3:6, 13, 22). And even today He is here to speak to every minister and church ministries who will honor, reverence and acknowledge Him.

"He who has an ear, let him hear what the Spirit says to the churches."

The Holy Spirit desires to direct and govern leadership decisions and ministries in the churches.

DR. ABRAHAM PETERS

1. He desires to assist in evangelism (Acts 8:29). He will lead us to divine appointments.

Now an angel of the Lord spoke to Philip, saying, "Arise and go toward the south along the road which goes down from Jerusalem to Gaza." This is desert. 27 So he arose and went. And behold, a man of Ethiopia, a eunuch of great authority under Candace the queen of the Ethiopians, who had charge of all her treasury, and had come to Jerusalem to worship, 28 was returning. And sitting in his chariot, he was reading Isaiah the prophet. 29 Then the Spirit said to Philip, "Go near and overtake this chariot." 30 So Philip ran to him, and heard him reading the prophet Isaiah, and said, "Do you understand what you are reading?" 31 And he said, "How can I, unless someone guides me?" And he asked Philip to come up and sit with him. Acts 8:26-31

2. He desires to direct believers to His prepared people (Acts 10:19-20; 11:12).

While Peter thought about the vision, the Spirit said to him, "Behold, three men are seeking you. Arise therefore, go down and go with them, doubting nothing; for I have sent them." Acts 10:19-20

Then the Spirit told me to go with them, doubting nothing. Moreover these six brethren accompanied me, and we entered the man's house. Acts 11:12

God still wants to do these things today. As Peter followed the leading of the Holy Spirit that went against his personal comfort, he experienced one of the greatest Holy Ghost meetings of his life (Acts 11:44-48).

3. He desires to govern the policy of the church (Acts 15:28).

The leadership of the church had met in an atmosphere of prayer concerning certain policies having to do with the coming in of the Gentiles into the churches. When they made their decision it was done under the auspices and approval of the Holy Spirit. This is how Christ governs the church. This is how the local church functions as a "theocracy."

For it seemed good to the Holy Spirit, and to us, to lay upon you no greater burden than these necessary things...

4. He desires to order the missionary activity of the church (Acts 16:6-10).

Now when they had gone through Phrygia and the region of Galatia, they were forbidden by the Holy Spirit to preach the word in Asia. 7 After they had come to Mysia, they tried to go into Bithynia, but the Spirit did not permit them. 8 So passing by Mysia, they came down to Troas. 9 And a vision appeared to Paul in the night. A man of Macedonia stood and pleaded with him, saying, "Come over to Macedonia and help us." 10 Now after he had seen the vision, immediately we sought to go to Macedonia, concluding that the Lord had called us to preach the gospel to them.

Paul had some natural inclinations about where he should preach next. But he was sensitive to the Holy Spirit. The Holy Spirit had other plans. As Paul followed the leading of the Holy Spirit many great churches were established.

5. He desires to prepare us for impending danger (Acts 20:22-24).

Paul was always ready for what the world would throw at him because he was in step with the Holy Spirit.

And see, now I go bound in the spirit to Jerusalem, not knowing the things that will happen to me there, except that the Holy Spirit testifies in every city, saying that chains and tribulations await me. But none of these things move me; nor do I count my life dear to myself, so that I may finish my race with joy, and the ministry which I received from the Lord Jesus, to testify to the gospel of the grace of God.

The Holy Spirit teaches us what to say in difficult situations (Matthew 10:16-20; John 14:26; 16:14).

Behold, I send you out as sheep in the midst of wolves. Therefore be wise as serpents and harmless as doves. But beware of men, for they will deliver you up to councils and scourge you in their synagogues. You will be brought before governors and kings for My sake, as a testimony to them and to the Gentiles. But when they deliver you up, do not worry about how or what you should speak. For it will be given to you in that hour what you should speak; for it is not you who speak, but the Spirit of your Father who speaks in you. Matthew 10:16-20

The Holy Spirit helps preachers and teachers know what to say (1 Corinthians 2:12-13).

Now we have received, not the spirit of the world, but the Spirit who is from God, that we might know the things that have been freely given to us by God. These things we also speak, not in words which man's wisdom teaches but which the Holy Spirit teaches, comparing spiritual things with spiritual.

The Holy Spirit empowers the preaching of the Gospel (Romans 15:18-19; 1 Corinthians 2:4-5; 2 Corinthians 3:3; 1 Thessalonians 1:5; 1 Peter 1:12).

For I will not dare to speak of any of those things which Christ has not accomplished through me, in word and deed, to make the Gentiles obedient--in mighty signs and wonders, by the power of the Spirit of God, so that from Jerusalem and round about to Illyricum I have fully preached the gospel of Christ. Romans 15:18-19

And my speech and my preaching were not with persuasive words of human wisdom, but in demonstration of the Spirit and of power, that your faith should not be in the wisdom of men but in the power of God. 1 Corinthians 2:4-5

...clearly you are an epistle of Christ, ministered by us, written not with ink but by the Spirit of the living God, not on tablets of stone but on tablets of flesh, that is, of the heart. 2 Corinthians 3:3

For our gospel did not come to you in word only, but also in power, and in the Holy Spirit and in much assurance, as you know what kind of men we were among you for your sake. 1 Thessalonians 1:5

To them it was revealed that, not to themselves, but to us they were ministering the things which now have been reported to you through those who have preached the gospel to you by the Holy Spirit sent from heaven--things which angels desire to look into. 1 Peter 1:12

The Holy Spirit prepares the hearts of the sinner for the preaching of the Gospel (John 16:8-11).

And when He [the Holy Spirit] has come, He will convict the world of sin, and of righteousness, and of judgment: of sin, because they do not believe in Me; of righteousness, because I go to My Father and you see Me no more; of judgment, because the ruler of this world is judged. John 16:8-11

The Holy Spirit works miracles in the Church to facilitate His purposes (Acts 8:39; 1 Corinthians 12:10; Romans 15:18-19).

Now when they came up out of the water, the Spirit of the Lord caught Philip away, so that the eunuch saw him no more; and he went on his way rejoicing. Acts 8:39

The Holy Spirit heals the Church (Romans 15:18-19; 1 Corinthians 12:9, 28, 30). He does this principally by placing the gifts of healing and healing ministries in the Church.

The Holy Spirit creates an atmosphere for fellowship in the Church (2 Corinthians 13:14; Philippians 2:1).

Therefore if there is any consolation in Christ, if any comfort of love, if any fellowship of the Spirit, if any affection and mercy... Philippians 2:1

The Holy Spirit is working to prepare the Church to be the Bride of Christ when He returns   (Ephesians 5:25-32).

DR. ABRAHAM PETERS

CHAPTER FIVE

THE WORK OF THE HOLY SPIRIT IN THE BELIEVER

Fellowship With The Holy Spirit

We are living in the age of the Holy Spirit. That means that the principle worker in the Godhead that we as believers interface with is the Holy Spirit. We could say that we owe everything to the Holy Spirit.

The Holy Spirit is responsible for our being Christians.

The Holy Spirit is the agent by which the Father draws us (John 6:44; Luke 14:1623 [the Holy Spirit is the Servant]).

No one can come to Me unless the Father who sent Me draws him; and I will raise him up at the last day. John 6:44

Then He said to him, "A certain man gave a great supper and invited many, 17 and sent his servant at supper time to say to those who were invited, 'Come, for all things are now ready.' 18 But they all with one accord began to make excuses. The first said to him, 'I have bought a piece of ground, and I must go and see it. I ask you to have me excused.' 19 And another said, 'I have bought five yoke of oxen, and I am going to test them. I ask you to have me excused.' 20 Still another said, 'I have married a wife, and therefore I cannot come.' 21 So that servant came and reported these things to his master. Then the master of the house, being angry, said to his servant, 'Go out quickly into the streets and lanes of the city, and bring in here the poor and the maimed and the lame and the blind.' 22 And the servant said, 'Master, it is done as you commanded, and still there is room.' 23 Then the master said to the servant, 'Go out into the highways and hedges, and compel them to come in, that my house may be filled.'" Luke 14:16-23

DR. ABRAHAM PETERS

The Holy Spirit causes the believer to acknowledge Jesus as Lord (1 Corinthians 12:3).

Therefore I make known to you that no one speaking by the Spirit of God calls Jesus accursed, and no one can say that Jesus is Lord except by the Holy Spirit.

The Holy Spirit is responsible for the regeneration of the human spirit (John 1:1213; 3:5-6).

Jesus answered, "Most assuredly, I say to you, unless one is born of water and the Spirit, he cannot enter the kingdom of God. That which is born of the flesh is flesh, and that which is born of the Spirit is spirit. John 3:5-6

The Holy Spirit indwells the spirit of the believer (John 14:17; Romans 8:9; 1 Corinthians 3:16; 6:17; 2 Corinthians 6:16; Galatians 2:20; 2 Timothy 1:14; 1 John 2:27).

So then, those who are in the flesh cannot please God. But you are not in the flesh but in the Spirit, if indeed the Spirit of God dwells in you. Now if anyone does not have the Spirit of Christ, he is not His. Romans 8:8-9

Do you not know that you are the temple of God and that the Spirit of God dwells in you? 1 Corinthians 3:16

That good thing which was committed to you, keep by the Holy Spirit who dwells in us. 2 Timothy 1:14

The Holy Spirit unites us with Christ (1 Corinthians 6:17; 12:13; 1 John 4:13).

But he who is joined to the Lord is one spirit with Him. 1 Corinthians 6:17

For by one Spirit we were all baptized into one body--whether Jews or Greeks, whether slaves or free--and have all been made to drink into one Spirit. 1 Corinthians 12:13

By this we know that we abide in Him, and He in us, because He has given us of His Spirit. 1 John 4:13

The Holy Spirit gives assurance of salvation (Romans 8:15-16; Galatians 4:6).

The Spirit Himself bears witness with our spirit that we are children of God... Romans 8:16

The Holy Spirit is responsible for establishing us as Christians.

The baptism of the Holy Spirit is part of the Christian's foundation and his or her "power from on high" (Acts 1:4-5, 8; 2:4).

But you shall receive power when the Holy Spirit has come upon you; and you shall be witnesses to Me in Jerusalem, and in all Judea and Samaria, and to the end of the earth. Acts 1:8

The Holy Spirit fills the believer continually (Ephesians 5:18).

DR. ABRAHAM PETERS

And do not be drunk with wine, in which is dissipation; but be filled with the Spirit, speaking to one another in psalms and hymns and spiritual songs, singing and making melody in your heart to the Lord... Ephesians 5:18-19

The Holy Spirit sets us free from the law of sin and death enabling the believer to put to death the deeds of the flesh (Romans 8:2, 13).

For if you live according to the flesh you will die; but if by the Spirit you put to death the deeds of the body, you will live. Romans 8:13

The Holy Spirit sanctifies us, sets us apart and makes us holy (1 Corinthians 6:11; 2 Thessalonians 2:13; 1 Peter 1:2).

As for us, we always thank God for you, dear brothers and sisters loved by the Lord. We are thankful that God chose you to be among the first to experience salvation, a salvation that came through the Spirit who makes you holy and by your belief in the truth. 2 Thessalonians 2:13, NLT

The Holy Spirit transforms us into the image of Christ (2 Corinthians 3:18).

But we all, with unveiled face, beholding as in a mirror the glory of the Lord, are being transformed into the same image from glory to glory, just as by the Spirit of the Lord.

The Holy Spirit renews the believer (Titus 3:5).

Fellowship With The Holy Spirit

Not by works of righteousness which we have done, but according to His mercy He saved us, through the washing of regeneration and renewing of the Holy Spirit...

The Holy Spirit produces Christ-like fruit in the life of the believer (Galatians 5:22-23).

The Holy Spirit strengthens the believer in the inner person (Ephesians 3:16; cf. 2 Corinthians 4:16).

For this reason I bow my knees to the Father of our Lord Jesus Christ, from whom the whole family in heaven and earth is named, that He would grant you, according to the riches of His glory, to be strengthened with might through His Spirit in the inner man...
Ephesians 3:14-16

The Holy Spirit speaks to the believer (Acts 8:29; 1 Timothy 4:1; Revelation 2:7, 11, 17, 29).

The Holy Spirit leads the believer (Romans 8:14; Galatians 5:16, 25).

For as many as are led by the Spirit of God, these are sons of God. Romans 8:14

The Holy Spirit teaches the believer and leads him into truth (John 16:13; 1 John 2:27).

However, when He, the Spirit of truth, has come, He will guide you into all truth; for He will not speak on His own authority, but whatever He hears He will speak; and He will tell you things to come. John 16:13

But the anointing which you have received from Him abides in you, and you do not need that anyone teach you; but as the same anointing teaches you concerning all things, and is true, and is not a lie, and just as it has taught you, you will abide in Him. 1 John 2:27

The Holy Spirit reveals the deep things of God to the believer (John 16:14; 1 Corinthians 2:9-14).

But as it is written: "Eye has not seen, nor ear heard, nor have entered into the heart of man the things which God has prepared for those who love Him." 10 But God has revealed them to us through His Spirit. For the Spirit searches all things, yes, the deep things of God. 11 For what man knows the things of a man except the spirit of the man which is in him? Even so no one knows the things of God except the Spirit of God. 12 Now we have received, not the spirit of the world, but the Spirit who is from God, that we might know the things that have been freely given to us by God. 13 These things we also speak, not in words which man's wisdom teaches but which the Holy Spirit teaches, comparing spiritual things with spiritual. 14 But the natural man does not receive the things of the Spirit of God, for they are foolishness to him; nor can he know them, because they are spiritually discerned. 1 Corinthians 2:9-14

The Holy Spirit opens the believer's understanding to the things of God (1 Corinthians 2:12).

The Holy Spirit reveals the future to the believer (Luke 2:26; John 16:13; Acts 20:23; 21:11; Revelation 1:10).

And behold, there was a man in Jerusalem whose name was Simeon, and this man was just and devout, waiting for the Consolation of Israel, and the Holy Spirit was upon him. And it had been revealed to him by the Holy Spirit that he would not see death before he had seen the Lord's Christ. Luke 2:25-26

When he had come to us, he took Paul's belt, bound his own hands and feet, and said, "Thus says the Holy Spirit, 'So shall the Jews at Jerusalem bind the man who owns this belt, and deliver him into the hands of the Gentiles.'" Acts 21:11

The Holy Spirit helps and guides in prayer and intercession (Romans 8:26-27; Ephesians 6:18; Jude 20).

Likewise the Spirit also helps in our weaknesses. For we do not know what we should pray for as we ought, but the Spirit Himself makes intercession for us with groanings which cannot be uttered. Now He who searches the hearts knows what the mind of the Spirit is, because He makes intercession for the saints according to the will of God. Romans 8:26-28

The Holy Spirit inspires the believer's worship (John 4:24; Philippians 3:3; 1 Corinthians 14:15).

For we are the circumcision, who worship God in the Spirit, rejoice in Christ Jesus, and have no confidence in the flesh...
Philippians 3:3

The Holy Spirit comforts (John 15:26; Acts 9:31).

Then the churches throughout all Judea, Galilee, and Samaria had peace and were edified. And walking in the fear of the Lord and in the comfort of the Holy Spirit, they were multiplied. Acts 9:31

The Holy Spirit seals the believer (Ephesians 1:13; 4:30; 2 Corinthians 1:21-22).

And do not grieve the Holy Spirit of God, by whom you were sealed for the day of redemption. Ephesians 4:30

The Holy Spirit teaches how to answer persecutors (Matthew 10:19-20; Mark 13:11; Luke 12:11-12; Acts 4:8; 7:55).

But when they arrest you and deliver you up, do not worry beforehand, or premeditate what you will speak. But whatever is given you in that hour, speak that; for it is not you who speak, but the Holy Spirit. Mark 13:11

The Holy Spirit abides with us forever (John 14:16).

And I will pray the Father, and He will give you another Helper, that He may abide with you forever—

The Holy Spirit is the driving force behind our ministry as Christians.

The Holy Spirit calls believers to special service (Acts 13:2-4).

The Holy Spirit imparts spiritual gifts to the believer (1 Corinthians 12:7-11).

The Holy Spirit guides believers in their ministry (Acts 8:29; 16:6-7).

The Holy Spirit empowers the believer for witness (Acts 1:8; 1Thessalonians 1:5; 1 Corinthians 2:1-5).

The Holy Spirit gives us the boldness that we need to fulfill our ministry (Acts 4:31).

And being let go, they went to their own companions and reported all that the chief priests and elders had said to them. 24 So when they heard that, they raised their voice to God with one accord and said: "Lord, You are God, who made heaven and earth and the sea, and all that is in them, 25 who by the mouth of Your servant David have said: 'Why did the nations rage, and the people plot vain things? 26 The kings of the earth took their stand, and the rulers were gathered together against the LORD and against His Christ.' 27 For truly against Your holy Servant Jesus, whom You anointed, both Herod and Pontius Pilate, with the Gentiles and the people of Israel, were gathered together 28 to do whatever Your hand and Your purpose determined before to be done. 29 Now, Lord, look on their threats, and grant to Your servants that with all boldness they may speak Your word, 30 by stretching out Your hand to heal, and that signs and wonders may be done through the name of Your holy Servant Jesus." 31 And when they had prayed, the place where they were assembled together was shaken; and they were all filled with the Holy Spirit, and they spoke the word of God with boldness.

Jesus has given a big challenge to the Church. He has given all of us a big challenge personally. If you are like me, when we fully understand what God wants us to do, it can be quite intimidating.

1. The work that the Lord wants us to do can be intimidating. Why?

   We know how weak we really are.
   We know the thoughts that we think.
   We know the unbelief with which we wrestle at times.
   We know the inner struggles that we have.
   We know our own failures from the past.
   We know how hostile the world is to what we are doing.
   We know how large the work is that God wants us to do.

2. We need the boldness of the Holy Spirit in the face of intimidation.

   To be bold is to be brave, courageous, fearless, open and daring.
   The opposite of boldness is cowardice, silence, faintheartedness, fearfulness, timidity, and chicken-heartedness.

   It takes boldness to share the gospel to hostile people.
   It takes boldness to step out into new areas of endeavor.
   It takes boldness to go against the tide of culture.

3. Our boldness will be dependent on the five things.

These are the same five things that gave boldness to the early church.

    a. Their boldness was dependent upon their relationship to Jesus (Acts 4:13).

Now when they saw the boldness of Peter and John, and perceived that they were uneducated and untrained men, they marveled. And they realized that they had been with Jesus.

    b. Their boldness was dependent upon their personal experience of salvation (Acts 4:19-20).

But Peter and John answered and said to them, "Whether it is right in the sight of God to listen to you more than to God, you judge. For we cannot but speak the things which we have seen and heard."

    c. Their boldness was dependent upon their understanding of their message (Acts 4:12).

Nor is there salvation in any other, for there is no other name under heaven given among men by which we must be saved.

    d. Their boldness was dependent upon their heart of love and compassion for the lost (2 Corinthians 5:14).

For the love of Christ compels us...

e. Their boldness was dependent upon the continual infilling of the Holy Spirit (Acts 4:31).

And when they had prayed, the place where they were assembled together was shaken; and they were all filled with the Holy Spirit, and they spoke the word of God with boldness.

CHAPTER SIX

THE OFFENSES AGAINST THE HOLY SPIRIT

One of the proofs that we used to substantiate the personhood of the Holy Spirit was that the Holy Spirit as a person could be offended. What are the ways in which we can actually offend the Holy Spirit? The word offend means "to give displeasure to, to displease, to affront or to anger." In its various uses, it can also mean "to transgress or violate." So what are the ways in which we give displeasure to the Holy Spirit? What are the ways we transgress or violate our relationship to Him? How do we actually cause the Holy Spirit to be angered?

We can grieve the Holy Spirit (Ephesians 4:30).

And do not grieve the Holy Spirit of God, by whom you were sealed for the day of redemption.

And do not bring sorrow to God's Holy Spirit by the way you live. Remember, he is the one who has identified you as his own, guaranteeing that you will be saved on the day of redemption. – NLT

The word that is used in this passage for "grieve" literally means "to make sorry, to cause heaviness or sadness, or to offend."

The immediate context of this verse has to do with how we treat other people, especially other members of the Body of Christ (Ephesians 4:25-32). We grieve the Holy Spirit when we do the following:

1. Lie to one another (vs. 25).
2. Hold our anger and fail to resolve conflict with one another, giving the devil a place to work in our lives (vs. 26-27).

3. Defraud one another by taking what is not our own (vs. 28).
4. Speak evil to and about one another (vs. 29, 31).

We have to remember that every believer is indwelt by the Spirit of God, so that what we do against one another, we actually do against the Holy Spirit within them. This same principle holds true in how we treat our spouse and other family members.

We can rebel against or vex the Holy Spirit (Isaiah 63:10).

But they rebelled and grieved [vexed, KJV] *His Holy Spirit; so He turned Himself against them as an enemy, and He fought against them.*

The word used for "rebelled" in this passage also means to be contentious and disobedient. The word used for "grieved" means to "to hurt, to vex, to cause pain, to torture." In the context of this passage we have the people of God repeating their usual cycle where they forget all of the wonderful things that God has done for them and persist in a lifestyle of disobedience, even to the point of going after other gods. In such cases, God can even become our enemy and fight against us.

At times Israel was guilty of this as illustrated in Exodus 32:7-10.

And the LORD said to Moses, "Go, get down! For your people whom you brought out of the land of Egypt have corrupted themselves. They have turned aside quickly out of the way which I commanded them. They have made themselves a molded calf, and worshiped it and sacrificed to it, and said, 'This is your god, O Israel, that brought you out of the land of Egypt!'" And the LORD

> *said to Moses, "I have seen this people, and indeed it is a stiff-necked people! Now therefore, let Me alone, that My wrath may burn hot against them and I may consume them. And I will make of you a great nation."*

All of the resistance that we feel in our lives may not be from the devil. If we are rebelling against the Holy Spirit, we may actually be fighting against God (Acts 5:39). When you wrestle with God, you always end up the loser.

We can lie to the Holy Spirit (Acts 5:1-4).

> *But a certain man named Ananias, with Sapphira his wife, sold a possession. And he kept back part of the proceeds, his wife also being aware of it, and brought a certain part and laid it at the apostles' feet. But Peter said, "Ananias, why has Satan filled your heart to lie to the Holy Spirit and keep back part of the price of the land for yourself? While it remained, was it not your own? And after it was sold, was it not in your own control? Why have you conceived this thing in your heart? You have not lied to men but to God."*

In this context Ananias and Sapphira made a commitment to God (the Holy Spirit) to perform a certain deed. In a real sense they made a personal covenant, vow or promise to God. However, when it came time to make good on the vow, they only completed part of it. How often do we make vows to the Lord in a time of worship or emotional highs? How often to we perform those vows? Ecclesiastes 5:2-7 speaks directly to this offense against the Holy Spirit.

> *Do not be rash with your mouth, and let not your heart utter anything hastily before God. For God is in heaven, and you on earth; therefore let your words be few. 3 For a dream comes through much activity, and a fool's voice is known by his many words. 4 When you make a vow to God, do not delay to pay it; for He has no pleasure in fools. Pay what you have vowed-- 5 Better not to vow than to vow and not pay. 6 Do not let your mouth cause your flesh to sin, nor say before the messenger of God that it was an error. Why should God be angry at your excuse and destroy the work of your hands. 7 For in the multitude of dreams and many words there is also vanity. But fear God.*

Why is it that we have so great hesitation in lying to people or failing to meet our commitments to people, but we can so easily renege on our vows to God?

We can tempt the Holy Spirit (Acts 5:9).

> *And Peter said, "How could the two of you even think of doing a thing like this-conspiring together to test [tempt, KJV] the Spirit of the Lord? Just outside that door are the young men who buried your husband, and they will carry you out, too."* –NLT

In a sense what Ananias and Saphira did was put the Holy Spirit to the test. Does the Holy Spirit really know what is in our hearts? Will the Holy Spirit really do anything about it? We put the Holy Spirit to the test when we knowingly do things that are wrong and yet still expect God to fulfill all of His promises to us.

We can resist the Holy Spirit (Acts 7:51).

DR. ABRAHAM PETERS

You stiff-necked and uncircumcised in heart and ears! You always resist the Holy Spirit; as your fathers did, so do you.

The context of this verse is the sermon given by Stephen to the same Jewish leaders who condemned Jesus to death. He is now facing death, but before he is stoned by the mob, he gave one last appeal to the nation. He demonstrates through a recounting of their history that they have rejected most of God's attempts to speak to them. They rejected the prophets, they rejected Jesus and now they are rejecting him. Whenever they did not like the message they got rid of the messenger. The word "stiff-necked" means "stubborn, obstinate and headstrong." The word "resist" means "to strive against, oppose or be adverse to." The leaders of the people were always running in the opposite direction of the Holy Spirit.

"You stubborn people! You are heathen at heart and deaf to the truth. Must you forever resist the Holy Spirit? But your ancestors did, and so do you!" –NLT

God has a plan for our lives. God has our destiny marked out. The Holy Spirit is the one who is given the task of assisting us in reaching that destiny. But how often do we resist His message and choose to run in the opposite direction?

We can harden our hearts against the Holy Spirit (Hebrews 3:7-15).

That is why the Holy Spirit says, "Today you must listen to his voice. 8 Don't harden your hearts against him as Israel did when they rebelled, when they tested God's patience in the wilderness. 9 There your ancestors tried my patience, even though they saw my miracles for forty years. 10 So I was angry with them, and I said,

'Their hearts always turn away from me. They refuse to do what I tell them.' 11 So in my anger I made a vow: 'They will never enter my place of rest.'" 12 Be careful then, dear brothers and sisters. Make sure that your own hearts are not evil and unbelieving, turning you away from the living God. 13 You must warn each other every day, as long as it is called "today," so that none of you will be deceived by sin and hardened against God. 14 For if we are faithful to the end, trusting God just as firmly as when we first believed, we will share in all that belongs to Christ. 15 But never forget the warning: "Today you must listen to his voice. Don't harden your hearts against him as Israel did when they rebelled."
–NLT

Even though the Holy Spirit is trying to do His work in our lives, we can harden our heart so that His voice is no longer heard by us. The more you harden your heart the harder it becomes and the more difficult it is to turn around. Pharaoh is an example of a man who resisted the work of the Holy Spirit and became a vessel of dishonor (Exodus 5:1-2, 9; 7:3-4, 22; 8:15, 32; 9:7, 12, 35; 10:1, 20, 27; 11:10; 14:4, 8). His heart was so hard that he and his great army eventually sunk like a stone (Exodus 15:5).

We can insult or despise the Holy Spirit (Hebrews 10:29).

Of how much worse punishment, do you suppose, will he be thought worthy who has trampled the Son of God underfoot, counted the blood of the covenant by which he was sanctified a common thing, and insulted the Spirit of grace?

The context of this passage is talking about people who were the objects of God's grace. They are people who have been pulled out of the fire by the work of the Holy Spirit only to return to their sin. These are people who know the truth and yet they reject that truth and willfully sin. It is an insult to the Holy Spirit when we so despise what He has done for us that we return to the old ways. Peter addressed this very thing in 2 Peter 2:20-22.

And when people escape from the wicked ways of the world by learning about our Lord and Savior Jesus Christ and then get tangled up with sin and become its slave again, they are worse off than before. It would be better if they had never known the right way to live than to know it and then reject the holy commandments that were given to them. They make these proverbs come true: "A dog returns to its vomit," and "A washed pig returns to the mud."
–NLT

We can quench the Holy Spirit (1 Thessalonians 5:19).

Do not quench the Spirit.

Do not put out the light of the Spirit. –TCNT

Do not extinguish the Spirit's fire. –Ber

Do not stifle the voice of the Spirit. –ALT

Do not suppress the Spirit. –MSG

The word for "quench" in the Bible always refers to the extinguishing of a flame. The Holy Spirit is the flame in our lives. The Holy Spirit is the "Spirit of Burning" who lights our flame and inspires our service. This is not a fire that we want to quench, extinguish, suppress, stifle or put out. We want to fan this fire and feed this fire in our lives. The Holy Spirit wants to move in our lives. He is constantly urging or prompting us to action. We want to be those who follow those prompting.

We can blaspheme the Holy Spirit (Matthew 12:22-32; Mark; 3:28-29; Luke 12:10).

Therefore I say to you, every sin and blasphemy will be forgiven men, but the blasphemy against the Spirit will not be forgiven men. Anyone who speaks a word against the Son of Man, it will be forgiven him; but whoever speaks against the Holy Spirit, it will not be forgiven him, either in this age or in the age to come. All of the other offences can eventually lead to this offense. Matthew 12:31-32

Assuredly, I say to you, all sins will be forgiven the sons of men, and whatever blasphemies they may utter; but he who blasphemes against the Holy Spirit never has forgiveness, but is subject to eternal condemnation. Mark 3:28-29

And anyone who speaks a word against the Son of Man, it will be forgiven him; but to him who blasphemes against the Holy Spirit, it will not be forgiven. Luke 12:10

This particular passage has aroused significant debate throughout history. The only way to understand what Jesus was saying is by understanding the full context of His statement and to whom He was speaking.

DR. ABRAHAM PETERS

1. The Audience

Jesus was speaking to the religious leaders of the day who should have been the most prepared and open to the message of the Gospel. However, in the face of the awesome teaching and miracles of Jesus they were totally unconvinced and were resistant to the notion of Jesus as the Messiah.

2. The Context

Jesus followed up on His baptism in Jordan with a tremendous ministry in Israel. He shared some of the clearest teaching on the laws of the kingdom; He opened the eyes of the blind; He cleansed lepers; He even raised people from the dead.

In the face of all of that the religious leaders refused to believe and they even accused Jesus of doing what He was doing in the power of Beelzebub (Matthew 12:24).

3. The Warning

At this point Jesus does two things.

    a. He gives the religious leaders a stern warning about blasphemy against the Holy Spirit.

Since we are living in the age of the Spirit, it is the work of the Holy Spirit to bring us to God. If we reject the Holy Spirit, we reject the very agent of our salvation. The ultimate rejection of the Holy Spirit is to shun His work in our lives and persist in unbelief in the face of abundant witness.

    b. He immediately changes His mode of teaching.

From this point in Matthew's Gospel Jesus changed His method of teaching. In chapter 13, Jesus began speaking in parables because of the hardness of heart among the religious leaders. At first the disciples didn't understand why Jesus changed his teaching. Jesus explained His actions clearly in Matthew 13:10-17.

4. The Unpardonable Sin

The only sin for which people will be damned, the only sin that everyone in hell will have in common is persistent unbelief (Luke 12:46). Unfortunately, if we continually harden our hearts to the work of the Holy Spirit there could come a day when we are no longer able to respond. There may come a time when we are no longer able to come to a place of repentance (Hebrews 6:4-6). God's Spirit will not always strive with men (Genesis 6:3). God eventually will give people over to their own lusts (Romans 1:18-32). At this point they become a vessel of dishonor that God will use much like He did Pharaoh.

The unpardonable sin is not...

Making a careless statement in a fit of rage or an accidental slip of the tongue.

Ascribing "speaking in tongues" to the work of the devil.

Knowingly doing something that you know you should not.

Easy to commit. If you even care whether or not you have committed it, you have not committed it.

The unpardonable sin is the culmination of all of the above offenses against the Holy Spirit. It is a knowledgeable and deliberate sin. It is not a sin of ignorance. Paul spoke of his own experience in this area (1 Timothy 1:12-13).

And I thank Christ Jesus our Lord who has enabled me, because He counted me faithful, putting me into the ministry, although I was formerly a blasphemer, a persecutor, and an insolent man; but I obtained mercy because I did it ignorantly in unbelief.

Blasphemy against the Holy Spirit is the incorrigible hardening of the heart against the work of the Holy Spirit and is caused by repeated, willful refusal to partake of God's way of salvation, coupled with a persistence to follow the ways of darkness. It can only be committed by someone to whom the deity of Jesus Christ has been internally revealed (Hebrews 3:12-13).

Beware, brethren, lest there be in any of you an evil heart of unbelief in departing from the living God; but exhort one another daily, while it is called "Today," lest any of you be hardened through the deceitfulness of sin.

5. Characteristics of an Unpardonable Sinner

- No godly sorrow
- No repentance
- No desire for God
- No desire to change
- Hardness of heart
- Willful disobedient

6. **Guidelines for Judgment**

   a. God practices His own guideline of forgiveness (Luke 17:3-4).

Take heed to yourselves. If your brother sins against you, rebuke him; and if he repents, forgive him. And if he sins against you seven times in a day, and seven times in a day returns to you, saying, "I repent," you shall forgive him.

   b. Jesus will not cast away those who come to Him (John 6:37).

All that the Father gives Me will come to Me, and the one who comes to Me I will by no means cast out.

   c. Whoever calls on the name of the Lord will be saved (Romans 10:13).

   d. Judgment will be based on how we end up not on what we turned away from (Ezekiel 18:21-32).

How can we ensure that we do not offend the Holy Spirit?

Thankfully, it is also possible to please the Holy Spirit (Acts 15:28).

When we keep our hearts and our hears open to the Lord and live in a state of obedience to what the Holy Spirit is saying, we are sure to please the Holy Spirit.

DR. ABRAHAM PETERS

CHAPTER SEVEN

THE BAPTISM OF THE HOLY SPIRIT

What the Old Testament promise in regard to the outpouring of the Holy Spirit An outpouring was promised to the Seed of Jacob (Isaiah 44:3).

For I will pour water on the thirsty land, and streams on the dry ground; I will pour out my Spirit on your offspring, and my blessing on your descendants. Isaiah 44:3

God would use other tongues to speak to His people (Isaiah 28:11-12; 1 Corinthians 14:21).

Very well then, with foreign lips and strange tongues God will speak to this people, to whom he said, "This is the resting place, let the weary rest"; and, "This is the place of repose"--but they would not listen. Isaiah 28:11-12

I thank my God I speak with tongues more than you all; yet in the church I would rather speak five words with my understanding, that I may teach others also, than ten thousand words in a tongue. Brethren, do not be children in understanding; however, in malice be babes, but in understanding be mature. In the law it is written: "With men of other tongues and other lips I will speak to this people; and yet, for all that, they will not hear Me," says the Lord. Therefore tongues are for a sign, not to those who believe but to unbelievers; but prophesying is not for unbelievers but for those who believe. 1 Corinthians 14:18-22

God promised to pour out His Spirit on all flesh in the last days (Joel 2:28-29).

And afterward, I will pour out my Spirit on all people. Your sons and daughters will prophesy, your old men will dream dreams, your young men will see visions. Even on my servants, both men and women, I will pour out my Spirit in those days. Joel 2:28-29

The relation of Christ to the baptism of the Holy Spirit

Jesus was baptized in the Holy Spirit at Jordan. The Spirit came and remained on Him (Matthew 3:16-17; Mark 1:10-11; Luke 3:21-22; John 1:19-34).

As soon as Jesus was baptized, he went up out of the water. At that moment heaven was opened, and he saw the Spirit of God descending like a dove and lighting on him. And a voice from heaven said, "This is my Son, whom I love; with him I am well pleased." Matthew 3:16-17

As Jesus was coming up out of the water, he saw heaven being torn open and the Spirit descending on him like a dove. And a voice came from heaven: "You are my Son, whom I love; with you I am well pleased." Mark 1:10-11

When all the people were being baptized, Jesus was baptized too. And as he was praying, heaven was opened and the Holy Spirit descended on him in bodily form like a dove. And a voice came from heaven: "You are my Son, whom I love; with you I am well pleased." Luke 3:21-22

Now this was John's testimony when the Jews of Jerusalem sent priests and Levites to ask him who he was. He did not fail to confess, but confessed freely, "I am not the Christ." They asked him, "Then who are you? Are you Elijah?" He said, "I am not." "Are you the Prophet?" He answered, "No." Finally they said, "Who are you? Give us an answer to take back to those who sent us. What do you say about yourself?" John replied in the words of Isaiah the prophet, "I am the voice of one calling in the desert, 'Make straight the way for the Lord.'" Now some Pharisees who had been sent questioned him, "Why then do you baptize if you are not the Christ, nor Elijah, nor the Prophet?" "I baptize with water," John replied, "but among you stands one you do not know. He is the one who comes after me, the thongs of whose sandals I am not worthy to untie." This all happened at Bethany on the other side of the Jordan, where John was baptizing. The next day John saw Jesus coming toward him and said, "Look, the Lamb of God, who takes away the sin of the world! This is the one I meant when I said, 'A man who comes after me has surpassed me because he was before me.' I myself did not know him, but the reason I came baptizing with water was that he might be revealed to Israel." Then John gave this testimony: "I saw the Spirit come down from heaven as a dove and remain on him. I would not have known him, except that the one who sent me to baptize with water told me, 'The man on whom you see the Spirit come down and remain is he who will baptize with the Holy Spirit.'" John 1:19-34

It is part of the ministry of Jesus to baptize with the Holy Spirit (John 1:33; Compare to John 4:2).

I would not have known him, except that the one who sent me to baptize with water told me, "The man on whom you see the Spirit come down and remain is he who will baptize with the Holy Spirit." John 1:33

It should be noted that to avoid confusion about the baptism to which God was referring in the above passage, Jesus did not personally baptize anyone in water.

Therefore, when the Lord knew that the Pharisees had heard that Jesus made and baptized more disciples than John (though Jesus Himself did not baptize, but His disciples). John 4:2

Jesus prophesied that this baptism would be a believer's experience (John 7:38-39).

"Whoever believes in me, as the Scripture has said, streams of living water will flow from within him." By this he meant the Spirit, whom those who believed in him were later to receive. Up to that time the Spirit had not been given, since Jesus had not yet been glorified. John 7:38-39

In order for Christ to fulfill this ministry, He had to leave the earth (John 16:7).

But I tell you the truth: It is for your good that I am going away. Unless I go away, the Counselor will not come to you; but if I go, I will send him to you. John 16:7

It is given on the basis of the finished work of Calvary and the exaltation of Christ. He received it from the Father and has given it to us (Acts 2:33; See also John 7:37-39).

Exalted to the right hand of God, he has received from the Father the promised Holy Spirit and has poured out what you now see and hear. Acts 2:33

Christ gave His disciples instructions prior to their receiving the baptism of the Holy Spirit (Acts 1:4-5; Luke 24:49).

On one occasion, while he was eating with them, he gave them this command: "Do not leave Jerusalem, but wait for the gift my Father promised, which you have heard me speak about. For John baptized with water, but in a few days you will be baptized with the Holy Spirit." Acts 1:4-5

"I am going to send you what my Father has promised; but stay in the city until you have been clothed with power from on high."
Luke 24:49

What the baptism of the Holy Spirit is:

It is the promise of the Father (Acts 1:4-5).

And being assembled together with them, He commanded them not to depart from Jerusalem, but to wait for the Promise of the Father, "which," He said, "you have heard from Me; for John truly baptized with water, but you shall be baptized with the Holy Spirit not many days from now." –NKJV

It is an endowment with power to do the commands of Christ (Acts 1:8; Luke 24:49).

"But you will receive power when the Holy Spirit comes on you; and you will be my witnesses in Jerusalem, and in all Judea and Samaria, and to the ends of the earth." Acts 1:8

DR. ABRAHAM PETERS

"I am going to send you what my Father has promised; but stay in the city until you have been clothed with power from on high."
Luke 24:49

It is a definite experience of which we can know that we have or have not received (Acts 19:2).

And asked them, "Did you receive the Holy Spirit when you believed?" They answered, "No, we have not even heard that there is a Holy Spirit." Acts 19:2

It takes place at a given point in time (Acts 1:5).

"For John baptized with water, but in a few days you will be baptized with the Holy Spirit." Acts 1:5

It is an operation of the Spirit distinct from and subsequent to the conversion experience or being born of the Spirit (Acts 8:12, 15-16; 19:1-2).

But when they believed Philip as he preached the good news of the kingdom of God and the name of Jesus Christ, they were baptized, both men and women. When they arrived, they prayed for them that they might receive the Holy Spirit, because the Holy Spirit had not yet come upon any of them; they had simply been baptized into the name of the Lord Jesus. Acts 8:12, 15-16

While Apollos was at Corinth, Paul took the road through the interior and arrived at Ephesus. There he found some disciples and asked them, "Did you receive the Holy Spirit when you believed?"

Fellowship With The Holy Spirit

They answered, "No, we have not even heard that there is a Holy Spirit." Acts 19:1-2

Every true believer has the Holy Spirit, but not every believer has the baptism of the Holy Spirit (1 Corinthians 6:19; Romans 8:9; Acts 19:1-2).

Do you not know that your body is a temple of the Holy Spirit, who is in you, whom you have received from God? You are not your own. 1 Corinthians 6:19

You, however, are controlled not by the sinful nature but by the Spirit, if the Spirit of God lives in you. And if anyone does not have the Spirit of Christ, he does not belong to Christ. Romans 8:9

It is part of the proper Christian birth and separation from the old life (Acts 2:38).

On the Day of Pentecost after Peter had preached to the multitudes and the Holy Spirit had brought conviction to their hearts, the multitudes asked, "What must we do?"

Peter replied, "Repent and be baptized, every one of you, in the name of Jesus Christ for the forgiveness of your sins. And you will receive the gift of the Holy Spirit." Acts 2:38

Peter gave them the whole package that involved repentance, faith, water baptism, the baptism of the Holy Spirit and separation from the world (Acts 2:40). Synonymous phrases include baptized with the Holy Spirit, the Holy Spirit fell on them, the promise of the Father etc.

DR. ABRAHAM PETERS

How the Early Church did experience the baptism of the Holy Spirit

On the Day of Pentecost God poured out His Spirit upon the expectant disciples (Acts 2:1-13).

> *When the day of Pentecost came, they were all together in one place. Suddenly a sound like the blowing of a violent wind came from heaven and filled the whole house where they were sitting. They saw what seemed to be tongues of fire that separated and came to rest on each of them. All of them were filled with the Holy Spirit and began to speak in other tongues as the Spirit enabled them. Now there were staying in Jerusalem God-fearing Jews from every nation under heaven. When they heard this sound, a crowd came together in bewilderment, because each one heard them speaking in his own language. Utterly amazed, they asked: "Are not all these men who are speaking Galileans? Then how is it that each of us hears them in his own native language? Parthians, Medes and Elamites; residents of Mesopotamia, Judea and Cappadocia, Pontus and Asia, Phrygia and Pamphylia, Egypt and the parts of Libya near Cyrene; visitors from Rome (both Jews and converts to Judaism); Cretans and Arabs-we hear them declaring the wonders of God in our own tongues!" Amazed and perplexed, they asked one another, "What does this mean?" Some, however, made fun of them and said, "They have had too much wine."* Acts 2:1-13

The believers at Samaria received the Holy Spirit (Acts 8:14-17).

> *When the apostles in Jerusalem heard that Samaria had accepted the word of God, they sent Peter and John to them. When they*

arrived, they prayed for them that they might receive the Holy Spirit, because the Holy Spirit had not yet come upon any of them; they had simply been baptized into the name of the Lord Jesus. Then Peter and John placed their hands on them, and they received the Holy Spirit. Acts 8:14-17

The Holy Spirit fell on those that heard the Word in the house of Cornelius, a Gentile (Acts 10:44-48; 11:15-17).

While Peter was still speaking these words, the Holy Spirit came on all who heard the message. The circumcised believers who had come with Peter were astonished that the gift of the Holy Spirit had been poured out even on the Gentiles. For they heard them speaking in tongues and praising God. Then Peter said, "Can anyone keep these people from being baptized with water? They have received the Holy Spirit just as we have." So he ordered that they be baptized in the name of Jesus Christ. Then they asked Peter to stay with them for a few days. Acts 10:44-48

As I began to speak, the Holy Spirit came on them as he had come on us at the beginning. Then I remembered what the Lord had said: "John baptized with water, but you will be baptized with the Holy Spirit." So if God gave them the same gift as he gave us, who believed in the Lord Jesus Christ, who was I to think that I could oppose God? Acts 11:15-17

The Ephesians believers received the gift of the Holy Spirit (Acts 19:1-6).

While Apollos was at Corinth, Paul took the road through the interior and arrived at Ephesus. There he found some disciples and asked them, "Did you receive the Holy Spirit when you believed?"

They answered, "No, we have not even heard that there is a Holy Spirit." So Paul asked, "Then what baptism did you receive?" "John's baptism," they replied. Paul said, "John's baptism was a baptism of repentance. He told the people to believe in the one coming after him, that is, in Jesus." On hearing this, they were baptized into the name of the Lord Jesus. When Paul placed his hands on them, the Holy Spirit came on them, and they spoke in tongues and prophesied. Acts 19:1-6

Paul received the Holy Spirit (Acts 9:17-18).

Then Ananias went to the house and entered it. Placing his hands on Saul, he said, "Brother Saul, the Lord-Jesus, who appeared to you on the road as you were coming here-has sent me so that you may see again and be filled with the Holy Spirit." Immediately, something like scales fell from Saul's eyes, and he could see again. He got up and was baptized. Acts 9:17-18

What is the necessity of receiving the baptism of the Holy Spirit?

The baptism of the Holy Spirit is absolutely necessary for every Christian for the service that Christ demands and expects of us.

1. Christ commanded the disciples not to enter upon the work to which He had Himself called them until they were baptized with the Holy Spirit (Acts 1:4).

2. Jesus Christ Himself did not enter into His ministry until the Spirit of God come upon Him and He had been anointed with the Holy Spirit and power (Luke 3:21-22; 4:14, 18; John 1:29-34; 2:11; Acts 10:38).

The Spirit of the Lord is on me, because he has anointed me to preach good news to the poor. He has sent me to proclaim freedom for the prisoners and recovery of sight for the blind, to release the oppressed. Luke 4:18

3. When the apostles found believers in Christ they sought to discover whether they had been baptized in the Holy Spirit, and if not, they at once saw to it that they were (Acts 19:1-2).

With the baptism of the Holy Spirit comes spiritual authority to the believer (Acts 1:8).

But you will receive power when the Holy Spirit comes on you; and you will be my witnesses in Jerusalem, and in all Judea and Samaria, and to the ends of the earth. Acts 1:8

What is the evidence of the baptism of the Holy Spirit?

In all of the instances of people receiving the baptism of the Holy Spirit in the Bible, speaking with other tongues is either present or implied.

4. This was true at the initial outpouring on the day of Pentecost (Acts 2:4).

"And began to speak with other tongues, as the Spirit gave them utterance."Acts 2:4

5. This was true when the Samaritans were baptized in the Holy Spirit (Acts 8:14-21).

> *"And when Simon saw that through the laying on of hands the Holy Spirit was given..."* Acts 8:18

One has to wonder what Simon saw. Peter explains later that Simon had "neither part nor portion in this matter" (Acts 8:21, Greek, *logos*, which means utterance or speech).

6. This was true when Paul receive his Spirit baptism (Acts 9:17 with 1 Corinthians 14:18). Although there is not a specific reference to tongues at the time of Paul's baptism, it is clear that this was part of Paul's personal life experience.

> *I thank my God, I speak in tongues more than ye all.* 1 Corinthians 14:18

7. This was true when the Holy Spirit fell upon Cornelius and his household (Acts 10:44-48).

> *For they heard them speak with tongues and magnify God.* Acts 10:46

8. This was true when the men of Ephesus were baptized in the Holy Spirit (Acts 19:1-6).

> *And they spoke with tongues, and prophesied.* Acts 19:6

The Bible does not say that you must speak in tongues to have the baptism of the Holy Spirit, but it does teach us by illustration that if you have the baptism of the Holy Spirit, you will be given the immediate evidence of speaking in tongues. God chose this sign because He wants to purify us by getting a hold of our unruly member (James 3:1-12).

Not many of you should presume to be teachers, my brothers, because you know that we who teach will be judged more strictly. We all stumble in many ways. If anyone is never at fault in what he says, he is a perfect man, able to keep his whole body in check. When we put bits into the mouths of horses to make them obey us, we can turn the whole animal. Or take ships as an example. Although they are so large and are driven by strong winds, they are steered by a very small rudder wherever the pilot wants to go. Likewise the tongue is a small part of the body, but it makes great boasts. Consider what a great forest is set on fire by a small spark. The tongue also is a fire, a world of evil among the parts of the body. It corrupts the whole person, sets the whole course of his life on fire, and is itself set on fire by hell. All kinds of animals, birds, reptiles and creatures of the sea are being tamed and have been tamed by man, but no man can tame the tongue. It is a restless evil, full of deadly poison. With the tongue we praise our Lord and Father, and with it we curse men, who have been made in God's likeness. Out of the same mouth come praise and cursing. My brothers, this should not be. Can both fresh water and salt water flow from the same spring? My brothers, can a fig tree bear olives, or a grapevine bear figs? Neither can a salt spring produce fresh water. James 3:1-12

Who may receive the baptism of the Holy Spirit?

All believers in Christ are candidates (Acts 2:39; Mark 16:17).

The promise is for you and your children and for all who are far off-for all whom the Lord our God will call. Acts 2:39

DR. ABRAHAM PETERS

And these signs will accompany those who believe: In my name they will drive out demons; they will speak in new tongues. Mark 16:17

The fundamental conditions upon which the baptism of the Holy Spirit is given are repentance and faith in Jesus Christ as an all-sufficient Savior apart from the works of the law (Acts 2:38; 10:44).

Peter replied, "Repent and be baptized, every one of you, in the name of Jesus Christ for the forgiveness of your sins. And you will receive the gift of the Holy Spirit." Acts 2:38

While Peter was still speaking these words, the Holy Spirit came on all who heard the message. Acts 10:44

For those who believe on Christ the experimental reception of the baptism with the Holy Spirit is sometimes conditioned on the believer's knowledge that there is such a blessing and that it is for him in the here and now (Acts 19:2-6).

And asked them, "Did you receive the Holy Spirit when you believed?" They answered, "No, we have not even heard that there is a Holy Spirit."...When Paul placed his hands on them, the Holy Spirit came on them, and they spoke in tongues and prophesied. Acts 19:2, 6

God gives the Holy Spirit to them that obey Him. Obedience means absolute surrender to the Lordship of Christ (Acts 5:32).

Fellowship With The Holy Spirit

"We are witnesses of these things, and so is the Holy Spirit, whom God has given to those who obey him." When they heard this, they were furious and wanted to put them to death. Acts 5:32

How one does receive the baptism of the Holy Spirit

Fulfill the prerequisites for receiving the Holy Spirit as listed above. Remember that it is a free gift and not earned (Galatians 3:2).

I would like to learn just one thing from you: Did you receive the Spirit by observing the law, or by believing what you heard?

Ask Christ to give you this gift and He will (Acts 8:14; Luke 11:9-13).

When the apostles in Jerusalem heard that Samaria had accepted the word of God, they sent Peter and John to them. Acts 8:14

So I say to you: Ask and it will be given to you; seek and you will find; knock and the door will be opened to you. For everyone who asks receives; he who seeks finds; and to him who knocks, the door will be opened. "Which of you fathers, if your son asks for a fish, will give him a snake instead? Or if he asks for an egg, will give him a scorpion? If you then, though you are evil, know how to give good gifts to your children, how much more will your Father in heaven give the Holy Spirit to those who ask him!" Luke 11:9-13

Expect to receive this gift as hands are laid upon you (Acts 8:14-17; 9:17). Exercise your faith by speaking in an unknown language unto the Lord. Yield your unruly member as an instrument of righteousness, not fearing that the Lord will give you something else than that which you desire. Do not attempt to work up your emotions, relax in His presence. Once you have received the baptism of the Holy Spirit use your tongue often as it is a key to spiritual vitality.

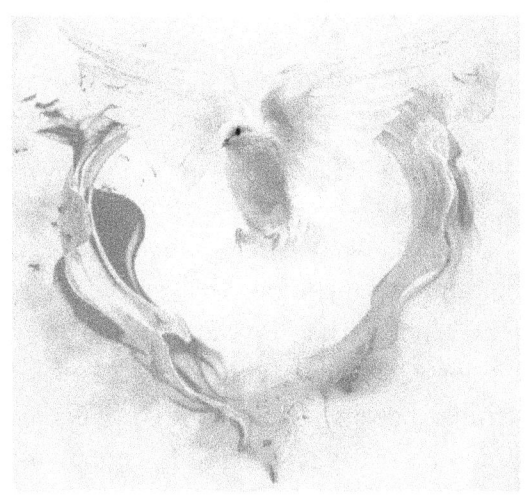

CHAPTER EIGHT

SPEAKING WITH OTHER TONGUES

Why "speaking with other tongues" is sometimes misunderstood: There are those who do not believe that this experience is for today (1 Corinthians 13:8-10). They believe that the Bible teaches that "tongues" have ceased.

Love never fails. But whether there are prophecies, they will fail; whether there are tongues, they will cease; whether there is knowledge, it will vanish away. For we know in part and we prophesy in part. But when that which is perfect has come, then that which is in part will be done away.

This comes from a misunderstanding of the context of 1 Corinthians 13. Paul was highlighting the importance of functioning in all of the gifts and ministries in a spirit of love and for the purpose of serving and edifying others. Love is something eternal that will last throughout eternity because God is love. This comes from a misunderstanding of what is referred to by "that which is perfect." In some people's mind the "perfect" in this passage refers to the New Testament Canon of Scripture. It is important to note that the Bible is only perfect in so far as it reflects the Perfect One, the Lord Jesus Christ.

Paul tells us very clearly the time when the perfect will come (Ephesians 4:13). It has to do with the completion of the Church that comes at the return of Christ. At this time the mortal gives way to the immortal and the imperfect gives way to that which is perfect. Our imperfect knowledge gives way to perfect knowledge (1 Corinthians 13:12). Our imperfect communication gives way to perfect communication and a new language of heaven.

There are those who do not believe that this experience is for everyone (1Corinthians12:28-30).

And God has appointed these in the church: first apostles, second prophets, third teachers, after that miracles, then gifts of healings, helps, administrations, varieties of tongues. Are all apostles? Are all prophets? Are all teachers? Are all workers of miracles? Do all have gifts of healings? Do all speak with tongues? Do all interpret?

This passage seems to indicate that all do not speak with other tongues. It also seems to indicate that all are not involved in healings and miracles. This has led people to conclude that this is an experience that is optional and, perhaps, not for them. This, however, seems to contradict what Jesus said (Mark 16:17-18) and what Peter said on the Day of Pentecost (Acts 2:39).

And these signs will follow those who believe: In My name they will cast out demons; they will speak with new tongues; they will take up serpents; and if they drink anything deadly, it will by no means hurt them; they will lay hands on the sick, and they will recover. Mark 16:17-18

For the promise is to you and to your children, and to all who are afar off, as many as the Lord our God will call. Acts 2:39

There are those who are troubled by what appears to be conflicting instructions on the subject (1 Corinthians 14:5-9, 18-19, 23).

But now, brethren, if I come to you speaking with tongues, what shall I profit you unless I speak to you either by revelation, by knowledge, by prophesying, or by teaching? 7 Even things without life, whether flute or harp, when they make a sound, unless they make a distinction in the sounds, how will it be known what is piped or played? 8 For if the trumpet makes an uncertain sound, who will prepare for battle? 9 So likewise you, unless you utter by the tongue words easy to understand, how will it be known what is spoken? For you will be speaking into the air. 1 Corinthians 14:6-9

I thank my God I speak with tongues more than you all; yet in the church I would rather speak five words with my understanding, that I may teach others also, than ten thousand words in a tongue.
1 Corinthians 14:18-19

Therefore if the whole church comes together in one place, and all speak with tongues, and there come in those who are uninformed or unbelievers, will they not say that you are out of your mind? 1 Corinthians 14:23

There are different expressions of "speaking with tongues" in the Church. The only way to resolve the apparent conflict in relation to the experience of speaking with other tongues is to realize that the Bible actually refers to three different expressions of speaking with tongues. In each verse the reader must determine from the context the expression of tongues to which it refers.

1. The Evidence: Speaking in tongues as a private prayer language (1 Corinthians 14:18).

2. The Gift: Speaking in tongues as one of the nine gifts of the Spirit (1 Corinthians 12:10).

3. The Ministry: Speaking in tongues as a ministry of some members of the Body of Christ (1 Corinthians 12:28-30).

Study the following chart for further distinctions between these three expressions.

DR. ABRAHAM PETERS

Speaking with Tongues
The Evidence, the Gift and the Ministry

Evidence	Gift	Ministry
Defined: The initial evidence of the Baptism of the Holy Spirit that becomes an ongoing ability used for the purpose of communion with God in private prayer and the edification of the one speaking.	Defined: One of the nine gifts of the Holy Spirit available to every believer from time to time at the impulse of the Spirit. It is most often used in conjunction with the Gift of Interpretation of Tongues and is used for the edification of the church.	Defined: A ministry that is given to some individual members in the Body of Christ to be used regularly in conjunction and harmony with the other body ministries for the purpose of ministering to the church and the world.
Characteristics: For all believers Permanent endowment To be used often To be used privately No one understands Communion with God Edification of speaker	Characteristics: Available to believers Temporary endowment To be used on occasion To be used publicly To be accompanied by interpretation	Characteristics: Available to a few Permanent ministry To be used regularly To be used publicly To be accompanied by interpretation Edification of the church

	Edification of the church	
Key Verses: Mark 16:17 Acts 10:46 Acts 19:6 I Corinthians 14:2, 4, 5, 6, 14, 18, 19, 23, 31	Key Verses: I Corinthians 12:10 I Corinthians 13:1, 8 I Corinthians 14:5, 13, 22, 26-27	Key Verses: I Corinthians 12:28, 30 I Corinthians 13:1, 8 I Corinthians 14:26-27

What occurred on the Day of Pentecost was the initial and special outpouring of the Holy Spirit in fulfillment of the prophecy of Joel (Joel 2:28-32). This was a unique experience at the Pentecostal inauguration of the Church and this can be duplicated in demonstration as the same Holy Spirit may chooses today (Acts 2:1-13).

Some of the unique features of this experience include the following:

1. The heavenly sound of a mighty wind.
2. The manifestation of fire and the tongues of fire.
3. The miracle of tongues being understood without interpretation.

Some of the reasons for Speaking in Tongues

A lot of times when "speaking with other tongues" is discussed, it is presented in a negative way. That is, people often ask the question, "Do I really need to speak with tongues?" They speak as if "tongues" were a negative option. However, when you see the tremendous spiritual benefits that come to a believer through the experience of speaking with other tongues the question will become, "Why wouldn't I want to speak with other tongues?"

It is one of the signs of a believer (Mark 16:17; John 7:38-39).

And these signs will accompany those who believe: In my name they will drive out demons; they will speak in new tongues. Mark 16:17

"Whoever believes in me, as the Scripture has said, streams of living water will flow from within him." By this he meant the Spirit, whom those who believed in him were later to receive. Up to that time the Spirit had not been given, since Jesus had not yet been glorified. John 7:38-39

By it God speaks to man (1 Corinthians 14:21; Isaiah 28:11-12).

In the Law it is written: "Through men of strange tongues and through the lips of foreigners I will speak to this people, but even then they will not listen to me," says the Lord. 1 Corinthians 14:21

Very well then, with foreign lips and strange tongues God will speak to this people, to whom he said, "This is the resting place, let the weary rest"; and, "This is the place of repose"--but they would not listen. Isaiah 28:11-12

By it man may speak to God (1 Corinthians 14:2).

For anyone who speaks in a tongue does not speak to men but to God. Indeed, no one understands him; he utters mysteries with his spirit. 1 Corinthians 14:2

It is a way to edify or build ourselves up (1 Corinthians 14:4; Jude 20).

He who speaks in a tongue edifies himself, but he who prophesies edifies the church. 1 Corinthians 14:4

But you, dear friends, build yourselves up in your most holy faith and pray in the Holy Spirit. Jude 20

It is a way to magnify, praise and bless God (Acts 10:45, 1 Corinthians 14:16).

The circumcised believers who had come with Peter were astonished that the gift of the Holy Spirit had been poured out even on the Gentiles. For they heard them speaking in tongues and praising God. Acts 10:45

Otherwise, if you bless with the spirit, how will he who occupies the place of the uninformed say "Amen" at your giving of thanks, since he does not understand what you say? 1 Corinthians 14:16

It is a means of spiritual worship (1 Corinthians 14:15, 17; John 4:24).

So what shall I do? I will pray with my spirit, but I will also pray with my mind; I will sing with my spirit, but I will also sing with my mind. 1 Corinthians 14:15

DR. ABRAHAM PETERS

For you indeed give thanks well... 1 Corinthians 14:17a

God is spirit, and his worshipers must worship in spirit and in truth. John 4:24

It is part of the spiritual weaponry of the believer (Ephesians 6:18).

And pray in the Spirit on all occasions with all kinds of prayers and requests. With this in mind, be alert and always keep on praying for all the saints. Ephesians 6:18

It is part of the power package of the believer.

But you will receive power when the Holy Spirit comes on you; and you will be my witnesses in Jerusalem, and in all Judea and Samaria, and to the ends of the earth. Acts 1:8

It helps us to pray according to the will of God (Romans 8:26; 1 Corinthians 14:14).

In the same way, the Spirit helps us in our weakness. We do not know what we ought to pray for, but the Spirit himself intercedes for us with groans that words cannot express. Romans 8:26

For if I pray in a tongue, my spirit prays, but my mind is unfruitful. 1 Corinthians 14:14

It is a spiritual blessing for which we should be thankful (1 Corinthians 14:18).

Thank God that I speak in tongues more than all of you. 1 Corinthians 14:18

It is spoken of as a "refreshing" or a "resting place" (Isaiah 28:11-12).

Very well then, with foreign lips and strange tongues God will speak to this people, to whom he said, "This is the resting place, let the weary rest"; and, "This is the place of repose"--but they would not listen. Isaiah 28: 11-12

In my book titled, Prayer: Communicating with God, Connecting with Heaven and Changing the World. The chapter seven on the Supernatural Prayer Language discussed much more on this significant subject. Also I recommend, Seventy Reasons for Speaking in Tongues: Your Own Built in Spiritual Dynamo by Dr. Bill Hamon.

DR. ABRAHAM PETERS

CHAPTER NINE

THE FRUIT OF THE SPIRIT

Fellowship With The Holy Spirit

I say then: Walk in the Spirit, and you shall not fulfill the lust of the flesh. 17 For the flesh lusts against the Spirit, and the Spirit against the flesh; and these are contrary to one another, so that you do not do the things that you wish. 18 But if you are led by the Spirit, you are not under the law. 19 Now the works of the flesh are evident, which are: adultery, fornication, uncleanness, lewdness, 20 idolatry, sorcery, hatred, contentions, jealousies, outbursts of wrath, selfish ambitions, dissensions, heresies, 21 envy, murders, drunkenness, revelries, and the like; of which I tell you beforehand, just as I also told you in time past, that those who practice such things will not inherit the kingdom of God. 22 But the fruit of the Spirit is love, joy, peace, longsuffering, kindness, goodness, faithfulness, 23 gentleness, self-control. Against such there is no law. 24 And those who are Christ's have crucified the flesh with its passions and desires. 25 If we live in the Spirit, let us also walk in the Spirit. Galatians 5:16-25

What do we mean when we speak of fruit?

God loves to teach us using things that are common in our everyday lives. He often draws symbols and metaphors from the world of nature to teach us of spiritual things. It is no different here when we talk about fruit. The idea of "fruit" is a metaphor taken from the world of agriculture. When the Bible talks of fruit it brings in the themes of planting, watering, fertilizing and harvesting. The word "fruit" literally means that which is produced by the inherent energy of a living organism. In the natural realm, fruit is usually thought of as the seed-bearing product of a plant. It should be noted that not all fruit is "good" fruit. Some fruit is beneficial. Some fruit is harmful or poisonous. The word is used metaphorically in this case of attitudes, works and deeds that result from the energy from within. These attitudes, works or deeds can be "good" or they can be "evil." Fruit is the visible expression of power working inwardly and invisibly. The character of the fruit is the evidence of the character of the power producing it.

Some of the biblical challenges regarding fruit in our lives

True fruit comes from a spirit of repentance in our lives (Matthew 3:8; Luke 3:8).

Then Jerusalem, all Judea, and all the region around the Jordan went out to him and were baptized by him in the Jordan, confessing their sins. But when he saw many of the Pharisees and Sadducees coming to his baptism, he said to them, "Brood of vipers! Who warned you to flee from the wrath to come? Therefore bear fruits worthy of repentance..." Matthew 3:5-8

True fruit can only come forth from a seed that has died (John 12:24-25).

Most assuredly, I say to you, unless a grain of wheat falls into the ground and dies, it remains alone; but if it dies, it produces much grain [KJV, fruit]. He who loves his life will lose it, and he who hates his life in this world will keep it for eternal life.

True fruit can only come forth from those who abide in Christ (John 15:5). He is the life force behind the fruit.

I am the vine, you are the branches. He who abides in Me, and I in him, bears much fruit; for without Me you can do nothing.

God has an expectation of fruit in our lives (Matthew 21:19; Luke 3:9; 13:6-9; John 15:16). When someone makes a big investment, they expect a return on the investment.

You did not choose Me, but I chose you and appointed you that you should go and bear fruit, and that your fruit should remain, that whatever you ask the Father in My name He may give you. John 15:16

He also spoke this parable: "A certain man had a fig tree planted in his vineyard, and he came seeking fruit on it and found none. Then he said to the keeper of his vineyard, 'Look, for three years I have come seeking fruit on this fig tree and find none. Cut it down; why does it use up the ground?' But he answered and said to him, 'Sir, let it alone this year also, until I dig around it and fertilize it. And if it bears fruit, well. But if not, after that you can cut it down.'" Luke 13:6-9

God expects the fruit from our lives to be excellent (John 15:1-2). God is never satisfied with some fruit. He wants us to move to "more" fruit and on to "much" fruit (John 15:5, 8).

I am the true vine, and My Father is the vinedresser. Every branch in Me that does not bear fruit He takes away; and every branch that bears fruit He prunes, that it may bear more fruit.

By this My Father is glorified, that you bear much fruit; so you will be My disciples. John 15:8

If we do not produce godly fruit there will be judgment (Matthew 3:10; John 15:2). Jesus actually cursed the fig tree that did not produce fruit (Matthew 21:18-20; Mark 11:12-14, 20-21).

And even now the ax is laid to the root of the trees. Therefore every tree which does not bear good fruit is cut down and thrown into the fire. Matthew 3:10

Fruit can come forth in measures (Matthew 13:8; Mark 4:7-8). God's desire is that we grow in the area of fruitfulness. Each of the individual aspects of the fruit of the Spirit can continue to grow throughout our lives.

But others fell on good ground and yielded a crop: some a hundredfold, some sixty, some thirty. Matthew 13:8

Fruit takes time and patience to produce (James 5:7-8). Fruit usually grows gradually. It starts out as a bud, then a flower, then a small, hard and unripened fruit. Eventually it comes to full fruit or full maturity. The process takes time. In this sense the fruit of the Spirit is different from the gifts of the Spirit. The Bible does not speak of the "gift" of love or the "gift" of selfcontrol. Gifts are given in a moment while fruit is developed over time.

Therefore be patient, brethren, until the coming of the Lord. See how the farmer waits for the precious fruit of the earth, waiting patiently for it until it receives the early and latter rain. You also be patient. Establish your hearts, for the coming of the Lord is at hand.

The way you know the nature of the tree is by examining the fruit (Matthew 7:15-20; 12:33).

Beware of false prophets, who come to you in sheep's clothing, but inwardly they are ravenous wolves. 16 You will know them by their fruits. Do men gather grapes from thornbushes or figs from thistles? 17 Even so, every good tree bears good fruit, but a bad tree bears bad fruit. 18 A good tree cannot bear bad fruit, nor can a bad tree bear good fruit. 19 Every tree that does not bear good fruit is cut down and thrown into the fire. 20 Therefore by their fruits you will know them. Matthew 7:15-20

Either make the tree good and its fruit good, or else make the tree bad and its fruit bad; for a tree is known by its fruit. Matthew 12:33

Those that bear the proper fruit are honored by the Lord (Matthew 21:43).

Therefore I say to you, the kingdom of God will be taken from you and given to a nation bearing the fruits of it.

How fruit come forth from one's life

In the Bible, the Church or the people of God are referred to as the garden of the Lord (Song. 4:12-15), the planting of the Lord (Isaiah 61:3b) or His husbandry (1 Corinthians 3:9).

That they may be called trees of righteousness, the planting of the LORD, that He may be glorified. Isaiah 61:3b

DR. ABRAHAM PETERS

For we are fellow workmen (joint promoters, laborers together) with and for God; you are God's garden and vineyard and field under cultivation, [you are] God's building. 1 Corinthians 3:9 Amp.

At times individuals in that garden are likened to plants or trees (Psalm 1:3; Psalm 92:12-14).

He shall be like a tree planted by the rivers of water, that brings forth its fruit in its season, whose leaf also shall not wither; and whatever he does shall prosper. Psalm 1:3

The righteous shall flourish like a palm tree, he shall grow like a cedar in Lebanon. Those who are planted in the house of the LORD shall flourish in the courts of our God. They shall still bear fruit in old age; they shall be fresh and flourishing... Psalm 92:12-14

1. Palm Trees (Psalm 92:12)
2. Cedar Trees (Psalm 92:12)
3. Willow Trees (Isaiah 44:4)

The trees in a garden can either bring forth good fruit or bad fruit (Matthew 7:17-18; Luke 6:43-45).

Even so, every good tree bears good fruit, but a bad tree bears bad fruit. A good tree cannot bear bad fruit, nor can a bad tree bear good fruit. Matthew 7:17-18

For a good tree does not bear bad fruit, nor does a bad tree bear good fruit. For every tree is known by its own fruit. For men do not

gather figs from thorns, nor do they gather grapes from a bramble bush. A good man out of the good treasure of his heart brings forth good; and an evil man out of the evil treasure of his heart brings forth evil. For out of the abundance of the heart his mouth speaks.
Luke 6:43-45

1. Jesus spoke of a good tree and a bad tree.
2. In order for there to be two types of trees there must be two types of seed.

3. Each of these trees is inspired by a power from within that produces fruit of like nature and character.

Take Note the following progressions:

THE BAD TREE is the result of BAD SEED and it produces BAD FRUIT that is inspired by THE FLESH

THE GOOD TREE is the result of GOOD SEED and it produces GOOD FRUIT that is inspired by
THE HOLY SPIRIT

It is the Spirit who gives life; the flesh profits nothing. John 6:63a

The kind of fruit which grows on the outside is a reflection of the nature of the tree itself. Apples grow on apple trees; pear trees produce pears. And the fruit of the Spirit which grows in your life is an outgrowth of the nature within. God's desire is that all of the trees of His garden bring forth good fruit (Ezekiel 47:7, 12).

> *When I returned, there, along the bank of the river, were very many trees on one side and the other...Along the bank of the river, on this side and that, will grow all kinds of trees used for food; their leaves will not wither, and their fruit will not fail. They will bear fruit every month, because their water flows from the sanctuary. Their fruit will be for food, and their leaves for medicine.*

Good fruit will only come forth if the conditions for good fruit are present. In order for a plant to bring forth good fruit several things need to be in place. There must be good seed. The good seed is the incorruptible seed of the Word of God (Mark 4:14; Luke 8:11; 1 Peter 1:23).

> *Now the parable is this: The seed is the word of God.* Luke 8:11

> *...having been born again, not of corruptible seed but incorruptible, through the word of God which lives and abides forever...* 1 Peter 1:23

There must be good soil (Ezekiel 17:8). The soil is our hearts.

> *It was planted in good soil by many waters, to bring forth branches, bear fruit, and become a majestic vine.*

Jesus spoke of four kinds of soil that could characterize our hearts. Each condition has a great deal to do with the issue of fruit bearing (Matthew 13:3-9, 18-23). It should be noted that we control the condition of our hearts. It should also be noted that the first three conditions that Jesus described bore no fruit at all.

The Wayside (Matthew 13:4, 19)

And as he sowed, some seed fell by the wayside; and the birds came and devoured them...When anyone hears the word of the kingdom, and does not understand it, then the wicked one comes and snatches away what was sown in his heart. This is he who received seed by the wayside.

Here is a person who hears the Word of God but whose heart (soil) is hard. Because of the hardness of the soil, the seed is not able to get below the surface. The word is "on" the heart but not "in" the heart. This becomes an easy target for the birds of the air to snatch the word away. The result is no germination of the seed and hence no fruit.

The Stony Ground (Matthew 13:5-6, 20-21)

Some fell on stony places, where they did not have much earth; and they immediately sprang up because they had no depth of earth. But when the sun was up they were scorched, and because they had no root they withered away... But he who received the seed on stony places, this is he who hears the word and immediately receives it with joy; yet he has no root in himself, but endures only for a while. For when tribulation or persecution arises because of the word, immediately he stumbles.

This soil represents a heart that is cluttered with hard places that should have been removed to prepare for the planting of the seed. As a result the soil is very shallow. This heart belongs to one who gets very excited about the word until they understand the implications of the word. They are superficial hearers and as soon as persecution or challenge comes to them, they give up. The result of this is also no fruit.

The Thorny Ground (Matthew 13:7, 22)

And some fell among thorns, and the thorns sprang up and choked them… Now he who received seed among the thorns is he who hears the word, and the cares of this world and the deceitfulness of riches choke the word, and he becomes unfruitful.

This soil represents a heart that wants it all and does not discriminate between good seed and bad seed. They are double minded individuals who want the best of the world and the best of Christianity. Unfortunately the bad seed chokes out the good seed. If the cares of life and the deceitfulness of riches are allowed to co-exist with the good seed, the good plants will be choked out. There is only so much nutrition for plants. In this case there was no lasting fruit.

The Good Ground (Matthew 13:8, 23)

But others fell on good ground and yielded a crop: some a hundredfold, some sixty, some thirty…But he who received seed on the good ground is he who hears the word and understands it, who indeed bears fruit and produces: some a hundredfold, some sixty, some thirty.

The good ground represents a heart that is soft and receptive to the Word of God. This is a heart that hears, understands and keeps the Word (Luke 8:15). This is the life that bears fruit.

There must be a watering of the seed (Job 14:9; Isaiah 44:4; Jeremiah 17:7-8; Ezekiel 19:10). The Holy Spirit is likened to rain (Acts 2:2:17). The word of God and doctrine is also likened to water rain or dew (Deuteronomy 32:1-2; Ephesians 5:26).

For I will pour water on him who is thirsty, and floods on the dry ground; I will pour My Spirit on your descendants, and My blessing on your offspring; they will spring up among the grass like willows by the watercourses. Isaiah 44:3-4

Blessed is the man who trusts in the LORD, and whose hope is the LORD. For he shall be like a tree planted by the waters, which spreads out its roots by the river, and will not fear when heat comes; but its leaf will be green, and will not be anxious in the year of drought, nor will cease from yielding fruit. Jeremiah 17:7-8

Your mother was like a vine in your bloodline, planted by the waters, fruitful and full of branches because of many waters. Ezekiel 19:10

There must be a fertilizing of the seed (Luke 13:6-9).

He also spoke this parable: "A certain man had a fig tree planted in his vineyard, and he came seeking fruit on it and found none. Then he said to the keeper of his vineyard, 'Look, for three years I have come seeking fruit on this fig tree and find none. Cut it down; why does it use up the ground?' But he answered and said to him, 'Sir, let it alone this year also, until I dig around it and fertilize it. And if it bears fruit, well. But if not, after that you can cut it down.'"

For each aspect of the fruit of the Spirit there is a fertilizer that helps to bring that quality forth. Unfortunately sometimes the fertilizer is not the fun part of fruit producing. If you want patience, the fertilizer is the trial of your faith (James 1:2-4). If you want love, God will put people in your life who are difficult to love. They are the fertilizer.

My brethren, count it all joy when you fall into various trials, knowing that the testing of your faith produces patience. But let patience have its perfect work, that you may be perfect and complete, lacking nothing.

There must be a maturing of the seed (John 15:1-7). The conditions for fruitfulness that are described in this passage are:

- Union with Christ.
- Purging by the Father.
- Abiding in Christ.
- Christ and His Word abiding in us.

The qualities or virtues known as the fruit of the Spirit are produced by the power within or the action of the Holy Spirit within the believer.

There must be a removal of all hindrances to growth and fruitfulness. This means that we have to continually dig up those spiritual weeds that want to contest what the Spirit is doing in our lives. One thing about the works of the flesh is that they do not have to be planted or desired. They just spring up when we let down our guard.

When all of these things are in order we should start seeing some fruit.

The fruit of the Spirit

The fruit of the Spirit is that which springs forth from the inner working of the Holy Spirit in our lives. The Spirit is behind the fruit; He produces it. It is His work not ours. Because it is a work of the Spirit there should be no striving, no worrying but a simple yielding to the Spirit of God.

An apple tree does not have to strive to produce apples. The fruit of the Spirit is not produced by self-effort, but is produced and grows on the basis of the quality of the life within—in this case, the Holy Spirit.

It is called the fruit of the Spirit because we cannot take the credit for it (Hoshea 14:8; Isaiah 51:3). It is a manifestation of His beauty not ours.

> *O Ephraim, what more have I to do with idols? I will answer him and care for him. I am like a green pine tree; your fruitfulness comes from me.* Hosea 14:8

It is the believer's relationship to the Lord that causes him or her to bear fruit (Isaiah 61:1-3). Strictly speaking, the Lord is the one who bears the fruit.

> *The Spirit of the Lord GOD is upon Me, because the LORD has anointed Me to preach good tidings to the poor; He has sent Me to heal the brokenhearted, to proclaim liberty to the captives, and the*

> *opening of the prison to those who are bound; to proclaim the acceptable year of the LORD, and the day of vengeance of our God; to comfort all who mourn, to console those who mourn in Zion, to give them beauty for ashes, the oil of joy for mourning, the garment of praise for the spirit of heaviness; that they may be called trees of righteousness, the planting of the LORD, that He may be glorified.*

The Spirit is working in us so that Christ and His virtues might be formed in us (Galatians 4:19; 1 Peter 2:9).

> *My little children, for whom I labor in birth again until Christ is formed in you...* Galatians 4:19

> *But you are a chosen generation, a royal priesthood, a holy nation, His own special people, that you may proclaim the praises of Him who called you out of darkness into His marvelous light...* 1 Peter 2:9

The word used in this verse for "praises" means "virtues, moral goodness or purity." The fruit of the Spirit is described in Galatians 5:22-23.

1. The fruit of the Spirit should be expected to grow, mature and ripen gradually.

2. The fruit of the Spirit is contrasted to the works of the flesh.

Fellowship With The Holy Spirit

The Spirit Produces	The Flesh Produces
LOVE	Hatred, Anger, Animosity, Hostility, Murder
JOY	Heaviness, Sorrow, Misery, Depression
PEACE	Strife, Contention, Restlessness, Anxiety
LONGSUFFERING	Impatience, Fretfulness, Hastiness
GENTLENESS	Pushiness, Harshness, Quarrelsomeness
GOODNESS	Wickedness, Jealousy, Sorcery, Immorality
FAITH	Doubt, Mistrust, Unbelief, Apprehension
MEEKNESS	Pride, Selfish Ambition, Intolerance
SELF-CONTROL	Addictions, Angry Outbursts, Unrestraint

The fruit of the Spirit is singular in number. The Bible does not speak of the "fruits" of the Spirit but the "fruit" of the Spirit.

1. Although these qualities can be studied separately, they are inseparable in the life of the believer. There is a unity among them. They represent one harmonious whole.

    a. They should be pictured like an orange rather than a bowl full of different kinds of fruit. One fruit with many segments (See Diagram).

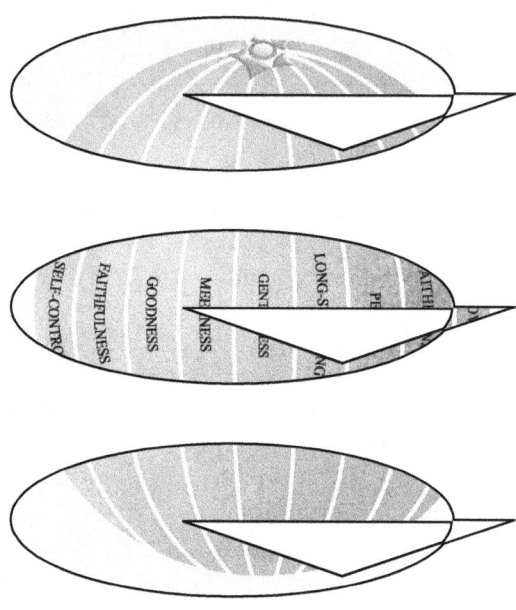

b. In some believers one grace may predominate the others yet all will be present in some measure if the Holy Spirit is operating in the life of the believer.

- The meekness of Moses (Numbers 12:3)
- The patience of Job (James 5:11)
- The love of the Apostle John (John 20:2; 21:7, 20)

These are seen in contrast to the works (plural) of the flesh (Galatians 5:19).

   c. The plural stresses the disorganization, fragmentation and the instability of the life lived under the dictates of the flesh.

d. The unregenerate life is fragmented and at odds with itself.

   e. The fruit of the Spirit as they are listed have a certain order to them.

2. The first one on the list is LOVE.

   a. This one is the foundation on which the other are built.

   b. This one encompasses the rest of the qualities (1 Corinthians 13:3). All of the others flow out of this one.

Paul makes it clear in 1 Corinthians 13 that love:

- suffers long;
- is kind;
- does not envy;
- does not parade itself;
- does not get 'puffed up';
- does not behave rudely;
- is not provoked;
- does not think evilly, nor rejoice in sin;
- rejoices in the truth;
- bears all things;
- believes all things;
- hopes all things;
- endures all things.

3. The rest of the fruit listed divide themselves into three groups of three.

a. My inner state of mind—Love, Joy, Peace

b. My attitudes toward others—Longsuffering, Gentleness, Goodness

c. My demonstration of trust in the Lord—Faith, Meekness, Self-Control

The fruit of the Spirit is supported by societal laws (Galatians 5:23b).

> *...against such there is no law.*

> *And no law exists against any of them.* –Phillips

> *Against such things there is no law [that can bring a charge].* – Amp.

> *Here there is no conflict with the law.* –NLT

> *There is no law against those who practice these things.* –Moffatt

> *There is no law against behaving in any of these ways.* –CEV

When Paul says that "against such things there is no law", he is referring to the fact that the societal authorities find it pretty hard to object to behavior that shows these characteristics. Even a staunch enemy of the church will likely find these qualities appealing. They are known to be positive characteristics by the general public in nearly every culture in every age.

What You can do to insure a place of fruitfulness in the Kingdom

Make sure that you have partaken of the good seed of the Word of God. It will produce after its own kind (Genesis 1:11).

> *Then God said, "Let the earth bring forth grass, the herb that yields seed, and the fruit tree that yields fruit according to its kind, whose seed is in itself, on the earth"; and it was so.*

Make sure that you sow plenty of seed for a large harvest (Mark 4:24). What kind of seed are you feeding on?

> *"If anyone has ears to hear, let him hear." Then He said to them, "Take heed what you hear. With the same measure you use, it will be measured to you; and to you who hear, more will be given."*

Yield your life totally to the Spirit of God (Romans 6:13, 19-22).

> *And do not present your members as instruments of unrighteousness to sin, but present yourselves to God as being alive from the dead, and your members as instruments of righteousness to God.* Romans 6:13

Prepare the ground of your heart before the Lord (2 Chronicles 30:18-19).

In 2 Chronicles 30 Hezekiah prayed for those who prepared their "heart to seek God."

4. Plow up the fallow ground (Hoshea 10:12).

Sow for yourselves righteousness; reap in mercy; break up your fallow ground, for it is time to seek the LORD, till He comes and rains righteousness on you.

5. Live by principle not by emotions (Psalm119).
6. Separate yourself from the cares of this life (Luke 21:34; Colossians 3:2-3; Titus 2:12; James 4:4).

If then you were raised with Christ, seek those things which are above, where Christ is, sitting at the right hand of God. Set your mind on things above, not on things on the earth. For you died, and your life is hidden with Christ in God. Colossians 3:1-3

7. Be both hearers and doers of the word (Ezekiel 33:32; Matthew 7:26; Luke 11:27; James 1:22-24).

Yield your members to the pruning process (John 15:2).

Plant yourself by the river (Psalm 92:13-14).

Those who are planted in the house of the LORD shall flourish in the courts of our
God. They shall still bear fruit in old age; they shall be fresh and flourishing...

But the godly will flourish like palm trees and grow strong like the cedars of Lebanon. For they are transplanted into the LORD's own house. They flourish in the courts of our God. Even in old age they will still produce fruit; they will remain vital and green. –NLT

CHAPTER TEN

THE GIFTS OF THE HOLY SPIRIT

DR. ABRAHAM PETERS

The Godhead is involved in giving in the plan of redemption.

1. The Father gave the Son (John 3:16).

For God so loved the world that He gave His only begotten Son, that whoever believes in Him should not perish but have everlasting life.

2. The Son gave the Holy Spirit (John 15:26; Acts 2:33).

But when the Helper comes, whom I shall send to you from the Father, the
Spirit of truth who proceeds from the Father, He will testify of Me.
John 15:26

3. The Spirit gives gifts (1 Corinthians 12:8-12).

But the manifestation of the Spirit is given to each one for the profit of all: for to one is given the word of wisdom through the Spirit, to another the word of knowledge through the same Spirit, to another faith by the same Spirit, to another gifts of healings by the same Spirit, to another the working of miracles, to another prophecy, to another discerning of spirits, to another different kinds of tongues, to another the interpretation of tongues. But one and the same Spirit works all these things, distributing to each one individually as He wills. For as the body is one and has many members, but all the members of that one body, being many, are one body, so also is Christ.

The Godhead also provides different spiritual equipment to enable the Church (1 Corinthians 12:1-6).

Now concerning spiritual gifts, brethren, I do not want you to be ignorant: 2 You know that you were Gentiles, carried away to these dumb idols, however you were led. 3 Therefore I make known to you that no one speaking by the Spirit of God calls Jesus accursed, and no one can say that Jesus is Lord except by the Holy Spirit. 4 There are diversities of gifts, but the same Spirit. 5 There are differences of ministries, but the same Lord. 6 And there are diversities of activities, but it is the same God who works all in all.

1 The Holy Spirit provides the gifts through which divine ability is imparted (vs. 4).

There are diversities of gifts, but the same Spirit.

1. The Lord Jesus provides ministries to believers including the five leadership and other body ministries (1 Corinthians 12:5). Christ gave these ministry gifts after He ascended (Ephesians 4:7-16). He distributed the fullness that was in Him to His body (Ephesians 1:20-23).

   There are differences of ministries, but the same Lord.

2. The Father God energizes the believer or provides the impetus to make the gifts and ministries effective (1 Corinthians 12:6). The word "operations" or "activities" is also rendered "workings".

And there are diversities of activities, but it is the same God who works all in all.

a. In Galatians 2:8 the same Greek word is used and rendered "worked effectively."

b. He works all things after the counsel of His own will (Ephesians 1:11, same word).

c. It is the proper motivation behind the gifts and ministries that make them work and produce the proper result.

Source	Holy Spirit	Jesus	Father
Grace Given	Gifts or Manifestations	Ministries or Functions	Motivations or Energies
Greek Word	*Charisma*	*Diakonia*	*Energeima*
English Equivalent	Gift of Grace or Favor	Ministry, Service or Function	Workings, Effects or Energies
Key Verses	I Corinthians 12:7-11	I Corinthians 12:12-30; Ephesians 4:7-16; Romans 12:1-8	I Corinthians 13-14
Examples	Word of Wisdom, Knowledge, Faith, Healings, Miracles, Prophecy, Tongues,	Apostle, Prophet, Evangelist, Pastor, Teacher, Giver, Shower of Mercy Exhorter,	Love Edification

	Interpretation, Discerning of Spirits	Helper, Healer, Etc.	
Distinctions	An outshining of the Holy Spirit made available to all believers when needed at the direction of the Holy Spirit.	A lifetime call or ministry that is to be recognized, developed and fulfilled by each member of the Body of Christ.	The effectual power that is to operate behind all of the gifts and ministries in the Body of Christ.

The "GIFTS" of the Spirit defined.

The Greek word for "gifts" is "χαρςσμα" (charisma).

1. This word occurs 17 times in the New Testament (Romans 1:11).

For I long to see you, that I may impart to you some spiritual gift, so that you may be established... Romans 1:11

2. This word is etymologically connected to "χαρςσ" (charis) meaning "grace or unmerited favor."

3. This word always refers to a free and unearned gift (Romans 5:15-16; 12:6; 1 Peter 4:10).

But the free gift is not like the offense. For if by the one man's offense many died, much more the grace of God and the gift by the grace of the one Man, Jesus Christ, abounded to many. Romans 5:15

*Having then gifts differing according to the grace that is given to us...*Romans 12:6a

4. This word is always referred to as coming from God as the source and the giver (James 1:17, Note: This is a different Greek word, but it expresses the idea).

Every good gift and every perfect gift is from above, and comes down from the Father of lights, with whom there is no variation or shadow of turning.

5. This word literally means "a gift freely and graciously given" or "a favor bestowed."

    a. It can refer to our eternal salvation (Romans 6:23).

For the wages of sin is death, but the gift of God is eternal life in Christ Jesus our Lord.

    b. It can refer to special endowments by God consistent with our calling (1 Corinthians 7:7). Paul spoke of his gift of singleness that was vital for him to do what God had called him to do.

For I wish that all men were even as I myself. But each one has his own gift from God, one in this manner and another in that.

    c. It can refer to our ministries from the Lord (Romans 11:29; 12:6; 1 Corinthians 12:28, 30, 31; 1 Timothy 4:14; 2 Timothy 1:6; 1 Peter 4:10).

For the gifts and the calling of God are irrevocable. Romans 11:29

As each one has received a gift, minister it to one another, as good stewards of the manifold grace of God. 1 Peter 4:10

    d. It can refer to the charismatic gifts of the Holy Spirit (1 Corinthians 1:7; 12:4, 9).

The "Gifts of the Spirit" are to be distinguished from other gifts of God. They are distinguished from the other gifts of God in at least two ways.

1. They are given by the Spirit (1 Corinthians 12:4, 7-11). These gifts are distinctly attributed to the Holy Spirit as opposed to the Lord Jesus or God the Father (1 Corinthians 12:1-6).

But the manifestation of the Spirit is given to each one for the profit of all: for to one is given the word of wisdom through the Spirit, to another the word of knowledge through the same Spirit, to another faith by the same Spirit, to another gifts of healings by the same Spirit, to another the working of miracles, to another prophecy, to another discerning of spirits, to another different kinds of tongues, to another the interpretation of tongues. But one and the same Spirit works all these things, distributing to each one individually as He wills. 1 Corinthians 12:7-11

2. They are a manifestation of the Spirit (1 Corinthians 12:7).

a. The word "manifestation" means "shining forth".

   b. These nine gifts are the ways in which the indwelling Spirit shines forth or reveals (manifests) Himself through believers.

   c. These "Gifts of the Spirit" are supernatural in character.

3. These are not simply an extension or refinement of natural abilities or powers.

   a. They are not natural abilities or aptitudes plus some help from God.

   b. The gifts of healing, for instance, do not refer to Christian doctors (a trade that is learned) but it is the supernatural manifestation of God's presence and power (Note: Doctors in a sense are indeed the gift of God, but these are not the kind of gifts that we are talking about here.).

4. These cannot be developed by man by a systematic approach or study.

These "Gifts of the Spirit" are distributed at the direction of the Holy Spirit (1 Corinthians 12:11).

But one and the same Spirit works all these things, distributing to each one individually as He wills.

These "Gifts of the Spirit" are not permanent endowments, but they are given by the Spirit to meet specific needs at specific times.

5. In the context where these gifts are described, Paul is talking about their gatherings. As they are gathered together, the Spirit will give someone an expression and He will give someone else another expression.
6. These "Gifts of the Spirit" are not to be confused with ministries.

    a. Ministries deal with a person's life as a whole. A man possesses a ministry ability from Christ and that ministry ability is irrevocable (Romans 11:29). Believers may disqualify themselves for a particular expression of that ministry, but the gifts enabling them to minister are still present in their lives.

    b. The list in 1 Corinthians 12:28-30 is referring to these ministry callings and not to the "gifts" of the Spirit.

These "Gifts of the Spirit" are resident in the Holy Spirit, the believer does not possess them as such. Hence…

7. No one has all nine gifts of the Spirit.

8. The Holy Spirit has all nine gifts of the Spirit.

9. The Holy Spirit is indwelling every believer.

10. The Holy Spirit may manifest any of these gifts through any believer at any time to meet any particular need.

11. Paul serves as a good example of someone who was yielded to the Spirit and was used of the Lord in many of the gifts.

DR. ABRAHAM PETERS

    a. Word of Knowledge (Acts 13:9-12)

Then Saul, who also is called Paul, filled with the Holy Spirit, looked intently at him and said, "O full of all deceit and all fraud, you son of the devil, you enemy of all righteousness, will you not cease perverting the straight ways of the Lord? And now, indeed, the hand of the Lord is upon you, and you shall be blind, not seeing the sun for a time." And immediately a dark mist fell on him, and he went around seeking someone to lead him by the hand. Acts 13:9-12

Note that this was the gift of the Word of Knowledge and the gift of miracles.

    b. A Word of Wisdom (Acts 23:6-10)

But when Paul perceived that one part were Sadducees and the other Pharisees, he cried out in the council, "Men and brethren, I am a Pharisee, the son of a Pharisee; concerning the hope and resurrection of the dead I am being judged!" 7 And when he had said this, a dissension arose between the Pharisees and the Sadducees; and the assembly was divided. 8 For Sadducees say that there is no resurrection--and no angel or spirit; but the Pharisees confess both. 9 Then there arose a loud outcry. And the scribes of the Pharisees' party arose and protested, saying, "We find no evil in this man; but if a spirit or an angel has spoken to him, let us not fight against God." 10 Now when there arose a great dissension, the commander, fearing lest Paul might be pulled to pieces by them, commanded the soldiers to go down and take him by force from among them, and bring him into the barracks.

c. Discerning of Spirits (Acts 16:16-18)

Now it happened, as we went to prayer, that a certain slave girl possessed with a spirit of divination met us, who brought her masters much profit by fortune-telling. This girl followed Paul and us, and cried out, saying, "These men are the servants of the Most High God, who proclaim to us the way of salvation." And this she did for many days. But Paul, greatly annoyed, turned and said to the spirit, "I command you in the name of Jesus Christ to come out of her." And he came out that very hour.

d. Faith (Romans 15:18-19)

For I will not dare to speak of any of those things which Christ has not accomplished through me, in word and deed, to make the Gentiles obedient--in mighty signs and wonders, by the power of the Spirit of God, so that from Jerusalem and round about to Illyricum I have fully preached the gospel of Christ.

e. Healing (Acts 14:8-10)

And in Lystra a certain man without strength in his feet was sitting, a cripple from his mother's womb, who had never walked. This man heard Paul speaking. Paul, observing him intently and seeing that he had faith to be healed, said with a loud voice, "Stand up straight on your feet!" And he leaped and walked.

f. Miracles (Acts 20:9-12)

And in a window sat a certain young man named Eutychus, who was sinking into a deep sleep. He was overcome by sleep; and as Paul continued speaking, he fell down from the third story and was taken up dead. But Paul went down, fell on him, and embracing him said, "Do not trouble yourselves, for his life is in him." Now when he had come up, had broken bread and eaten, and talked a long while, even till daybreak, he departed. And they brought the young man in alive, and they were not a little comforted.

    g. Others by implications: Tongues and Prophecy (1 Corinthians 14:6)

But now, brethren, if I come to you speaking with tongues, what shall I profit you unless I speak to you either by revelation, by knowledge, by prophesying, or by teaching?

The Gifts of the Spirit are supernatural endowments given to the believer at the direction of the Holy Spirit to meet particular needs at particular times.

The "Gifts" of the Spirit are for Today!

There are several arguments proposed against the validity of the "gifts" for today.

1. Some say that the Lord withdrew the gifts of the Spirit at the end of the apostolic age. The argument has these elements:

    a. Discernment was needed before the canon was complete so true and false revelation given in oral form could be judged.

b. Speaking with tongues is replaced by the canon of Scripture, the perfect (1Corinthians 13:8).

c. Miracles have ceased because "the particular purpose for which they were originally given (i.e. to authenticate the oral message) has ceased to exist".

d. Prophesying is just another word for inspired preaching, but again, since the canon has been established, there is no more need for futuristic prophecy.

e. Healings were needed in days when medicine was not well developed.

f. It is interesting that most people who deny the validity of the "gifts" for today like to keep faith, knowledge and wisdom in some form.

2. Some say that history proves that they ceased with the apostolic age.

3. Some say that the New Testament canon is now completed, and so ministry through spiritual gifts is no longer needed—we have the written word.

4. Some say that they are no longer needed today, because the world is now convinced of the truth of Christianity.

5. Some say, "If these gifts are for today, then why are they not manifested and possessed by our great church leaders?"

There are several things that can be said in the face of these arguments (Note: The following numbers correspond to the points in the previous section).

6. Nowhere are we ever told or instructed that these gifts would cease or that there is, in fact, a special apostolic age (Mark 16:17-18; Matthew 28:19-20; Acts 2:38-39; Romans 11:29; Hebrews 13:8).

> *And these signs will follow those who believe: In My name they will cast out demons; they will speak with new tongues; they will take up serpents; and if they drink anything deadly, it will by no means hurt them; they will lay hands on the sick, and they will recover.* Mark 16:17-18

Jesus didn't say, "These signs shall follow you until the year 100 A.D. and after that you are on your own!"

> *"Go therefore and make disciples of all the nations, baptizing them in the name of the Father and of the Son and of the Holy Spirit, teaching them to observe all things that I have commanded you; and lo, I am with you always, even to the end of the age." Amen.*
> Matthew 28:19-20

Jesus said that He would be with us "to the end of the age."

> *Then Peter said to them, "Repent, and let every one of you be baptized in the name of Jesus Christ for the remission of sins; and you shall receive the gift of the Holy Spirit. For the promise is to*

you and to your children, and to all who are afar off, as many as the Lord our God will call." Acts 2:38-39

For the gifts and the calling of God are irrevocable. Romans 11:29

Jesus Christ is the same yesterday, today, and forever. Hebrews 13:8

Throughout history there has always been a true remnant of believers who experienced these "gifts."
The main reason for their decline of the gifts of the Spirit was the love of many growing cold. It is a serious thing to accuse God of withdrawing these gifts if the real fact is that the Church lost them through lukewarmness!.

2   The New Testament Canon is not the "perfect" that is to come (1 Corinthians 13:10 with Ephesians 4:13).

The disciples themselves had inspired writings and yet God used the signs to confirm the Word, not supersede it. Not only that, the New Testament Canon was not complete until the 3rd or 4th Century A.D. long after the gifts ceased in the experience of the church.

3   The gifts of the Spirit are needed more than ever for the gospel to be confirmed with signs, wonders and mighty deeds. There is a smaller percentage of people in the world today that have received the gospel than there were in the days when the last apostle died.
4   Perhaps some resist the idea of the gifts of the Holy Spirit simply because they are not part of their experience or religious tradition

(Matthew 15:6; Romans 10:17). If you do not believe in something it is very difficult to experience something.

Thus you have made the commandment of God of no effect by your tradition. Matthew 15:6

These are gifts to the Church. We are the Church. These gifts should be active right up to the 2nd coming (Ephesians 4:13-16; 1 Corinthians 13:10).

The "Gifts" of the Spirit are necessary.
The Church of today is sorely in need of the spiritual power demonstrated in the book of Acts.

1. The Church in the Book of Acts referred to "special" miracles (Acts 19:11-12). Today any miracle is special.

   Now God worked unusual miracles by the hands of Paul, so that even handkerchiefs or aprons were brought from his body to the sick, and the diseases left them and the evil spirits went out of them.

2. The gifts are not extra adornments for the Church, but essential operations without which the Church cannot function properly.

3. God rules the Church, which is and should be supernatural. If the Church is not above and beyond the natural, then it has nothing more to offer than any good social organization or government program (Acts 1:8).

The gifts are part of the "signs" that are to follow believers. Believers are not to follow signs, signs are to follow them! (Mark 16:15-20).

4. They are God's way of confirming our witness in both word and deed.

5. They are part of our credentials as ambassadors of Jesus (See: Acts 8:5-8; Romans 15:17-20; 1 Corinthians 2:4-5; Hebrews 2:1-4).

Then Philip went down to the city of Samaria and preached Christ to them. And the multitudes with one accord heeded the things spoken by Philip, hearing and seeing the miracles which he did. For unclean spirits, crying with a loud voice, came out of many who were possessed; and many who were paralyzed and lame were healed. And there was great joy in that city. Acts 8:5-8

And my speech and my preaching were not with persuasive words of human wisdom, but in demonstration of the Spirit and of power, that your faith should not be in the wisdom of men but in the power of God. 1 Corinthians 2:4-5

Therefore we must give the more earnest heed to the things we have heard, lest we drift away. For if the word spoken through angels proved steadfast, and every transgression and disobedience received a just reward, how shall we escape if we neglect so great a salvation, which at the first began to be spoken by the Lord, and was confirmed to us by those who heard Him, God also bearing witness both with signs and wonders, with various miracles, and gifts of the Holy Spirit, according to His own will? Hebrews 2:1-4

Where the gifts are in evidence, growth occurs.

6. This happened with a positive expression of the gifts of the Spirit in the healing of the lame man (Connect Acts 3:6-10 with Acts 4:4).

Then Peter said, "Silver and gold I do not have, but what I do have I give you: In the name of Jesus Christ of Nazareth, rise up and walk." And he took him by the right hand and lifted him up, and immediately his feet and ankle bones received strength. So he, leaping up, stood and walked and entered the temple with them-- walking, leaping, and praising God. And all the people saw him walking and praising God. Then they knew that it was he who sat begging alms at the Beautiful Gate of the temple; and they were filled with wonder and amazement at what had happened to him.
Acts 3:6-10

The direct result of this miracle came later.

However, many of those who heard the word believed; and the number of the men came to be about five thousand. Acts 4:4

Men will often try to imitate these miraculous displays with well planned theatrics, but we can never duplicate the true effect that the gifts flowing as God intended will have.

2. This happened with a negative expression of the gifts of the Spirit in the judgment on Ananias and Saphira (Connect Acts 5:3-5 with Acts 5:12-16).

And through the hands of the apostles many signs and wonders were done among the people. And they were all with one accord in Solomon's Porch. Yet none of the rest dared join them, but the people esteemed them highly. And believers were increasingly added to the Lord, multitudes of both men and women, so that they brought the sick out into the streets and laid them on beds and couches, that at least the shadow of Peter passing by might fall on some of them. Also a multitude gathered from the surrounding cities to Jerusalem, bringing sick people and those who were tormented by unclean spirits, and they were all healed. Acts 5:12-16

The gifts help to establish, strengthen and edify the Body of Christ (Romans 1:11; 1 Corinthians 14:3-5; 1 Corinthians 14:12, 26; 1 Corinthians 12:7).

How is it then, brethren? Whenever you come together, each of you has a psalm, has a teaching, has a tongue, has a revelation, has an interpretation. Let all things be done for edification. 1 Corinthians 14:26

We are told to desire these gifts not just "tolerate" them (1 Corinthians 12:31; 14:1, 12).

Pursue love, and desire spiritual gifts, but especially that you may prophesy. 1 Corinthians 14:1

1. These gifts were to provide a spiritual capability for mightier works than the finest natural abilities could ever supply.

2. The New Testament believer is called to the highest order of ministry. The gifts of the Spirit are the supernatural tools with which he ministers.

DR. ABRAHAM PETERS

The gifts give expression to the principle of body ministry (1 Corinthians 12:12-27), each member contributing and flowing together to edify the whole.

The gifts are an indication and confirmation of the presence of God in our midst (1 Corinthians 14:25).

But if all prophesy, and an unbeliever or an uninformed person comes in, he is convinced by all, he is convicted by all. And thus the secrets of his heart are revealed; and so, falling down on his face, he will worship God and report that God is truly among you. 1 Corinthians 14:26-25

...and they will fall down on their knees and worship God, declaring, "God is really here among you." –NLT

...declaring that God is among you in very truth. –Amp

...publicly confessing that God is indeed among you. –Knox

The gifts are a witness to unbelievers (Acts 13:12; 1 Corinthians 14:25).

Then the proconsul believed, when he saw what had been done, being astonished at the teaching of the Lord. Acts 13:12

The "Gifts" of the Spirit in operation.

There is a madness which is of faith and a madness which is of fanaticism. The former is manifested in an utter devotion to God and His holy will (Mark 3:21; Acts 26:24). The latter is something which has plagued Christianity from apostolic days. The fear of the latter must never be allowed to drive us from practicing the former.

God and man work together as co-laborers in the operation of the gifts.

1. We can be sure that God will do His part.

    a. He distributes the gifts (1 Corinthians 12:11, 18, 28).

    b. He gives different gifts to different ones (Romans 12: 3, 6). We should not be jealous of one another.

2. We must be ready to do our part. Since these gifts are not initiated by man we do not decide to manifest a gift, but we can condition our vessel to be used.

    a. We should be totally yielded to the Lord. (Romans 6:13)

    And do not present your members as instruments of unrighteousness to sin, but present yourselves to God as being alive from the dead, and your members as instruments of righteousness to God.

    b. We should have a desire to be used in this realm. (1 Corinthians 14:1, 12, 19).

    c. We should learn all we can about the gifts (1 Corinthians 12:1). The Bible states that "My people are destroyed for lack of knowledge" (Hoshea 4:6).

DR. ABRAHAM PETERS

Now concerning spiritual gifts, brethren, I do not want you to be ignorant...
1 Corinthians 12:1

    d. We should pray to be used (1 Corinthians 14:13; Matthew 7:11).

If you then, being evil, know how to give good gifts to your children, how much more will your Father who is in heaven give good things to those who ask Him! Matthew 7:11

    e. We should keep our eyes on the giver and not the gift (avoid being gift conscious).

    f. We should maintain faith and dispel unbelief (Mark. 6:5-6; Matthew 21:21; James 5:15; Romans 12:6)

Now He could do no mighty work there, except that He laid His hands on a few sick people and healed them. And He marveled because of their unbelief. Then He went about the villages in a circuit, teaching. Mark 6:5-6

Jesus answered and said to them, "Assuredly, I say to you, if you have faith and do not doubt, you will not only do what was done to the fig tree, but also if you say to this mountain, 'Be removed and be cast into the sea,' it will be done." Matthew 21:21

    g. For those who have dormant gifts, we must not neglect them but stir them up (1 Timothy 4:14).

Do not neglect the gift that is in you, which was given to you by prophecy with the laying on of the hands of the eldership. 1 Timothy 4:14

    B. There are several principles that are important in the operation of the gifts.

Some people get offended when you start talking about guidelines for the operation of the gifts. They would have really gotten offended at Paul in I Corinthians 14. Paul was not afraid to give pastoral guidance to the operation of the gifts because the gifts always include the human element. Paul's concern was for more for the possible effect of the use of the gifts on the local church than for the feelings of the person administering the gift.

1. The Golden Rule governing the exercise of spiritual gifts is edification (1 Corinthinas 12:7; 14:3, 4, 5, 12, 17-26). The key word in 1 Corinthians 14 is "edify." It occurs seven times in the chapter in one form or another.

But the manifestation of the Spirit is given to each one for the profit of all... Corinthians 12:7
...for some useful purpose. –NEB

I wish you all spoke with tongues, but even more that you prophesied; for he who prophesies is greater than he who speaks with tongues, unless indeed he interprets, that the church may receive edification. 1 Corinthians 14:5

Even so you, since you are zealous for spiritual gifts, let it be for the edification of the church that you seek to excel. 1 Corinthians 14:12

How is it then, brethren? Whenever you come together, each of you has a psalm, has a teaching, has a tongue, has a revelation, has an interpretation. Let all things be done for edification. 1 Corinthians 14:26

Other phrases support the concept of edification and building...

...what shall I profit you unless I speak to you either by revelation, by knowledge, by prophesying, or by teaching? Vs. 6

...yet in the church I would rather speak five words with my understanding, that I may teach others also... Vs. 19

Questions to ask:

    a. Will this build up the people of God?

    b. Will it strengthen the local church?

    c. Will it bring encouragement to the saints (1 Corinthians 14:31)?

For you can all prophesy one by one, that all may learn and all may be encouraged.

2. The gifts of the Spirit must be tested against the Word of God (Isaiah 8:20).

To the law and to the testimony! If they do not speak according to this word, it is because there is no light in them.

    a. The gifts should confirm the word; never violate it (Galatians 1:8).

    b. The gifts are not infallible because they are operating through fallible vessels. They must be measured against the infallible measuring rod of the Word of God.

    c. Just because something sounds good or pleasant to our ears does not make it divine truth (Jeremiah 5:31; 2 Timothy 4:3).

The prophets prophesy falsely, and the priests rule by their own power; and My people love to have it so. But what will you do in the end? Jeremiah 5:31

For the time will come when they will not endure sound doctrine, but according to their own desires, because they have itching ears, they will heap up for themselves teachers... 2 Timothy 4:3

3. The gifts must be operated decently and in order (Colossians 2:5; 1 Corinthians 14:27, 29, 33, 40). Guidelines for the gifts are like banks to a river. As long as the banks are in place, the river brings life wherever it goes. Remove the banks and that same water becomes a flood and has the potential for great devastation.

    By establishing guidelines, Paul was not trying to discourage the gifts, he only wanted to see them regulated so that they would accomplish their intended purpose. Paul was not being insensitive to the Holy Spirit. He was not a "controller" on a "power trip" by establishing guidelines for the moving of the Spirit in the corporate setting. Paul was functioning out of the spirit of a true shepherd and was concerned about the benefit of the entire flock. The Holy Spirit is not quenched when we function with a sense of order and decorum.

For though I am absent in the flesh, yet I am with you in spirit, rejoicing to see your good order and the steadfastness of your faith in Christ. Colossians 2:5

Let all things be done decently and in order. 1 Corinthians 14:40

For the purpose of order in the corporate gathering, the person operating the gift should evaluate three things:

a. Evaluate the message. The message should be clear and must not bring confusion to what the Spirit is saying (1 Corinthians 14:31-33). God is not the author of confusion.

For you can all prophesy one by one, that all may learn and all may be encouraged. And the spirits of the prophets are subject to the prophets. For God is not the author of confusion but of peace, as in all the churches of the saints.

i. Is this flowing with what God is already saying?

ii. Is this edifying to the people of God?

    b. Evaluate the timing. It must fit in with what has gone before and prepare for what will follow.

    c. Evaluate the manner. Personal mannerisms should never detract from the message.

i. Is my voice clear and loud?

ii. Are my physical members in control?

4. The gifts must be operated without the vessel drawing undue attention to itself.

    a. We should seek to exalt Christ not ourselves (John 3:30). He must increase, I must decrease.

    b. We should exercise true humility in the way we function (Romans 12:3).

    c. We should follow the example of the apostles (Acts 3:3-4; 12; 4:21).

To the man in need the apostles said "Look at us" (Acts 3:3). To the admiring crowds they said, "Why look so intently at us, as though by our own power or godliness we had made this man walk?" (Acts 3:12). As a result of how they functioned, "all glorified God for what had been done" (Acts 4:21).

5. The one operating the gift should exercise self-control (1 Corinthians 14:32; Proverbs 25:28; 29:11, 20). The gifts are not

toys to be played with. They are serious responsibilities and those operating in them must have rule over their own spirit.

And the spirits of the prophets are subject to the prophets. 1 Corinthians 14:32

Whoever has no rule over his own spirit is like a city broken down, without walls. Proverbs 25:28

A fool vents all his feelings, but a wise man holds them back. Proverbs 29:11

Judge your own gift before you exercise it (Ecclesiastes 5:1-2; Proverbs 30:5-6).

Every word of God is pure; He is a shield to those who put their trust in Him. Do not add to His words, lest He rebuke you, and you be found a liar. Proverbs 30:5-6

    a. Avoid all distracting manifestations (screeching, shaking, etc.).

i. The Holy Spirit does not drive us out of control, otherwise some of Paul's admonitions would be senseless (1 Corinthians 14:28, 30).

ii. The Holy Spirit is a gentleman and is never rude or pushy.

6. Let the more mature or experienced set the flow and guidelines for what take place.

7. Observe the guidelines set by the leadership.

Remember that those in leadership are still responsible for the entire flock and have the right to decide what is interjected into any service (Acts 20:28-30). Every river must have banks to contain, guide and direct the water to the real place of need.

8. Do not be afraid to wait and watch, proving your own gift.

Watch others that move in the same realm checking what you had with what they ministered (1 Corinthians 12:1; 14:31). Not every one who had the same message needs to speak the message. God is more interested in the message being delivered than in who actually delivers the message.

9. The gifts must be balanced with the fruit of the Spirit (Galatians 5:22-23).

Some circles are characterized by and emphasis on the fruit of the Spirit to the point of neglect in relation to the gifts of the Spirit. With other groups the converse is true. We want to be well balanced in this area. We want to see the fruit of the Spirit working in perfect harmony with the gifts of the Spirit.

    a. Both the gifts and the fruit are necessary.

i. The fruit of the Spirit represents the character of God.

ii. The gifts of the Spirit represent the ability of God.

Divine ability without divine character is dangerous. Divine character without divine ability leaves one powerless to be effective in what God has called us unto.

    b. There was a perfect balance in Jesus (Compare Matthew 26:53 and Matthew 9:6). Jesus ministered out of a heart of compassion.

Jesus did not use His anointing for self preservation; He used it to minister to the needs and the suffering of others.

Or do you think that I cannot now pray to My Father, and He will provide Me with more than twelve legions of angels? Matthew 26:53

"But that you may know that the Son of Man has power on earth to forgive sins"--then He said to the paralytic, "Arise, take up your bed, and go to your house." Matthew 9:6

Contrast James and John who may have misused the gifts (Luke 9:54-56).

And when His disciples James and John saw this, they said, "Lord, do You want us to command fire to come down from heaven and consume them, just as Elijah did?" But He turned and rebuked them, and said, "You do not know what manner of spirit you are of. For the Son of Man did not come to destroy men's lives but to save them." And they went to another village.

        c. Each of the different aspect of the fruit of the Spirit will help to balance the application of the various gifts. Think of how the following aspects of the fruit of the Spirit might affect the operation of the gifts.

i. Love

Our motivation should be love for the brethren (Ephesians 4:15-16).

...but, speaking the truth in love, may grow up in all things into Him who is the head—Christ from whom the whole body, joined and knit together by what every joint supplies, according to the effective working by which every part does its share, causes growth of the body for the edifying of itself in love. Ephesians 4:15-16

- Are you adding this to build up others (1Thessalonians 3:12)?

And may the Lord make you increase and abound in love to one another and to all, just as we do to you...

- Are you interested in the well being of others (1 Corinthians 13)?

ii. Joy

Do you find joy in building the people of God (Psalms 27:4; 102:14)?

iii. Peace (James 3:18)

iv. Patience, Gentleness, Self-control, Kindness, Etc.

DR. ABRAHAM PETERS

There are some misconceptions regarding the gifts.

There are at least three misconceptions regarding the gifts that are often made.

A. The gifts of the Spirit are given as an indication of God's approval on your life or your assembly. This is not true because:

1. The gifts are not earned or deserved.
2. The gifts can be abused and misused.
3. God gives the gifts in order to meet the needs of His people not because of the worthiness of the vessel being used.
4. God will deal personally with those who misuse the gifts (Matthew 7:21-23).

    B. One's ability to function in the gifts of the Spirit are an indication of spiritual maturity. Again this is not true because:

1. The gifts of the Spirit are not earned or deserved.

2. Someone isn't "better" if they are used in a gift.

    a. The gifts are not spiritual merit badges.

    b. The Corinthian believers proved this point (1 Corinthians 3:1-3 with 1:4, 6-7). They came behind in no gift and yet they were carnal Christians.

    C. The gifts of the Spirit operate primarily in the context of the worship service in a local church.

The truth is that most of the time that the gifts of the Spirit were seen in operation in the life of Jesus and in the Early Church they took place outside of the context of a church meeting.

The gifts of the Spirit work best on the street and are tools that God places in our hands to minister in the world. The basic biblical rule when operating the Gifts of the Spirit, obey the moving of the Holy Spirit which operates according to the Word of God on the basis of love and edification.

DR. ABRAHAM PETERS

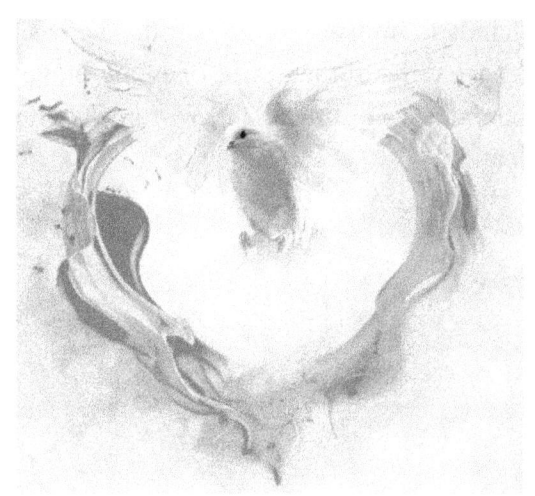

CHAPTER ELEVEN

THE WORD OF WISDOM AND THE WORD OF KNOWLEDGE

How we define "the word of knowledge'

The word of knowledge is the supernatural revelation of facts—past, present or future—which were not learned or developed through the efforts of the natural mind. It may be described as the mind of Christ being imparted to the mind of the believer. A word of knowledge is given by revelation in a moment of time.

The four kinds of knowledge

Natural Human Knowledge

This knowledge is sometimes referred to as "learning." It included true science and other fields of learning.

1. This knowledge is natural not supernatural.

2. This knowledge can be expanded through research, study and human effort (2 Timothy 2:15).

Be diligent to present yourself approved to God, a worker who does not need to be ashamed, rightly dividing the word of truth.

3. This knowledge can be a source of human pride (1 Corinthians 8:1).

Knowledge puffs up, but love edifies.

4. This knowledge will increase throughout the ages (Daniel 12:4).

But you, Daniel, shut up the words, and seal the book until the time of the end; many shall run to and fro, and knowledge shall increase.

Fallen Man's Supernatural Knowledge

There are two sources of spiritual power in the world—God and Satan. Just because something is supernatural, it does not mean it is from God. This knowledge is that which is obtained from the world of the occult. This includes information gained from supernatural sources other than the Holy Spirit of God. It includes interactions with witches, wizards, mediums, séances, divination, astrology, horoscopes, Ouija boards, fortune tellers and the like (1 Samuel 28:8; Isaiah 8:19-20).

> *And when they say to you, "Seek those who are mediums and wizards, who whisper* [KJV, peep] *and mutter," should not a people seek their God? Should they seek the dead on behalf of the living? To the law and to the testimony! If they do not speak according to this word, it is because there is no light in them.*
> Isaiah 8:19-20

5. This form of knowledge is a counterfeit to the true and is an abomination to the Lord (Leviticus 19:26; Deuteronomy 18:9-14; 1 Chronicles 10:13-14).

> *When you come into the land which the LORD your God is giving you, you shall not learn to follow the abominations of those nations. 10 There shall not be found among you anyone who makes his son or his daughter pass through the fire, or one who practices witchcraft, or a soothsayer, or one who interprets omens, or a*

sorcerer, 11 or one who conjures spells, or a medium, or a spiritist, or one who calls up the dead. 12 For all who do these things are an abomination to the LORD, and because of these abominations the LORD your God drives them out from before you. 13 You shall be blameless before the LORD your God. 14 For these nations which you will dispossess listened to soothsayers and diviners; but as for you, the LORD your God has not appointed such for you. Deuteronomy 18:9-14

So Saul died for his unfaithfulness which he had committed against the LORD, because he did not keep the word of the LORD, and also because he consulted a medium for guidance. But he did not inquire of the LORD; therefore He killed him, and turned the kingdom over to David the son of Jesse. 1 Chronicles 10:13-14

6. In the Old Testament those who practiced these things were to be put to death (Exodus 22:18; Leviticus 20:27).

You shall not permit a sorceress to live. Exodus 22:18

A man or a woman who is a medium, or who has familiar spirits, shall surely be put to death; they shall stone them with stones. Their blood shall be upon them. Leviticus 20:27

7. Seeking this type of knowledge will lead to defilement (Leviticus 19:31).

Give no regard to mediums and familiar spirits; do not seek after them, to be defiled by them: I am the LORD your God.

8. God is offended when we seek this type of knowledge (Leviticus 20:6).

And the person who turns to mediums and familiar spirits, to prostitute himself with them, I will set My face against that person and cut him off from his people.

If any among the people are unfaithful by consulting and following mediums or psychics, I will turn against them and cut them off from the community.–NLV

9. We can expect this type of activity to also increase throughout the ages (1 Timothy 4:1).

Now the Spirit expressly says that in latter times some will depart from the faith, giving heed to deceiving spirits and doctrines of demons...

True Intellectual or Spiritual Knowledge

This is spiritual knowledge that can only come to us through knowing God and His word. It is only as we understand this knowledge that we are in our "right mind."

10. This knowledge is that which comes to us when we are born again and have our eyes open to both see and enter the Kingdom of God (John 3:3, 5).

11. This is knowledge that comes to us from knowing God personally through Jesus Christ (John 17:3).

And this is eternal life, that they may know You, the only true God, and Jesus Christ whom You have sent.

12. This is knowledge of the ways of God that comes to us from the Holy Spirit who dwells within us (1 Corinthians 2:11-14).

For what man knows the things of a man except the spirit of the man which is in him? Even so no one knows the things of God except the Spirit of God. Now we have received, not the spirit of the world, but the Spirit who is from God, that we might know the things that have been freely given to us by God. These things we also speak, not in words which man's wisdom teaches but which the Holy Spirit teaches, comparing spiritual things with spiritual. But the natural man does not receive the things of the Spirit of God, for they are foolishness to him; nor can he know them, because they are spiritually discerned.

13. This knowledge comes to us by seeking the Lord in prayer and in His word (Exodus 33:13; Psalm 119:130).

Now therefore, I pray, if I have found grace in Your sight, show me now Your way, that I may know You and that I may find grace in Your sight. And consider that this nation is Your people. Exodus 33:13

The entrance of Your words gives light; it gives understanding to the simple. Psalm 119:130

14. This knowledge is eternal knowledge that will last forever (Matthew 24:35; 1 Peter 1:25).

DR. ABRAHAM PETERS

Heaven and earth will pass away, but My words will by no means pass away. Matthew 24:35

But the word of the LORD endures forever. 1 Peter 1:25

15. This knowledge is also on the increase (Isaiah 11:9b).

For the earth shall be full of the knowledge of the LORD as the waters cover the sea.

Divine Supernatural Knowledge

This is a word of knowledge as described above.

16. This is not psychic phenomenon, extrasensory perception, clairvoyance or any other thing that is forbidden by God.

17. This is not the result of human ability or pursuit.

18. This is a supernatural gift given by God in an instant of time.

19. This is the knowledge of a portion of information from God's total knowledge that can only be known divine impartation.

What are some examples of the "word of knowledge" in operation?

B. Samuel was able to tell Saul that his lost donkeys were found by a revelation from God (1 Samuel 9:15-20).

But as for your donkeys that were lost three days ago, do not be anxious about them, for they have been found. 1 Samuel 9:20a

C. Samuel was able to find Saul hidden in the baggage by a revelation from God (1 Samuel 10:21-23).

So they asked the LORD, "Where is he?" And the LORD replied, "He is hiding among the baggage." 1 Samuel 10:22, NLT

D. Nathan was able to know the secret sin of David by a revelation from God (2 Samuel 12:7-13).

Why, then, have you despised the word of the LORD and done this horrible deed? For you have murdered Uriah and stolen his wife…You did it secretly, but I will do this to you openly in the sight of all Israel. 2 Samuel 12:9, 12

E. The prophet Ahijah was able to see through the disguise of Jereboam's wife (even though he had poor eyesight) by a revelation from God (1 Kings. 14:1-6).

At that time Jeroboam's son Abijah became very sick. 2 So Jeroboam told his wife, "Disguise yourself so that no one will recognize you as the queen. Then go to the prophet Ahijah at Shiloh--the man who told me I would become king. 3 Take him a gift of ten loaves of bread, some cakes, and a jar of honey, and ask him what will happen to the boy." 4 So Jeroboam's wife went to Ahijah's home at Shiloh. He was an old man now and could no longer see. 5 But the LORD had told Ahijah, "Jeroboam's wife will come here, pretending to be someone else. She will ask you about her son, for he is very sick. You must give her the answer that I give you." 6 So when Ahijah heard her footsteps at the door,

> *he called out, "Come in, wife of Jeroboam! Why are you pretending to be someone else?" –NLT*

F. Elijah knew that Gehazi had asked for a reward from Naaman by a revelation from God (2 Kings. 5:20-27).

G. Jesus knew that Nathanael was sitting under a fig tree by a revelation from God (John 1:47-50).

H. Jesus knew that the woman at the well (whom He had never met) had five past husbands and that she was living with a man who was not her husband by a revelation from God (John 4:17-18, 29).

> *Jesus said to her, "Go, call your husband, and come here." The woman answered and said, "I have no husband." Jesus said to her, "You have well said, 'I have no husband,' for you have had five husbands, and the one whom you now have is not your husband; in that you spoke truly." The woman said to Him, "Sir, I perceive that You are a prophet"... "Come, see a Man who told me all things that I ever did. Could this be the Christ?" John 4:16-19, 29*

I. Jesus knew that Lazarus had died by a revelation from God (John 11:13-14).

J. Peter knew that Jesus was the Christ by a revelation from God (Matthew 16:16-17).

> *Simon Peter answered and said, "You are the Christ, the Son of the living God." Jesus answered and said to him, "Blessed are you,*

Simon Bar-Jonah, for flesh and blood has not revealed this to you, but My Father who is in heaven."

K. Peter knew about the conspiracy of Ananias and Saphira by a revelation from God (Acts 5:3).

L. Ananias knew where Saul (Paul) would be residing by a revelation from God (Acts 9:11-12, 17).

M. Peter knew that three men were seeking him by a revelation from God (Acts 10:17-23).

God still uses the word of knowledge today in ways that are consistent with His eternal purpose.

Guidelines for the operation of the "word of knowledge"

N. Ask God for insight as to why you were given this piece of information.

O. Ask God for wisdom as to how to act upon this information.

P. Ask God for direction concerning with whom this information should be shared.

Q. Ask God how this information can be used for the purpose of love and edification.

How we define "the word of wisdom"

Whereas the word of knowledge is informative, wisdom is directive.

The word of wisdom is the supernatural application of knowledge. It is knowing the divine course of action to be taken in regard to the natural or supernatural knowledge God has given. It is proper judgment for action.

The four kinds of wisdom

R. Natural Human Wisdom

Natural human wisdom is naturally applied knowledge. This wisdom is important but often is foolishness compared to God wisdom (1 Corinthians 1:18-31; 2:6; James 3:15).

> *However, we speak wisdom among those who are mature, yet not the wisdom of this age, nor of the rulers of this age, who are coming to nothing.* 1 Corinthians 2:6

S. Fallen Man's Supernatural Wisdom

This is the type of wisdom that is forbidden by God that was used by Satan to tempt man in the Garden of Eden (Genesis 3:6; Daniel 2:27-28).

> *Daniel answered in the presence of the king, and said, "The secret which the king has demanded, the wise men, the astrologers, the magicians, and the soothsayers cannot declare to the king. But there is a God in heaven who reveals secrets, and He has made known to King Nebuchadnezzar what will be in the latter days.*

Your dream, and the visions of your head upon your bed, were these..." Daniel 2:27-28

T. True Intellectual or Spiritual Wisdom

1. This is wisdom that comes down from above (1 Kings. 3:28; 1 Corinthians 2:7; James 3:17).

And all Israel heard of the judgment which the king had rendered; and they feared the king, for they saw that the wisdom of God was in him to administer justice. 1 Kings 3:28

2. This is the wisdom reflected in the Book of Proverbs (1 Kings. 4:29-34).

And God gave Solomon wisdom and exceedingly great understanding, and largeness of heart like the sand on the seashore. 30 Thus Solomon's wisdom excelled the wisdom of all the men of the East and all the wisdom of Egypt. 31 For he was wiser than all men--than Ethan the Ezrahite, and Heman, Chalcol, and Darda, the sons of Mahol; and his fame was in all the surrounding nations. 32 He spoke three thousand proverbs, and his songs were one thousand and five. 33 Also he spoke of trees, from the cedar tree of Lebanon even to the hyssop that springs out of the wall; he spoke also of animals, of birds, of creeping things, and of fish. 34 And men of all nations, from all the kings of the earth who had heard of his wisdom, came to hear the wisdom of Solomon.

3. We are told to get this type of wisdom by respecting the Lord and the Word of God (Job 28:28; Proverbs 4:7-8; 9:10).

DR. ABRAHAM PETERS

Wisdom is the principal thing; therefore get wisdom. And in all your getting, get understanding. Exalt her, and she will promote you; she will bring you honor, when you embrace her. Proverbs 4:7-8

The fear of the LORD is the beginning of wisdom, and the knowledge of the Holy One is understanding. Proverbs 9:10

4. This wisdom can be a stumbling block to the faith of some (1 Corinthians 1:18-25).

U. Divine Supernatural Wisdom

This gift of the word of wisdom is a sudden and miraculous giving of wisdom to be applied to a particular situation, answer a particular question or utilize a particular piece of knowledge.

1. It is not human ability.

2. It is a gift from God.

3. It is a small part of God's total wisdom (Romans 11:33-36; 16:27; 1 Timothy 1:17).

Now to the King eternal, immortal, invisible, to God who alone is wise, be honor and glory forever and ever. Amen. 1Timothy 1:17

Some biblical examples of the "word of wisdom" in operation?

V. Joseph had a word of wisdom as to how to save the world from the coming drought (Genesis 41:25-36).

So the advice was good in the eyes of Pharaoh and in the eyes of all his servants. And Pharaoh said to his servants, "Can we find such a one as this, a man in whom is the Spirit of God?" Genesis 41:37-38

W. Moses' mother had a word of wisdom as to how to save her baby from Pharaoh's sword (Exodus 2:1-10 with Hebrews 11:23).

X. Jethro had a word of wisdom for Moses as to how to oversee the nation of Israel (Exodus 18:13-26).

Y. Nathan used a word of wisdom as to how to approach David about his sin (2 Samuel 12:1-14). Note that he had the knowledge, but he used divine wisdom to apply the knowledge that he had received from God.

Z. Solomon had a word of wisdom for the two women who were fighting over the same baby (1 Kings. 3:16-28).

Jesus had words of wisdom when answering those who were trying to trap Him in His words (See Matthew 22:15-46).

1. When they questioned the source of His authority (Matthew 21:23-27).

Now when He came into the temple, the chief priests and the elders of the people confronted Him as He was teaching, and said, "By what authority are You doing these things? And who gave You this authority?" But Jesus answered and said to them, "I also will ask you one thing, which if you tell Me, I likewise will tell you by what authority I do these things: The baptism of John--where was it from? From heaven or from men?" And they reasoned among themselves, saying, "If we say, 'From heaven,' He will say to us, 'Why then did you not believe him?' But if we say, "From men,' we fear the multitude, for all count John as a prophet." So they answered Jesus and said, "We do not know." And He said to them, "Neither will I tell you by what authority I do these things."

2. When they asked about paying taxes to Caesar (Matthew 22:15-22).

Then the Pharisees went and plotted how they might entangle Him in His talk. And they sent to Him their disciples with the Herodians, saying, "Teacher, we know that You are true, and teach the way of God in truth; nor do You care about anyone, for You do not regard the person of men. Tell us, therefore, what do You think? Is it lawful to pay taxes to Caesar, or not?" But Jesus perceived their wickedness, and said, "Why do you test Me, you hypocrites? Show Me the tax money." So they brought Him a denarius. And He said to them, "Whose image and inscription is this?" They said to Him, "Caesar's." And He said to them, "Render therefore to Caesar the things that are Caesar's, and to God the things that are God's." When they had heard these words, they marveled, and left Him and went their way.

3. When He asked them about Christ being the Son of God (Matthew 22:41-46).

And no one was able to answer Him a word, nor from that day on did anyone dare question Him anymore. Matthew 22:46

Paul had a word of wisdom when he was before the Sanhedrin and realized that there was no way that he would get a fair hearing (Acts 23:1-10).

Paul had a word of wisdom concerning the safety of the crew during a violent storm (Acts 27:21-35).

God still uses the word of wisdom today in ways that are consistent with His eternal purpose. In fact, the word of wisdom heads the list of the gifts because this one is needed in operating all of the other gifts so that we can be sure we operate them in a way that truly reflects the love of God and edifies the body of Christ.

DR. ABRAHAM PETERS

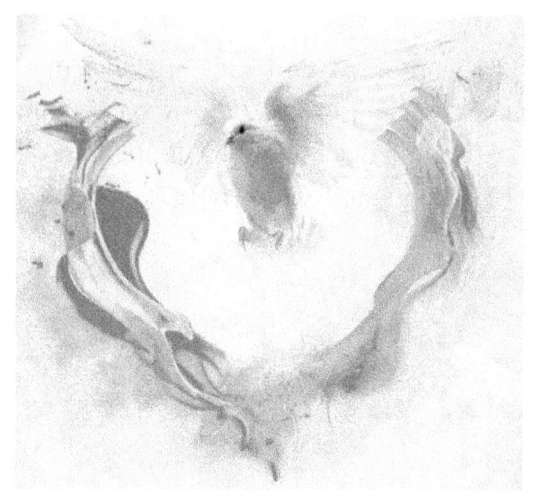

CHAPTER TWELVE

THE GIFT OF PROPHECY

Prophecy is one of the nine gifts of the Spirit (1 Corinthians 12:10).

As such, it is part of the spiritual equipment given by God to enable the Church.

...to another prophecy...

How the New Testament prophecy to be defined

Prophecy is the supernatural ability to receive a message initiated by God and the grace to speak it forth. It is not the same as "anointed preaching." It functions in two possible dimensions:

Forth Telling. This is the declarative aspect of prophecy where God delivers a message of edification, exhortation or comfort to His people.

Foretelling. This is the predictive aspect of prophecy where God delivers a message that involves the prediction of future events.

Prophecy is the principle expression resulting from the outpouring of the Holy Spirit for the entire Church Age (Acts 2:17-18).

And it shall come to pass in the last days, says God, that I will pour out of My Spirit on all flesh; your sons and your daughters shall prophesy, your young men shall see visions, your old men shall dream dreams. And on My menservants and on My maidservants I will pour out My Spirit in those days; and they shall prophesy.

DR. ABRAHAM PETERS

The various expressions of prophetic ministry that have been given to the Church

There are three primary expressions of prophetic ministry that have been given to the Church. All of them are to be used for the building of the Body of Christ.

A. There is the Gift of Prophecy (1 Corinthians 12:10).

B. There is the Ministry of Prophecy (Romans 12:6).

For I say, through the grace given to me, to everyone who is among you, not to think of himself more highly than he ought to think, but to think soberly, as God has dealt to each one a measure of faith. For as we have many members in one body, but all the members do not have the same function, so we, being many, are one body in Christ, and individually members of one another. Having then gifts differing according to the grace that is given to us, let us use them: if prophecy, let us prophesy in proportion to our faith; or ministry, let us use it in our ministering; he who teaches, in teaching; he who exhorts, in exhortation; he who gives, with liberality; he who leads, with diligence; he who shows mercy, with cheerfulness. Romans 12:1-8

C. There is the Ministry of a Prophet (Ephesians 4:11-12). This expression of prophecy is sometimes called "the Office of the Prophet."

And He Himself gave some to be apostles, some prophets, some evangelists, and some pastors and teachers, for the equipping of the saints for the work of ministry, for the edifying of the body of Christ...

Study the following chart in connection with these expressions of prophetic ministry:

Prophetic Expressions	The Gift of Prophecy	The Ministry of Prophecy	The Ministry of a Prophet
Defined	A gift of the Holy Spirit available to every believer from time to time at the impulse of the Spirit.	A consistent ministry given to some that serves as their primary function in the Body of Christ.	One of the five leadership/equipping ministries given to the church by Christ.
Key Verses	I Corinthians 12:10; 14:31, 39; Acts 19:6	Romans 12:6	Ephesians 4:11; 3:5; I Corinthians 12:28; 14:37; Acts 12:2728; 13:1; 15:32; 21:10
Distinctions	A temporary gift given in a moment for a specific situation. Operates in the realm of edification, exhortation and comfort.	A permanent ministry that functions at different levels. Operates in the realm of edification, exhortation and comfort.	A permanent ministry that functions at the highest level. Operates in the realm of guidance, rebuke, impartation, correction and revelation

Why prophecy is very important for the Church of today

D. Prophecy was an important expression and a normal activity in the Early Church (1 Corinthians 14).

1. Prophecy seems to have been considered a most significant gift (1 Corinthians 14:1; 1 Thessalonians 5:20).

Pursue love, and desire spiritual gifts, but especially that you may prophesy. 1 Corinthians 14:1

2. The prophetic ministry is specifically mentioned more than any other ministry in both the Old and the New Testament writings.

E. Prophecy is for the purpose of establishing, strengthening and comforting the local church (1 Corinthians 14:3-5).

But he who prophesies speaks edification and exhortation and comfort to men. He who speaks in a tongue edifies himself, but he who prophesies edifies the church. I wish you all spoke with tongues, but even more that you prophesied; for he who prophesies is greater than he who speaks with tongues, unless indeed he interprets, that the church may receive edification.

1. Prophecy is for the purpose of edification.

It is given by God with a view of building up the people of God and strengthening the local church. It is not given as a weapon to cut people down or sow division in the local assembly.

2. Prophecy is for the purpose of exhortation.

It is given by God with a view to bringing exhortation and comfort to the people of God. This would involve stirring people up and encouraging them toward the fulfillment of God's purposes in their lives. It is not for the purpose of rebuke and correction.

3. Prophecy is for the purpose of comfort.

It is given by God with a view to comfort the people of God and the local assembly in times of affliction, suffering, trials or persecution. It is not to bring judgment or condemnation.

Take note that those who function in the ministry of a prophet may actually go beyond these three areas to include direction or correction, but any prophetic ministry must always function in love for the purpose of edification.

F. Prophecy has the power to convince, convict, and reveal the secrets of the heart (1 Corinthians 14:24-25).

But if all prophesy, and an unbeliever or an uninformed person comes in, he is convinced by all, he is convicted by all. And thus the secrets of his heart are revealed; and so, falling down on his face, he will worship God and report that God is truly among you.

G. Prophecy can be a witness to unbelievers of the living presence of God (1 Corinthians 14:24-25).

H. Prophecies can be a significant tool for spiritual warfare (1Timothy 1:18; 4:14).

DR. ABRAHAM PETERS

This charge I commit to you, son Timothy, according to the prophecies previously made concerning you, that by them you may wage the good warfare... 1 Timothy 1:18

I. Prophecy is something that we are to desire—not just tolerate (1 Corinthians 14:1, 39).

Therefore, brethren, desire earnestly to prophesy, and do not forbid to speak with tongues. 1 Corinthians 14:39

Some biblical observations about prophecy

J. Prophecy is to be initiated by God (Jeremiah 23:16-22; Ezekiel 13:1-3).

And the word of the LORD came to me, saying, "Son of man, prophesy against the prophets of Israel who prophesy, and say to those who prophesy out of their own heart, 'Hear the word of the LORD!'" Thus says the Lord GOD: "Woe to the foolish prophets, who follow their own spirit and have seen nothing!" Ezekiel 13:1-3

K. Prophecy is God speaking to His people through a person (Exodus 4:15-16; 6:28-7:2).

God defined prophecy by using Moses' relationship to Aaron. God puts His words in the mouth of His prophets the same way Moses' put his words in the mouth of Aaron. The prophet speaks the words given by God, just as Aaron spoke the words that were given him by Moses.

> *Now you shall speak to him and put the words in his mouth. And I will be with your mouth and with his mouth, and I will teach you what you shall do. So he shall be your spokesman to the people. And he himself shall be as a mouth for you, and you shall be to him as God.* Exodus 4:15-16

> *So the LORD said to Moses: "See, I have made you as God to Pharaoh, and Aaron your brother shall be your prophet. You shall speak all that I command you. And Aaron your brother shall tell Pharaoh to send the children of Israel out of his land."* Exodus 7:1-2

L. Prophecy can function at different levels of faith (Romans 12:6).

> *Having then gifts differing according to the grace that is given to us, let us use them: if prophecy, let us prophesy in proportion to our faith...*

It is critical that we do not try to go past our faith or grace level in the area of prophecy.

How someone can function in the gift of prophecy

While the gift of prophecy is not earned or deserved, we can position ourselves to be more prepared to be used by God in this gift.

M. There are things that you can do as a lifestyle.

1. Fill your heart with the word of God (Colossians 3:16).

> *Let the word of Christ dwell in you richly in all wisdom, teaching and admonishing one another in psalms and hymns and spiritual songs, singing with grace in your hearts to the Lord.*

2. Be filled with the Spirit continually (Ephesians 5:18-19).

   > *And do not be drunk with wine, in which is dissipation; but be filled with the Spirit, speaking to one another in psalms and hymns and spiritual songs, singing and making melody in your heart to the Lord...*

3. Exercise your prayer language to build up your spirit (Jude 20-21).

   > *But you, beloved, building yourselves up on your most holy faith, praying in the Holy Spirit, keep yourselves in the love of God, looking for the mercy of our Lord Jesus Christ unto eternal life.*

4. Become an ardent worshipper of the Lord (Revelation 19:10).

Worship is a context that promotes prophetic sensitivity.

   > *And I fell at his feet to worship him. But he said to me, "See that you do not do that! I am your fellow servant, and of your brethren who have the testimony of Jesus. Worship God! For the testimony of Jesus is the spirit of prophecy."*

5. Become practiced in listening to the Holy Spirit in personal prayer times.

N. There are things that you can do in a specific setting.

1. Desire to be used in prophecy (1 Corinthians 14:31, 39).

2. Yield yourself to the Lord (Romans 6:13; 12:1-2).

   And do not present your members as instruments of unrighteousness to sin, but present yourselves to God as being alive from the dead, and your members as instruments of righteousness to God. Romans 6:13

3. Be sensitive to the prompting (nudging) of the Holy Spirit (2 Peter 1:21).

   ...for prophecy never came by the will of man, but holy men of God spoke as they were moved by the Holy Spirit.

4. Ask God for confirmation of the word you have received (2 Corinthians 13:1).

   By the mouth of two or three witnesses every word shall be established.

5. Check your heart's motivation (Jeremiah 23:16; 1 Corinthians 13:2). Make sure you do not have a personal agenda.

   Do not listen to the words of the prophets who prophesy to you. They make you worthless; they speak a vision of their own heart, not from the mouth of the LORD. Jeremiah 23:16

   And though I have the gift of prophecy, and understand all mysteries and all knowledge, and though I have all faith, so that I could remove mountains, but have not love, I am nothing. 1 Corinthians 13:2

6. Judge your own word before you give it (1 Thessalonians 5:20-21).

Do not despise prophecies. Test all things; hold fast what is good.

7. Look for the right opening or opportunity to share the word.

8. Ask God for direction as to how this word should be shared.

   a. In written form.
   b. In the form of a prayer or exhortation.
   c. Publicly to the local church.
   d. Privately to the leadership.

Some cautions or guidelines when it comes to prophecy

Some people get offended when you start talking about guidelines for the operation of the gifts. They would have really gotten offended at Paul in 1 Corinthians 14.

O. Some biblical guidelines

1. Stay within your realm of grace, faith and God-appointed sphere (Romans 12:16; 2 Corinthians 10:13-18).

2. Exercise self-control (1 Corinthians 14:32; Proverbs 25:28; 29:11, 20).

And the spirits of the prophets are subject to the prophets. 1 Corinthians 14:32

Whoever has no rule over his own spirit is like a city broken down, without walls. Proverbs 25:28

A fool vents all his feelings, but a wise man holds them back. Proverbs 29:11

3. Allow your ministry to be judged (1 Corinthians 14:29).

    Let two or three prophets speak, and let the others judge.

4. Observe the guidelines set by the leadership. Every river must have banks to contain, guide and direct the water to the real place of need.

5. If a word has been delivered by others do not feel that you must also speak (1 Corinthians 14:30).

    But if anything is revealed to another who sits by, let the first keep silent.

6. Quit when the Spirit quits (Proverbs 30:5-6).

    Every word of God is pure; He is a shield to those who put their trust in Him. Do not add to His words, lest He rebuke you, and you be found a liar.

P. Some practical guidelines

1. Use modern language when speaking (avoid King James English).

2. Speak loud and clear enough for the message to be understood (1 Corinthians 14:8).

For if the trumpet makes an uncertain sound, who will prepare for battle?

Paul summarizes the purpose for guidelines in 1 Corinthians 14:40:

Let all things be done decently and in order.

Judging Prophecy

Prophecy is a precious gift of the Spirit that has been given to the church for the blessing of God's people. When it is functioning as God designed, it has a tremendous ability to bless, strengthen, encourage, motivate, inspire, lift, envision and challenge. But, at the same time, prophecy that is abused or given in an unbiblical way can do serious damage, bring confusion and unrest, and misguide or mislead believing people who are sincerely looking for direction, divine counsel and a "word from God" for their life.

For this reason, Paul indicates in 1 Corinthians 14:29 that prophecy is to be judged.

Let two or three prophets speak, and let the others judge.

It is not easy to think in terms of judging prophecy for a several reasons. Because prophecy is a gift of the Spirit. For this reason, it is easy for us to feel that if we judge this prophecy, we are in some way judging the Spirit of God. No one wants to put him or herself in such a position. Because of the manner in which prophecy is usually given. When a person gives a prophecy, it is usually given in the first person as if God Himself was speaking (and indeed He is). Because it is difficult to judge the gift without feeling that you are judging the person exercising the gift.

Judging prophecy is very difficult for people to do, because it is difficult to judge the word without judging the person who is giving the word. No one wants to seem argumentative or to call another person into question. However, if prophecy is not judged, we do open ourselves up to being seriously misled in our walk with the Lord.

Why it is important that prophecy be judged

Prophecy is not on the same level with the written word of God. God makes it clear that prophecy is not to be viewed as infallible. This means that it is not to be taken on the same level as the written word of God. Prophecy comes through people who are fallible. Christ was the only infallible ministry. Every person born into the world must contend with sinful tendencies that can flavor any action that they take.

Prophecy by its very nature is highly subjective. When we deal in the area of prophecy we are dealing in the feeling realm. Feelings can be affected by many things. The Bible indicates that there will be false teachers, pastoral hirelings, false apostles and false prophets.

We are instructed to test ministries (Revelation 2:2). Jesus commended the Ephesians church for testing apostles.

I know your works, your labor, your patience, and that you cannot bear those who are evil. And you have tested those who say they are apostles and are not, and have found them liars...

Even pure ministries can "miss" God. Even valid ministries who have good hearts can "miss it" when it comes to giving counsel or uttering prophecy, because it is so easy to get emotionally involved in situations and find oneself sharing one's own words or desires rather than a pure word from God.

For all these reasons people can be affected by many different things that could have a bearing on a prophecy when given. For this reason godly people need to be discriminating as they listen to prophetic words and make a decision as to whether these words are indeed from God in part or in full.

The tests for prophetic utterance

There are eight tests for prophecy.

A. Test #1 – The written word of God, the Bible.

The written Word of God is the ultimate criterion for judging prophecy (2 Timothy 3:16). If the prophetic word is not in harmony with the Scripture it is to be rejected (Isaiah 8:19-20). Failure to do this can cause people to run the risk of placing prophecy on the same level as the written Word of God. This will cause instability and will open the person up to being seriously misled.

If they do not speak according to this word, it is because there is no light in them.   Isaiah 8:20

B. Test #2 – The spirit or the manner in which the word is given.

The spirit in which the "word" is ministered can also be an indicator of its authenticity. While God has used the manner and mannerisms of prophets in unusual ways at times, the general rule is that prophecy will minister edification, exhortation and comfort (1Corinthians 14:3) and lead to peace (1Corinthians 14:33).

For God is not the author of confusion but of peace, as in all the churches of the saints.   1 Corinthians 14:33

The Holy Spirit may bring a rebuke, but most often it will be done in a pastoral way. Often when a word is harsh in its delivery it is because the person doing the prophesying is personally upset about something and is letting his or her own feelings, attitude or emotions about the matter enter into their message. Because of this, the "quickening" that the person feels may or may not be brought on by the initiative of the Holy Spirit (Acts 21:4).

C. Test #3 – The conduct and personal life of the person prophesying.

God can certainly overrule the nature of the person prophesying and cause a true word to come forth from any vessel. If He can overrule the nature of a donkey, He can work through anyone. However, God's usual method of working is to speak through vessels who have set themselves aside in holiness and dedication to the Lord.

When a prophet has a lifestyle that is ungodly, it brings the words that they speak into question (Jeremiah 23:15-16; 2 Peter 2:2). Ministries who have learned a life of daily obedience to God have also learned to hear the "still small voice" of the Spirit. Their words can be trusted more readily. The gifts of the Spirit must be motivated and impelled by the fruit of the Spirit. This will help ensure that the fruit of the prophecy is in line with the fruit of the Spirit.

D. Test #4 – The inner witness of the Holy Spirit.

Since every true believer is inhabited by the Spirit of God and there is only one Holy Spirit, the Spirit of God within the believer should attest to the Spirit of God in the prophet (1 Corinthians 2:11-14).

The inner peace of the Holy Spirit in this sense is a guiding force to help us discern whether or not this is a true word for us. God is not the author of confusion. If there is a lot of confusion in a person's spirit after the prophecy is given, the prophecy should be "put on the shelf" until peace returns (1 Corinthians 14:33).

The believer should be cautioned, however, not to take any prophecy lightly. They should spend specific time in prayer regarding its content and ask the Lord whether there might be any truth to it.

E. Test #5 – The confirmation of other witnesses.

If a word is to be established, it should be confirmed "in the mouth of two or three witnesses" (2 Corinthians 13:1). Even Jesus was willing to have his words examined in this way (John 5:31-47).

These "witnesses" could include several things. One witness could be other prophetic ministries. Another witness could be pastors and other church leaders. Another witness could be parents and those that God has put over our lives. Even circumstances and other events in our lives that are almost like "divine coincidences" can bear witness to the authenticity of a prophetic word.

F. Test #6 – The edification experienced by the word given

If a prophetic utterance is from the Lord, it should build up, admonish and encourage the people of God (1 Corinthians 14:3). If it does not accomplish this, it must be rejected. If the word is confusing, condemning, discouraging and brings a heaviness to an otherwise peaceful, uplifting setting, it is probably not from the Lord.

This is not to say that there is never a time or place for prophecy that is correctional in nature. But prophecy of this nature should be carefully screened by the leadership of the church and should still be ministered in a pastoral way so that the listener can more easily receive it.

G. Test #7 – The fulfillment of the word given

If the prophetic word that is given is predictive in nature and it does not come to pass, the prophecy is not a true prophecy. This sounds so obvious, but it is amazing how people will try to "weasel out" of an inaccurate or presumptuous prophecy by accusing God of changing His mind, by blaming others for a lack of faith or prayer or by the claim that the Lord was only testing them.

The more a person brings forth inaccurate words, the more their prophecies will be considered suspect. Prophets whose words did not come to pass were not to be feared (Deuteronomy 18:20-22). In the Old Testament the erring prophet could actually be put to death. Today, we will most likely just ask them not to prophesy in the future.

But the prophet who presumes to speak a word in My name, which I have not commanded him to speak, or who speaks in the name of other gods, that prophet shall die. And if you say in your heart, "How shall we know the word which the LORD has not spoken?"—when a prophet speaks in the name of the LORD, if the thing does not happen or come to pass, that is the thing which the LORD has not spoken; the prophet has spoken it presumptuously; you shall not be afraid of him.

H. Test #8 – The prophecy's exaltation of JESUS CHRIST.

If prophecy is to be proper in all of its aspects, it must ultimately exalt the Lord and bring glory to Him and Him alone (1 Peter 4:1). The result of prophecy is that people should see Jesus and be drawn to Him (1 Corinthians 14:24-25). Indeed John proclaims in the Book of Revelation that the "testimony of Jesus" is the spirit of prophecy (Revelation 19:10), or as one translation says, "It is the truth concerning Jesus that inspires all prophecy" (Knox).

In the Old Testament even if the prophets words were true and came to pass, but the net result was that people were turned away from the Lord by their ministry, that prophet was to be considered false (Deuteronomy 13:1-5).

If there arises among you a prophet or a dreamer of dreams, and he gives you a sign or a wonder, 2 and the sign or the wonder comes to pass, of which he spoke to you, saying, "Let us go after other gods"--which you have not known—"and let us serve them," 3 you shall not listen to the words of that prophet or that dreamer of dreams, for the LORD your God is testing you to know whether you love the LORD your God with all your heart and with all your soul. 4 You shall walk after the LORD your God and fear Him, and keep His commandments and obey His voice; you shall serve Him and hold fast to Him. 5 But that prophet or that dreamer of dreams shall be put to death, because he has spoken in order to turn you away from the LORD your God, who brought you out of the land of Egypt and redeemed you from the house of bondage, to entice you from the way in which the LORD your God commanded you to walk. So you shall put away the evil from your midst.

The caution here is that we must never let anything be the center of the prophetic experience but Jesus. We must not let our focus be on the individual through whom the prophecy comes, or on an institution, or on a method or style. All prophecy should inspire the worship of Jesus.

Who is to judge prophecy?

There are various levels of judgment that should be operating in relation to prophecy. Each level of judgment should minimize the need for deeper levels of judgment. When everyone takes their God-given responsibility for the prophetic, we can grow in our confidence that prophecy will always edify and build up the people of God. We should be just as willing or eager to be judged as we are willing and eager to prophesy!

A. Judgment Level #1 – The one giving the prophecy.

The Bible clearly teaches that the "spirits of the prophets are subject to the prophets" (1 Corinthians 14:32). The Spirit of God does not overrule the will of man. When someone prophesies, they cannot say, "The Spirit made me do it." They cannot blame the Spirit of God for forcing them to prophesy in either an inopportune time or in an inappropriate manner. The Bible clearly teaches that we are responsible for what we say and do. Other translations of this same passage help us to understand more fully what is being said in this passage.

> *"Remember that a person who has a message from God has the power to stop himself and wait his turn."* –Living Bible

And the gift of prophecy does not take from the prophets the control of their own spirits. In other words, people have total control of themselves when they give a prophetic utterance. It was the prophets who were associated with pagan temples that claimed they were overtaken by the gods and prophesied with an ecstatic frenzy. True prophets are to exercise control of their prophetic gift.

When speaking in relation to the experience of communion, Paul said that if we would judge ourselves we would not be judged (1 Corinthians 11:31). While Paul was not speaking specifically about prophecy, self-analysis is clearly the first level of judgment that must take place in respect to any prophecy. This self-judgment should take place before the prophecy is given.

The individual needs to render judgment on the content of his or her own word when measured against the word of God. Before they prophesy, they need to ask themselves some important questions.

1. Is this word consistent with what the Bible says? Does it contradict the Scripture or violate any biblical principles?

2. Will this word bring edification, exhortation or comfort?

3. For whom is this word to be given? Is this a personal word for me or is it for the entire church?

4. Am I a committed member of this church with a demonstrated love for and loyalty to the individual members of this congregation?

5. Why do I want to give this word at this time? Is it in my heart to strengthen the church and its leadership?

6. What is my personal attitude toward the congregation at this time? The pastor? The leadership?

7. Is there any bitterness or lack of forgiveness in my spirit that might taint the word that is to be given?

8. Is this word consistent with what God has been saying to the Church in this season? In this service?

9. What seems to be the best time, place and context for this word to be given? Public setting? Private setting?

10. What is the tone in which this word should be spoken?

11. What is the manner in which the word is to be given? Orally to the pastor? Orally to the congregation? In writing to the pastor? Prophesied, exhorted or prayed?

12. Is this the type of word that the pastor should be aware of before it is given to the congregation?

13. Am I overstepping my authority in this congregation to give a word of this nature?

14. Will this word put the pastor and leadership on the spot in front of the congregation? Am I painting myself or anyone else in a corner with this word?

15. Am I using prophecy to bring a rebuke that I feel is needed, to speak my mind concerning the program or the vision of the church, or to get a major concern that I have off of my chest?

16. Am I willing to allow this word of mine to be judged by others without feeling like everyone must agree with my personal analysis of it?

17. Am I willing not to give this word if the leadership of the church feels that it is inappropriate?

18. If this is a personal word for an individual, am I willing to request the presence of an appropriate person to listen to and judge this word?

19. If my prophetic utterance proves to be inaccurate or does not come to pass, am I willing to take personal responsibility for it without blaming others for the result? Would I be willing to make a public statement acknowledging my error?

All of these questions will help the prophet minimize mistakes in the area of prophecy. But if this is to truly take place, a heartfelt desire for the serious evaluation of prophecy must be in the spirit of everyone who seeks to prophesy.

Judgment Level #2 – Other prophetic ministries.

The New Testament seems to have prophets working together in tandem with either apostolic ministries or other prophetic ministries (Acts 13:1; 15:32). Paul indicates that in the context of prophetic ministry, the prophets should serve as a check and a balance to each other. "Let two or three prophets speak, and let the others judge" (1 Corinthians 14:29).

There is no question that those who have been called by God to be prophetic voices to God's people have a special sensitivity to what God wants to say to His people. As prophetic ministries function together in the same setting, they should have a similar sensing of what God is trying to communicate to a person or to a congregation.

This is one reason why Paul undoubtedly encourages only two or three to speak, because in any given context they would all be receiving a similar message. How many times does a message have to be spoken before it is in effect delivered? The Bible answers this question also when it declares repeatedly that in the "mouth of two or three witnesses let every word be established" (2 Corinthians 13:1).

Judgment Level #3 – The leadership of the church.

Ultimately, it is the responsibility of the leadership of the local church to render a judgment concerning any given prophecy. The Senior Pastor and the elders of the church have a God-given responsibility to feed, care for and protect the flock of God which is under their charge.

Paul makes this responsibility clear when he addresses the Ephesians elders in his meeting with them in Miletus (Acts 20:28-31). The elders were instructed to be overseers and watchmen, guarding against anything that would hurt or damage the people of God.

The Bible also instructs members of the congregation to submit to the elders of the church (1 Peter 5:5; Hebrews 13:17). The reason for this submission to the elders is that ultimately God holds elders accountable for what takes place in the congregation under their charge. We make the task of the elders easier when we recognize their authority and receive whatever correction they may want to give us with a good spirit.

Really, Is prophetic ministry worth the effort?

With so much being said about judging prophecy, it makes one wonder whether or not we should just "scrap" the idea of having prophetic ministry. Maybe it would just be easier to eliminate it altogether. God forbid that we should ever think this way! We could say the same thing about raising children, building a home, cultivating friendships and even getting married. Just because something carries with it some challenges, it is no reason to do away with it. The problems associated with prophecy should never cause us to get to a place where we "despise prophecies" (1 Thessalonians 5:20).

The fact is that the blessing of the prophetic ministry so far out weighs any negative aspects of prophecy that eliminating this great gift from the church cannot even be considered. Churches that have no prophetic vision are missing a wonderful element of the whole Christian experience. Rather than seeking to eliminate the prophetic because of a few potential problems, we must seek how to harness this ministry for the ultimate purpose of strengthening the church of Jesus Christ.

A. We are instructed to not despise prophecies (1 Thessalonians 5:20).

B. We are to earnestly desire to prophesy (1 Corinthians 14:1).

When we prophesy within the framework provided to us by the Word of God, prophecy edifies or builds up the church (1 Corinthians 14:4). If the church is going to be what God has called it to be, it will not get there without prophets and prophecy being fully released. If you would love to go deeper in the studying of prophetic ministry, I recommend my book: AWAKENING THE PROPHET IN YOU: UNDERSTANDING THE PROPHETIC MINISTRY

CHAPTER THIRTEEN

THE POWER GIFTS: FAITH, HEALING AND MIRACLE

What the power gifts have in common: They are all supernatural in nature.

1. The faith that is listed among the gifts of the Spirit is a supernatural faith.

2. The gifts of healing are supernatural and not accomplished by the work of medical science.

3. The working of miracles is referring to happenings that only God can do.

They are all somewhat dependent upon each other.

It is hard to separate these three gifts of the Spirit. It takes supernatural faith to operate in the supernatural realms of divine healing and miracles. Very often the supernatural impartation of faith leads to an act of faith which often includes miracles and healing. It is also hard to distinguish whether something related to physical healing is the "gifts of healing" in operation or the "working of miracles."

They all operate at the impetus and direction of the Holy Spirit.

As with all of the gifts of the Spirit, these power gifts operate at the discretion of the Holy Spirit through the vessels of His choosing.

They are all part of the "power" that is to be part of the experience of the church (Acts 1:8).

The operation of these gifts is an indicator of the supernatural power that has been placed in the hands of the Church. They are the ability of God working through the hands of man or the Body of Christ.

They are all gifts and, therefore, they are undeserved and unearned by those who function in them.

They are all needed if the church is to be what God intended for it to be.

What the gift of faith is and how it does operate

The gift of faith must be distinguished from other realms of faith in the Bible.

There are at least four realms of faith in the Christian experience. There is saving faith (Ephesians 2:8-9; Romans 3:28; 5:1-2; Galatians 3:23, 26).

> *For by grace you have been saved through faith, and that not of yourselves; it is the gift of God, not of works, lest anyone should boast.* Ephesians 2:8-9

> *Therefore, having been justified by faith, we have peace with God through our Lord Jesus Christ, through whom also we have access by faith into this grace in which we stand, and rejoice in hope of the glory of God.* Romans 5:1-2

Saving faith is that faith imparted to us by God that enables us to receive Christ for who He is presented to be in the Gospel.

There is the fruit of faith (Romans 1:16-17; Galatians 2:20; 5:22).

For I am not ashamed of the gospel of Christ, for it is the power of God to salvation for everyone who believes, for the Jew first and also for the Greek. For in it the righteousness of God is revealed from faith to faith; as it is written, "The just shall live by faith."
Romans 1:16-17

I have been crucified with Christ; it is no longer I who live, but Christ lives in me; and the life which I now live in the flesh I live by faith in the Son of God, who loved me and gave Himself for me.
Galatians 2:20

The fruit of faith is the faith for living that grows gradually in us as we yield to the power of the Holy Spirit dwelling within us.

There is ministering faith (Romans 12:3-6; Acts 6:5, 8; 2 Corinthians 11:12-16; 2 Thessalonians 1:11-12).

For I say, through the grace given to me, to everyone who is among you, not to think of himself more highly than he ought to think, but to think soberly, as God has dealt to each one a measure of faith. For as we have many members in one body, but all the members do not have the same function, so we, being many, are one body in Christ, and individually members of one another. Having then gifts differing according to the grace that is given to us, let us use them: if prophecy, let us prophesy in proportion to our faith... Romans 12:3-6

Faith to minister is that measure of Christ's faith that is given to us enabling us to function in the ministry to which we have been called.

DR. ABRAHAM PETERS

There is the gift of faith (Mark. 11:20-24; 1 Corinthians 12:9; 13:2; Romans 4:18-21).

So Jesus answered and said to them, "Have faith in God. For assuredly, I say to you, whoever says to this mountain, 'Be removed and be cast into the sea," and does not doubt in his heart, but believes that those things he says will be done, he will have whatever he says. Therefore I say to you, whatever things you ask when you pray, believe that you receive them, and you will have them." Mark 11:22-24

And though I have the gift of prophecy, and understand all mysteries and all knowledge, and though I have all faith, so that I could remove mountains, but have not love, I am nothing. 1 Corinthians 13:2

The gift of faith is a temporary and supernatural impartation of faith to believe for the impossible in a specific situation at a specific moment in time. The gift of faith can be defined as small portion of God's total faith given to a believer and applied to a specific situation. God is the source of all faith. He leads the list of the heroes of faith in the faith chapter of the Bible (Hebrews 11:3; Psalm 33:6, 9).

By faith we understand that the worlds were framed by the word of God, so that the things which are seen were not made of things which are visible. Hebrews 11:3

By the word of the LORD the heavens were made, and all the host of them by the breath of His mouth....For He spoke, and it was done; He commanded, and it stood fast. Psalm 33:6, 9

To operate in the gift of faith we tap into the "faith of God" (Mark 11:22-24).

To operate in the gift of faith we must function under God's initiative (John 5:19; 14:10-11).

> *Then Jesus answered and said to them, "Most assuredly, I say to you, the Son can do nothing of Himself, but what He sees the Father do; for whatever He does, the Son also does in like manner."* John 5:19

Jesus operated in the gift of faith.

Jesus often declared the impossible that God would do even before it happened.

The raising of Lazarus from the dead (John 11:11).

> *These things He said, and after that He said to them, 'Our friend Lazarus sleeps, but I go that I may wake him up."*

Jesus spoke words of faith about Lazarus long before He worked the miracle of raising him from the dead.

The cleansing of the leper (Matthew 8:1-3). Jesus acted in boldness, confidence and a spirit of faith when He told the leper that He was willing to heal him, and then did!

The healing of the blind man (John 9:1-7). Jesus functioned in the gift of faith when he declared that the man born blind would bring glory to God by virtue of his healing. Then he exercised further faith when He put clay on his eyes and told Him to go wash.

His own resurrection from the dead (John 2:19-22).

> *Jesus answered and said to them, "Destroy this temple, and in three days I will raise it up." Then the Jews said, "It has taken forty-six years to build this temple, and will You raise it up in three days?" But He was speaking of the temple of His body. Therefore, when He had risen from the dead, His disciples remembered that He had said this to them; and they believed the Scripture and the word which Jesus had said.*

Jesus made a bold declaration of faith about His death and resurrection very early in His ministry.

Elijah operated in the gift of faith as he challenged the 450 prophets of Baal on Mt. Carmel (1 Kings. 18:21-40). Elijah was no stranger to receiving a word from the Lord. He no doubt received orders from above when he challenged the prophets of Baal. Notice the supernatural faith in the prophet Elijah.

He set forth an impossible challenge to the prophets of Baal (fire from heaven). He mocked the prophets' appeals to their false gods (painting himself into a corner).

> *And so it was, at noon, that Elijah mocked them and said, "Cry aloud, for he is a god; either he is meditating, or he is busy, or he is on a journey, or perhaps he is sleeping and must be awakened."*

He dug a trench around the altar and poured 12 barrels of water on the sacrifice and the wood until the trench was full of water (increasing the impossible nature of what he was doing). After all of this Elijah demonstrated that faith does not require a lot of noise, violent activity or outward show, but a simple prayer of faith based on the revealed word and will of God.

The Early Church practiced the gift of faith.

Peter exercised the gift of faith in anticipation of the healing of the lame man (Acts 3:1-7). God gave Peter a supernatural impartation of faith to be able to look the lame man in the eye and announce to him that he was going to be healed.

Peter declared judgment on Sapphira before it happened (Acts 5:9-10). God gave Peter a bold faith to announce to Sapphira that she was about to die for what her and her husband had done (not the positive miracle that most of us are looking for). Paul was able to declare what God was about to do through him in relation to Elymas the sorcerer (Act 13:8-11).

What the "gifts of healing" is and how it does operate

The "gifts of healing" is one of the ways that God has made provision for His people to receive healing for the body. There are several ways in which people can receive healing. There are natural means, including diet, exercise, relieving stress, proper rest and a disciplined life (Proverbs 17:22; 1 Timothy 4:8; Philippians 4:6; 2 Timothy 2:24). There is the medical profession, which is certainly used of God to help deal with sickness and disease (Matthew 9:12).

There are spiritual avenues of healing that God has put in the Church.

a. Simple prayer to God by the sick person (James 5:13-14; Hebrews 11:6).

b. The laying on of the hands of other believers (Mark 16:17).

c. Anointing with oil by church leadership (James 5:14).

d. Through the word of power (Matthew 8:5-13; Psalm 107:20).

e. Through the Table of the Lord (1 Corinthians 11:23-32).

f. Through special and miraculous means (Mark 7:31-37; 8:22-26; John 9:17; Acts 19:11-12; 5:15-16).

g. Through dealing with any demonic bondage that might be causing the infirmity (Luke 13:11-12).

h. Being ministered to by someone who has the ministry of healing (1 Corinthians 12:28).

   i. Being ministered to by someone operating in the gifts of healing (1 Corinthians 12:9).

The "gifts of healing" are a supernatural impartation of the ability of God to bring healing to an individual in an instant of time. It is often accompanied by the gift of faith. It is not to be confused with the "ministry" of healing (1 Corinthians 12:28).

And God has appointed these in the church: first apostles, second prophets, third teachers, after that miracles, then gifts of healings, helps, administrations, varieties of tongues. Are all apostles? Are

> *all prophets? Are all teachers? Are all workers of miracles? Do all have gifts of healings? Do all speak with tongues? Do all interpret? But earnestly desire the best gifts. And yet I show you a more excellent way.* 1 Corinthians 12:28-31

In Paul's discussion of the various ministries that function in the Body of Christ, he includes those who have been given the ministry of healing. Evidently there will be those in the Body of Christ who share in Christ's ministry of healing as their primary ministry function. Not everyone will function in this ministry. However, every believer can be used in the "gifts of healing" as described earlier in the chapter. It is not a gift that receives gradual results (Matthew 8:3; Mark 1:31).

> *Then Jesus put out His hand and touched him, saying, "I am willing; be cleansed." Immediately his leprosy was cleansed.*
> Matthew 8:3

> *So He came and took her by the hand and lifted her up, and immediately the fever left her. And she served them.* Mark 1:31

When Jesus functioned in this gift the result was always immediate. On one occasion when the result was incomplete, he was not satisfied with the result. He prayed again and the complete healing followed (Mark 8:22-25). Some of the other avenues of healing may see a more gradual recovery.

> *Then He came to Bethsaida; and they brought a blind man to Him, and begged Him to touch him. So He took the blind man by the hand and led him out of the town. And when He had spit on his eyes and put His hands on him, He asked him if he saw anything.*

DR. ABRAHAM PETERS

And he looked up and said, "I see men like trees, walking." Then He put His hands on his eyes again and made him look up. And he was restored and saw everyone clearly.

It is not the "gift of healing" but the "gifts of healing." The "gifts of healing" is the only gift of the Spirit that is referenced in the plural form. It is found in the plural because: There are many different diseases that need to be healed (Matthew 10:1; Luke 4:40).

And when He had called His twelve disciples to Him, He gave them power over unclean spirits, to cast them out, and to heal all kinds of sickness and all kinds of disease. Matthew 10:1

When the sun was setting, all those who had any that were sick with various diseases brought them to Him; and He laid His hands on every one of them and healed them.

There may be some who have an impartation of faith for a certain type of disease (1 Corinthians 12:28). For this reason there may be those who have greater faith or sensitivity to certain types of diseases. The gifts of healing operated in the life and ministry of Jesus.

Jesus healed all manner of sick people (Matthew 4:23-24). His healing ministry included dealing with leprosy, blindness, deafness, dumbness, paralysis, epilepsy, fever, and internal hemorrhaging.

And Jesus went about all Galilee, teaching in their synagogues, preaching the gospel of the kingdom, and healing all kinds of sickness and all kinds of disease among the people. Then His fame went throughout all Syria; and they brought to Him all sick people

> who were afflicted with various diseases and torments, and those who were demon-possessed, epileptics, and paralytics; and He healed them.

The gifts of healing operated in the life and ministry of the Early Church. Peter and John ministered healing to the lame man (Acts 3:1-8).

> "Silver and gold I do not have, but what I do have I give you: In the name of Jesus Christ of Nazareth, rise up and walk." And he took him by the right hand and lifted him up, and immediately his feet and ankle bones received strength. So he, leaping up, stood and walked and entered the temple with them--walking, leaping, and praising God. Acts 3:6-8

Philip saw multitudes healed under his ministry (Acts 8:6-8).

> And the multitudes with one accord heeded the things spoken by Philip, hearing and seeing the miracles which he did. For unclean spirits, crying with a loud voice, came out of many who were possessed; and many who were paralyzed and lame were healed. And there was great joy in that city.

Ananias prayed for Saul to receive his sight and he did (Acts 9:17-18).

> And Ananias went his way and entered the house; and laying his hands on him he said, "Brother Saul, the Lord Jesus, who appeared to you on the road as you came, has sent me that you may receive your sight and be filled with the Holy Spirit."

Immediately there fell from his eyes something like scales, and he received his sight at once; and he arose and was baptized.

Peter was used by God to heal Aeneas from paralysis (Acts 9:32-35).

There he found a certain man named Aeneas, who had been bedridden eight years and was paralyzed. And Peter said to him, "Aeneas, Jesus the Christ heals you. Arise and make your bed." Then he arose immediately. So all who dwelt at Lydda and Sharon saw him and turned to the Lord.

Paul and Barnabas saw strong signs and wonders in their ministry including the healing of a lame man in Lystra (Acts 14:3, 8-10).

Therefore they stayed there a long time, speaking boldly in the Lord, who was bearing witness to the word of His grace, granting signs and wonders to be done by their hands. Acts 14:3

And in Lystra a certain man without strength in his feet was sitting, a cripple from his mother's womb, who had never walked. This man heard Paul speaking. Paul, observing him intently and seeing that he had faith to be healed, said with a loud voice, "Stand up straight on your feet!" And he leaped and walked. Acts 14:8-10

Paul ministered to Publius and his fever left him (Acts 28:8-9). Others were also healed of various diseases.

And it happened that the father of Publius lay sick of a fever and dysentery.

Paul went in to him and prayed, and he laid his hands on him and healed him. So when this was done, the rest of those on the island who had diseases also came and were healed.

The gifts of healing operate on the basis of the compassion of Christ (Matthew 20:34; Mark 1:41; Luke 7:12-15).

So Jesus had compassion and touched their eyes. And immediately their eyes received sight, and they followed Him. Matthew 20:34

And when He came near the gate of the city, behold, a dead man was being carried out, the only son of his mother; and she was a widow. And a large crowd from the city was with her. When the Lord saw her, He had compassion on her and said to her, "Do not weep." Then He came and touched the open coffin, and those who carried him stood still. And He said, "Young man, I say to you, arise." So he who was dead sat up and began to speak. And He presented him to his mother. Luke 7:12-15

What the gift of the working of miracles is and how it does operate

When we think of "miracles" it is easy to think of miracles as our culture would interpret a miracle. The word "miracle" is used in our culture in many ways that are foreign to the biblical usage. We speak of a recovery from a serious illness and the "miracle of modern medicine." We speak of a person who has been through a lot as a "walking miracle."

1. We speak of the "miracle" of the human body.

2. We look at all of creation and speak of the "miracle" of the universe.

3. We speak of advances in medicine as "miracle drugs."

4. We speak of anything that we do not understand as a "miracle" (e.g. television, electricity, computers, air travel), even though these things function on the basis of natural laws.

All of these reflect that the idea of a miracle is always relative to a person's knowledge and experience. The English word "miracle" comes from a Latin word *"mirar"* which means "to wonder." A miracle is something that moves us to wonder. Why would we wonder?

    a. Because we cannot do it ourselves.

    b. Because we cannot understand how it is done.

A miracle is something which no man can perform and which no man can explain or understand. A miracle is God's power invading man's world. The gift of the Spirit known as "the working of miracles" is the impartation of divine ability or power to perform the impossible. It is tapping into the omnipotence or the power of God. The Holy Spirit is referred to as the "power of the highest" (Luke 1:35b).

The Holy Spirit will come upon you, and the power of the Highest will overshadow you... Jesus operated under the influence of the "power" of the Holy Spirit (Acts 10:38).

How God anointed Jesus of Nazareth with the Holy Spirit and with power, who went about doing good and healing all who were oppressed by the devil, for God was with Him.

Jesus told His followers that miraculous signs would follow them (Mark 16:16-18). They were not to follow after miraculous signs (which is the tendency of many people today).

And these signs will follow those who believe: In My name they will cast out demons; they will speak with new tongues; they will take up serpents; and if they drink anything deadly, it will by no means hurt them; they will lay hands on the sick, and they will recover.

Jesus told the disciples that they would receive "power" when the Holy Spirit came upon them (Acts 1:8).

But you shall receive power when the Holy Spirit has come upon you…

The apostles in the Early Church gave witness with great "power" (Acts 4:33).

And with great power the apostles gave witness to the resurrection of the Lord Jesus. And great grace was upon them all.

Paul preached the gospel with the demonstration of the Holy Spirit and "power" (1Corinthians 2:4-5).

And my speech and my preaching were not with persuasive words of human wisdom, but in demonstration of the Spirit and of power, that your faith should not be in the wisdom of men but in the power of God.

Paul told Timothy that we have received the "spirit of power" (2 Timothy 1:7).

For God has not given us a spirit of fear, but of power and of love and of a sound mind.

It is not to be confused with a ministry of or workers of miracles (1 Corinthians 12:28). As with the gifts of healing, in Paul's discussion of the various ministries that function in the Body of Christ, he includes those who have been given the ministry of "workers of miracles." Evidently there will be those in the Body of Christ who share in Christ's ministry of miracles as their primary ministry function. Not everyone will function in this ministry. However, every believer can be used in the "working of miracles" as one of the nine gifts of the Spirit.

Jesus functioned in the working of miracles. All of these miracles defied natural laws.

Jesus turned water into wine (John 2:1-11). Defying the laws of chemistry.

Jesus walked on water (John 6:19). Defying the laws of gravity.

Jesus calmed the winds and the sea (Matthew 8:23-27).

Jesus raised people from the dead (Matthew 9:18-26; John 11:38-44).

Jesus multiplied loaves and fish to feed multitudes (Matthew 15:32-39; John 6:114).

Jesus cursed a fig tree and it withered away (Matthew 21:18-22).

The Early Church functioned in the working of miracles. Many signs and wonders were done by the apostles (Acts 5:12).

And through the hands of the apostles many signs and wonders were done among the people. And they were all with one accord in Solomon's Porch.

The shadow of Peter fell on sick people and they were healed (Acts 5:14-16).

And believers were increasingly added to the Lord, multitudes of both men and women, so that they brought the sick out into the streets and laid them on beds and couches, that at least the shadow of Peter passing by might fall on some of them. Also a multitude gathered from the surrounding cities to Jerusalem, bringing sick people and those who were tormented by unclean spirits, and they were all healed.

Stephen did many signs and wonders (Acts 6:8).

And Stephen, full of faith and power, did great wonders and signs among the people.

Philip was miraculously transported (Acts 8:39-40).

DR. ABRAHAM PETERS

Now when they came up out of the water, the Spirit of the Lord caught Philip away, so that the eunuch saw him no more; and he went on his way rejoicing. But Philip was found at Azotus. And passing through, he preached in all the cities till he came to Caesarea.

The apostles saw people raised from the dead (Acts 9:40-43; 19:7-12).

Then Peter arose and went with them. When he had come, they brought him to the upper room. And all the widows stood by him weeping, showing the tunics and garments which Dorcas had made while she was with them. But Peter put them all out, and knelt down and prayed. And turning to the body he said, "Tabitha, arise." And she opened her eyes, and when she saw Peter she sat up. Then he gave her his hand and lifted her up; and when he had called the saints and widows, he presented her alive. And it became known throughout all Joppa, and many believed on the Lord. Acts 9:39-42

Paul smote Elymas with blindness (Acts 13:8-12; Compare II Kings 6:18).

But Elymas the sorcerer (for so his name is translated) withstood them, seeking to turn the proconsul away from the faith. Then Saul, who also is called Paul, filled with the Holy Spirit, looked intently at him and said, "O full of all deceit and all fraud, you son of the devil, you enemy of all righteousness, will you not cease perverting the straight ways of the Lord? And now, indeed, the hand of the Lord is upon you, and you shall be blind, not seeing the sun for a time." And immediately a dark mist fell on him, and he went around seeking someone to lead him by the hand. Then the proconsul believed, when he saw what had been done, being astonished at the teaching of the Lord.

Handkerchiefs were taken from Paul's body and people were healed (Acts 19:11-12).

Now God worked unusual miracles by the hands of Paul, so that even handkerchiefs or aprons were brought from his body to the sick, and the diseases left them and the evil spirits went out of them.

Paul shook off a poisonous snake and was not harmed (Acts 28:3-6). However, it appears to have been a bad experience for the snake.

But when Paul had gathered a bundle of sticks and laid them on the fire, a viper came out because of the heat, and fastened on his hand. So when the natives saw the creature hanging from his hand, they said to one another, "No doubt this man is a murderer, whom, though he has escaped the sea, yet justice does not allow to live." But he shook off the creature into the fire and suffered no harm. However, they were expecting that he would swell up or suddenly fall down dead. But after they had looked for a long time and saw no harm come to him, they changed their minds and said that he was a god.

Jesus indicated that those who followed Him would do "greater works" than the works that He did (John 14:11-12).

Believe Me that I am in the Father and the Father in Me, or else believe Me for the sake of the works themselves. Most assuredly, I say to you, he who believes in Me, the works that I do he will do also; and greater works than these he will do, because I go to My Father.

What the purpose in God's mind is for displaying His awesome power

God has His reasons for the display of signs, wonders and miracles. It is not to exalt people or impress people with His awesome power. It is to separate Himself from all other gods (Exodus 15:11; 9:14; 18:11).

...for at this time I will send all My plagues to your very heart, and on your servants and on your people, that you may know that there is none like Me in all the earth. Exodus 9:14

Then Jethro rejoiced for all the good which the LORD had done for Israel, whom He had delivered out of the hand of the Egyptians. And Jethro said, "Blessed be the LORD, who has delivered you out of the hand of the Egyptians and out of the hand of Pharaoh, and who has delivered the people from under the hand of the Egyptians. Now I know that the LORD is greater than all the gods; for in the very thing in which they behaved proudly, He was above them." Exodus 18:9-11

It is to show forth His glory (John 2:11; Exodus 9:16; 8:19; 10:2; Matthew 15:30-31).

This beginning of signs Jesus did in Cana of Galilee, and manifested His glory; and His disciples believed in Him. John 2:11

But indeed for this purpose I have raised you up, that I may show My power in you, and that My name may be declared in all the earth. Exodus 9:16

Then great multitudes came to Him, having with them the lame, blind, mute, maimed, and many others; and they laid them down at Jesus' feet, and He healed them. So the multitude marveled when they saw the mute speaking, the maimed made whole, the lame walking, and the blind seeing; and they glorified the God of Israel. Matthew 15:30-31

It is to attest to the divine origin of His servants (John 3:2; Exodus 3:12; 2 Corinthians 12:12).

This man came to Jesus by night and said to Him, "Rabbi, we know that You are a teacher come from God; for no one can do these signs that You do unless God is with him." John 3:2

It is to inspire the faith of unbelievers (John 11:47-48; 20:30-31).

Then the chief priests and the Pharisees gathered a council and said, "What shall we do? For this Man works many signs. If we let Him alone like this, everyone will believe in Him, and the Romans will come and take away both our place and nation." John 11:47-48

And truly Jesus did many other signs in the presence of His disciples, which are not written in this book; but these are written that you may believe that Jesus is the Christ, the Son of God, and that believing you may have life in His name. John 20:30-31

DR. ABRAHAM PETERS

It is to build the faith of future generations (Exodus 10:1-2; Psalm 71:17-18; Psalm 78:4).

Now the LORD said to Moses, "Go in to Pharaoh; for I have hardened his heart and the hearts of his servants, that I may show these signs of Mine before him, and that you may tell in the hearing of your son and your son's son the mighty things I have done in Egypt, and My signs which I have done among them, that you may know that I am the LORD." Exodus 10:1-2

We will not hide them from their children, telling to the generation to come the praises of the LORD, and His strength and His wonderful works that He has done. Psalm 78:4.

CHAPTER FOURTEEN

THE DISCERNING OF SPIRITS, TONGUES AND INTERPRETATION OF TONGUES

What the gift of "discerning of spirits" is and how it does operate

The discerning of spirits is one of God's answers to dealing with the world of evil spirits. It is one of the ways in which God guards and protects His people.

1. There is such a thing as the spirit world (Revelation 16:14).

2. The spirit world consists of good spirits and wicked spirits.

    a. Good spirits include God and the angelic orders.

    b. Wicked spirits include the devil and his demonic hoards.

Devils (Matthew 10:8; 12:27-28; Mark 6:13; 1 Corinthians 10:20-21; James 2:19).
Demons (Matthew 8:30; Mark 5:12; Luke 8:29; Revelation 16:14; 18:2).
Unclean spirits (Matthew 12:43; Luke 4:33; 9:42; Acts 8:7).
Seducing spirits (1 Timothy 4:1).
Principalities and Powers (Romans 8:38; Ephesians 6:12; Colossians 1:16).
Rulers of Darkness (Ephesians 6:12).

3. Jesus demonstrated power over the demonic world (Matthew 8:16; Luke 6:17-18).

When evening had come, they brought to Him many who were demon possessed. And He cast out the spirits with a word, and healed all who were sick...Matthew 8:16

And He came down with them and stood on a level place with a crowd of His disciples and a great multitude of people from all Judea and Jerusalem, and from the seacoast of Tyre and Sidon, who came to hear Him and be healed of their diseases, as well as those who were tormented with unclean spirits. And they were healed. Luke 6:17-18

    a. His ministry was given in part to set spiritual captives free (Luke 4:18; Acts 10:38).

The Spirit of the LORD is upon Me, because He has anointed Me to preach the gospel to the poor; He has sent Me to heal the brokenhearted, to proclaim liberty to the captives and recovery of sight to the blind, to set at liberty those who are oppressed... Luke 4:18

...how God anointed Jesus of Nazareth with the Holy Spirit and with power, who went about doing good and healing all who were oppressed by the devil, for God was with Him. Acts 10:38

    b. He destroyed the works of darkness wherever He went (Luke 13:32).

- He delivered two men who were demon-possessed (Matthew 8:28-34).

- He delivered the demon-possessed, blind and mute man (Matthew 12:22).

Then one was brought to Him who was demon-possessed, blind and mute; and He healed him, so that the blind and mute man both spoke and saw.

- He delivered the man in the synagogue who had an unclean spirit (Mark 1:21-28; Luke 4:31-37).

Then they went into Capernaum, and immediately on the Sabbath He entered the synagogue and taught. And they were astonished at His teaching, for He taught them as one having authority, and not as the scribes. Now there was a man in their synagogue with an unclean spirit. And he cried out, saying, "Let us alone! What have we to do with You, Jesus of Nazareth? Did You come to destroy us? I know who You are--the Holy One of God!" But Jesus rebuked him, saying, "Be quiet, and come out of him!" And when the unclean spirit had convulsed him and cried out with a loud voice, he came out of him. Then they were all amazed, so that they questioned among themselves, saying, "What is this? What new doctrine is this? For with authority He commands even the unclean spirits, and they obey Him." And immediately His fame spread throughout all the region around Galilee.

- He quieted the mouth of demons not allowing them to speak (Mark 1:32-34; Luke 4:40-41).

When the sun was setting, all those who had any that were sick with various diseases brought them to Him; and He laid His hands on every one of them and healed them. And demons also came out of many, crying out and saying, "You are the Christ, the Son of God!" And He, rebuking them, did not allow them to speak, for they knew that He was the Christ. Luke 4:40-41

- He cast out a demon from a mute man and he spoke immediately (Luke 11:14).

- He delivered the daughter of the woman of Canaan from demon possession without even being on site (Matthew 15:21-28; Mark 7:24-30).

4. The believer has been given authority by God over evil spirits.

   a. The disciples of Jesus were given this authority when Jesus sent them out two by two (Matthew 10:1-8; Mark 3:14-15; 6:7, 13; Luke 9:1).

And when He had called His twelve disciples to Him, He gave them power over unclean spirits, to cast them out, and to heal all kinds of sickness and all kinds of disease..."And as you go, preach, saying, 'The kingdom of heaven is at hand.' Heal the sick, cleanse the lepers, raise the dead, cast out demons. Freely you have received, freely give." Matthew 10:1, 7-8

And He called the twelve to Himself, and began to send them out two by two, and gave them power over unclean spirits...And they cast out many demons, and anointed with oil many who were sick, and healed them. Mark 6:7, 13

   b. The seventy were given this authority when Jesus sent them out (Luke 10:17-20).

Then the seventy returned with joy, saying, "Lord, even the demons are subject to us in Your name." And He said to them, "I saw

Satan fall like lightning from heaven. Behold, I give you the authority to trample on serpents and scorpions, and over all the power of the enemy, and nothing shall by any means hurt you. Nevertheless do not rejoice in this, that the spirits are subject to you, but rather rejoice because your names are written in heaven."

    c. The church and all future generations of believers are given this authority to equip them to confront the works of darkness (Mark 16:17-18).

And these signs will follow those who believe: In My name they will cast out demons; they will speak with new tongues; they will take up serpents; and if they drink anything deadly, it will by no means hurt them; they will lay hands on the sick, and they will recover.

5. The Early church demonstrated power over the demonic world.

    a. The shadow of Peter relieved people of demonic activity in their lives (Acts 5:16).

Also a multitude gathered from the surrounding cities to Jerusalem, bringing sick people and those who were tormented by unclean spirits, and they were all healed.

    b. Handkerchiefs were taken from Paul and laid on those with demons and they were delivered (Acts 19:11-12).

...so that even handkerchiefs or aprons were brought from his body to the sick, and the diseases left them and the evil spirits went out of them.

6. The preaching of the Gospel is a most powerful weapon against the demonic world (Acts 8:5-8).

Then Philip went down to the city of Samaria and preached Christ to them. And the multitudes with one accord heeded the things spoken by Philip, hearing and seeing the miracles which he did. For unclean spirits, crying with a loud voice, came out of many who were possessed; and many who were paralyzed and lame were healed. And there was great joy in that city.

B. The discerning of spirits is not what it is often purported to be.

1. It is not the ability to sense what is about to happen.

2. It is not impressions in our spirit regarding people and their motives.

3. It is not the gift of "discernment."

Discernment is keenness in judgment or insight. It is the ability to perceive what is actually taking place in a given situation and separate the good from the bad. Discernment is a wonderful quality and it usually grows as we grow in wisdom and understanding.

4. It is not dealing with the overt or obvious demonic situation (Mark 5:1-20).

There is no need for the discerning of spirits when a man comes out of a cave screaming, pulling his hair out, cutting himself with knives, dragging chains and foaming at the mouth. The discerning of spirits is needed when there is no visible evidence of demonic activity.

C. The discerning of spirits is the supernatural ability of God to identify the spirit behind an activity and the authority to deal with it.

1. Discerning of spirits is a supernatural ability from God.

This means that apart from a revelation from God, the source of the problem can not be known. It other words, the root of the problem will not be obvious to the natural man.

2. Discerning of spirits as it functions includes the ability to challenge the spirit behind the activity. There is no point in identifying the spirit and not being able to deal with the spirit.

D. Jesus functioned in the gift of discerning of spirits.

1. Jesus discerned that the young boy's epilepsy was connected with the demonic (Matthew 17:14-18; Mark 9:14-29). He identified the demonic influence as a deaf and mute spirit (not merely a mute spirit as his father had identified). He rebuked the demon and the boy was immediately delivered.

2. Jesus discerned that the woman's illness was associated with a "spirit of infirmity." He loosed her from the demonic hold and set her free (Luke 13:1013).

E. The Early Church functioned in the gift of discerning of spirits.

Paul discerned the spirit behind the words of the slave girl (Acts 16:16-18).

Now it happened, as we went to prayer, that a certain slave girl possessed with a spirit of divination met us, who brought her masters much profit by fortunetelling. This girl followed Paul and us, and cried out, saying, "These men are the servants of the Most High God, who proclaim to us the way of salvation." And this she did for many days. But Paul, greatly annoyed, turned and said to the spirit, "I command you in the name of Jesus Christ to come out of her." And he came out that very hour.

F. The church of this generation needs the gift of the discerning of spirits.

As we draw nearer to the return of Christ we can expect the devil do everything that he can to capture the "chosen generation." He will only become more active as his end draws near.

The people of this generation are in search of a spiritual encounter. Unfortunately, many of them are giving themselves over to the world of the demonic through the occult, Ouija boards, séances, tarot cards, fortune telling, mediums and the like.

What the gift of tongues is and how it does operate

G. The gift of tongues must be distinguished from the other aspects of "tongues" in the New Testament.

1. Tongues as the evidence (Acts 10:44-45).

All believers who are baptized in the Holy Spirit receive the evidence of speaking with other tongues. This experience is maintained in the believer's life as a prayer language for the purpose of communication with God.

2. Tongues as the gift (1 Corinthians 12:10).

The gift of tongues as a manifestation of the Spirit can operate through any believer at the discretion of the Holy Spirit as a temporary endowment to meet a specific need at a specific time.

3. Tongues as a ministry (1 Corinthians 12:28-30).

Evidently there will be those who have this divine ability as a ministry in the Body of Christ. This ministry aspect of tongues is reserved for a small group of people with that particular function.

H. The gift of tongues is the God-given ability to speak in a language that is not known by the person who is doing the speaking.

1. It may be a tongue or a language of men (1 Corinthians 13:1).

Though I speak with the tongues of men and of angels, but have not love, I have become sounding brass or a clanging cymbal.

That is, it is an actual human language that is spoken somewhere on the earth. It is simply unknown to the person who is doing the speaking.

a. When the apostles spoke in tongues on the day of Pentecost they apparently spoke in languages that were understood in various places of the world, but these languages were not known to the apostles themselves (Acts 2:4-13).

And they were all filled with the Holy Spirit and began to speak with other tongues, as the Spirit gave them utterance. 5 And there were dwelling in Jerusalem Jews, devout men, from every nation under heaven. 6 And when this sound occurred, the multitude came together, and were confused, because everyone heard them speak in his own language. 7 Then they were all amazed and marveled, saying to one another, "Look, are not all these who speak Galileans? 8 And how is it that we hear, each in our own language in which we were born? 9 Parthians and Medes and Elamites, those dwelling in Mesopotamia, Judea and Cappadocia, Pontus and Asia, 10 Phrygia and Pamphylia, Egypt and the parts of Libya adjoining Cyrene, visitors from Rome, both Jews and proselytes, 11 Cretans and
Arabs--we hear them speaking in our own tongues the wonderful works of
God." 12 So they were all amazed and perplexed, saying to one another, "Whatever could this mean?" 13 Others mocking said, "They are full of new wine."

When they heard this sound, they came running to see what it was all about, and they were bewildered to hear their own languages being spoken by the believers. They were beside themselves with wonder. "How can this be?" they exclaimed. "These people are all from Galilee, and yet we hear them speaking the languages of the lands where we were born!" Acts 2:6-8, NLT

b. People have been known to have spoken in actual languages that they themselves did not understand.

- There is the story of one man who was praying at an altar in tongues and a man who knew Hebrew heard him and understood him. It became a major sign in his life that led him to the Lord.

- There is another story of a man who was captured by a man-eating tribe. He did not know the language but was able to preach for an hour in a language which he did not know. Not only did it save his life, but much of the tribe turned to the Lord.

2. It may be a tongue or a language of angels (1 Corinthians 13:1).

That is, it is not a language that is actually known or spoken on the earth. It is a spiritual language that can only be understood with the accompanying gift of the interpretation of tongues.

C. The gift of tongues usually operates with the gift of interpretation.

1. This is true especially when it is operated in conjunction with a church gathering (1 Corinthians 14:13, 27).

2. This is not necessarily true when it is operated in a known language to the hearers (Acts 2:4-13). In this case, tongues can actually be a miraculous sign to the unbeliever (1 Corinthians 14:21-22).

It is written in the Scriptures, "I will speak to my own people through unknown languages and through the lips of foreigners. But even then, they will not listen to me," says the Lord. So you see that speaking in tongues is a sign, not for believers, but for unbelievers; prophecy, however, is for the benefit of believers, not unbelievers.

D. The gift of tongues is to be guarded when used in a corporate gathering of the saints.

1. Persons who deliver a tongue in the corporate gathering must pray to interpret the tongue as well (1 Corinthians 14:13).

Therefore let him who speaks in a tongue pray that he may interpret.

A message in tongues can be interpreted by three possible people—

a. The person giving the message in tongues operating through the gift of the interpretation of tongues (1 Corinthians 14:5, 13).

b. Any believer operating in the gift of the interpretation of tongues (1 Corinthians 12:10).

c. A person who has the ministry of an interpreter of tongues (1 Corinthians 14:28).

2. The gift of tongues without interpretation will not edify the church (1 Corinthians 14:2, 6-13).

Dear brothers and sisters, if I should come to you talking in an unknown language, how would that help you? But if I bring you some revelation or some special knowledge or some prophecy or some teaching--that is what will help you. 7 Even musical instruments like the flute or the harp, though they are lifeless, are examples of the need for speaking in plain language. For no one will recognize the melody unless the notes are played clearly. 8 And if the bugler doesn't sound a clear call, how will the soldiers know they are being called to battle? 9 And it's the same for you. If you talk to people in a language they don't understand, how will they know what you mean? You might as well be talking to an empty room. 10 There are so many different languages in the world, and all are excellent for those who understand them, 11 but to me they mean nothing. I will not understand people who speak those languages, and they will not understand me. 12 Since you are so eager to have spiritual gifts, ask God for those that will be of real help to the whole church. 13 So anyone who has the gift of speaking in tongues should pray also for the gift of interpretation in order to tell people plainly what has been said. 1 Corinthians 14:6-13, NLT

3. The gift of tongues without interpretation will be a bad witness to the unbeliever (1 Corinthians 14:23).

Therefore if the whole church comes together in one place, and all speak with tongues, and there come in those who are uninformed or unbelievers, will they not say that you are out of your mind?

E. The gift of tongues when coupled with the interpretation of tongues has the same benefit as prophecy (1 Corinthians 14:5).

I wish you all spoke with tongues, but even more that you prophesied; for he who prophesies is greater than he who speaks with tongues, unless indeed he interprets, that the church may receive edification.

What the gift of the interpretation of tongues is and how it does operate

The gift of the interpretation of tongues is the God-given ability to understand and interpret a message from a language that is not known by the person who is doing the interpretation.

1. It is a supernatural ability.

2. It is not the same as the learned, human ability to translate a message from one language to another. Daniel seemed to have functioned in this gift when he interpreted the writing on the wall (Daniel 5:13-29).

The gift of the interpretation of tongues is to be distinguished from the ministry of interpretation of tongues (1 Corinthians 14:27-28).

If anyone speaks in a tongue, let there be two or at the most three, each in turn, and let one interpret. But if there is no interpreter, let him keep silent in church, and let him speak to himself and to God.

3. The gift of the interpretation of tongues is a gift that can operate through any believer at the discretion of the Holy Spirit.

4. Evidently there are those who have this ministry as part of their function in the Body of Christ.

Cultivating a Relationship with the Holy Spirit

How what we have learned prepared has us for a deeper relationship with the Spirit

We have learned that the Holy Spirit is God. Because He is God all of the attributes of deity are His. When He is living in us, we realize the awesomeness of that which we have at our disposal. We have learned that the Holy Spirit is a person. Because He is a person, He can be related to as a person. This has both positive and negative aspects to it. We can have intimate fellowship with the Holy Spirit, but we can also offend the Holy Spirit who dwells within us.

We have learned that the Holy Spirit is the principal worker in the Church Age. Because He is the principal worker in this age, it is critical that we do not reject what the Holy Spirit is trying to do in our lives. We need to have a spirit of cooperation as the Spirit does His work in us.

We have learned that the Holy Spirit can be offended. The Holy Spirit is dove-like and can be offended by us especially when we participate in things that are against His holy nature or when we resist what He is trying to accomplish in our lives.

We have learned that the Holy Spirit is dwelling within us. The Holy Spirit is within us. We do not have to go and search for Him. The Power of the Highest is within us. He is the "Greater" who is in us compared to the one who is in the world.

We have learned that the Holy Spirit is our Comforter, Advocate and Helper. We are not alone as we seek to fulfill God's plans and purpose for our lives. We have someone to comfort us when we need it. We have someone to stick up for us when we are not able to speak for ourselves. We have a helper to come along the side of us whenever we need Him.

We have learned that the Holy Spirit would like to produce His fruit in us. As we yield to the power of the Holy Spirit within, we are transformed from glory to glory and we begin to take on the divine attributes of Jesus. The Holy Spirit is the one who is causing Christ to be formed in us.

We have learned that the Holy Spirit is the power source for all that we do. The Holy Spirit is the Spirit of power and might. Even though no human being has the power to do what God has designed for him to do, the Holy Spirit provides the power to do what man cannot do.

We have learned that the Holy Spirit has given us supernatural gifts that can assist us in fulfilling our supernatural mission. We have learned that the Holy Spirit was given to us so that we could fulfill or finish the work that was begun by Jesus.

What we must do to take full benefit of what is available to us through the Holy Spirit

We must live our lives yielded to the inner voice of the Holy Spirit.

1. As He convicts us of sin (John 16:8-11).
2. As He leads us into truth (John 16:13).
3. As He purifies or sanctifies our soul (2 Thessalonians 2:13).
4. As He guides us in our daily lives (Galatians 5:25).
5. As He prompts us to operate in the gifts of the Spirit (1 Corinthians 12:7-11).

We must ask for the assistance of this Holy Spirit. We need his assistance when we:

6. Read the Bible (1 Corinthians 2:11-14).
7. Worship God (John 4:24; Philippians 3:3).
8. Pray for difficult situations (Romans 8:26-27).
9. Share our faith (Acts 1:8).
10. Pray for and minister to the needy (Luke 4:18; Acts 10:38).

We must pursue a personal relationship with the Holy Spirit (2 Corinthians 13:14).
Relationships take work. Our relationship with the Holy Spirit is no different.

11. We must avoid those things which cause the Spirit grief (Ephesians 4:30).
12. We must consciously welcome the Holy Spirit into our daily life.
13. We must continually be filled with the Holy Spirit (Ephesians

Fellowship With The Holy Spirit

PART TWO

KNOWING

AND

HEARING

THE

VOICE OF

GOD

DR. ABRAHAM PETERS

CHAPTER FIFTEEN

KNOWING THE WILL OF GOD

"What is God's will for me?" This question is perhaps the one most often asked by believers. It is also a question that frequently confronts Christian leaders as men and women turn to them for guidance in decision making. In everyday situations of life, believers are constantly making choices which determine whether or not they will do the perfect will of God. It is essential to know God's voice, understand His will, and make right decisions each day. It is important because each minor decision affects the finding of God's will for a lifetime.

Man must make choices in relationship to God's will. This plan was instituted by God when Adam and Eve were placed in the Garden of Eden (Genesis 1-3). God's will for Adam and Eve was to name the animals, tend the Garden, have companionship with each other, and reproduce to populate the earth. Most important, they were to maintain intimate fellowship with God. Adam and Eve were also warned about what was <u>not</u> God's will. They were forbidden to eat of the tree of the knowledge of good and evil.

Including the story of Adam and Eve, the entire Bible is a history of decisions which individuals and nations made in relation to God's will. You can learn from both the successes and failures of these men and women. One of the most exciting revelations in the Bible is that God has a definite plan for every individual for this life and eternity. In order to fulfill these plans you must come to know God's voice. You must learn how He has communicated in times past and how He speaks today.

This section explains how God speaks to man and how to find God's will for your life. Guidelines are given on knowing the voice of God and determining His will. The pattern of God's will and Scriptural examples of how God reveals His will are discussed.

A Scriptural model for decision making is explained. Guidelines are presented on overcoming wrong decisions, what to do if you have missed the will of God, and handling questionable practices. Six stages of revelation of a plan of God are also identified.

This book focuses on what Jesus taught to equip men and women to reach their world with the Gospel. One of the great truths He revealed was that God does speak to men:

I am the good shepherd and know my sheep, and am known of mine. . .

And other sheep I have which are not of this fold: them also I must bring, and they shall hear my voice, and there shall be one fold and one shepherd.

My sheep hear my voice, and I know them, and they follow me. (John 10:14,16,27)

God has a plan for intimate relationship with mankind. Man is known by God and can know Him personally. You *can* know the voice of God!

KNOWING THE VOICE OF GOD

My sheep hear my voice, and I know them, and they follow me. (John 10:27)

First: That there is a God.
Second: That He communicates with man.
Third: That man can recognize His voice when He speaks.
Fourth: That God has something to say.

Let us examine each of these statements:

First: This course is based upon the truth that there is a God who is revealed to man through the written record of His Word, the Holy Bible.

Second: The Bible is the inspired written record of God's communication to man. It details the ways which God spoke to man and the response of individuals and nations to the voice of God. The Bible often repeats the phrase ". . . and the Lord said" and incidents where He spoke to man. This confirms that God communicates with men and women.

For an example, read the story of Balaam in Numbers chapter 22. God spoke to Balaam, but he refused to listen. God wanted to communicate to this man so much that He actually resorted to using a donkey. Balaam was:

. . . rebuked for his iniquity; the dumb ass speaking with man's voice forbad the madness of the prophet. (II Peter 2:16)

Third: The Bible verifies that believers can know the voice of God. Jesus said:

I am the good shepherd and know my sheep, and am known of mine. . .

And other sheep I have, which are not of this fold: them also I must bring, and they shall hear my voice, and there shall be one fold, and one shepherd.

My sheep hear my voice, and I know them, and they follow me. . . (John 10:14,16,27)

Fourth: God has something important to say to mankind. We are warned:

Wherefore (as the Holy Ghost saith), Today if ye will hear His voice, Harden not your hearts, as in the provocation, in the day of temptation in the wilderness. . .

While it is said, Today if ye will hear His voice, harden not your hearts, as in the provocation. . . (Hebrews 3:7,15)

The "temptation in the wilderness" and the "provocation" (provoking) of God mentioned in these verses refer to the disobedience of the nation of Israel.

After Israel was delivered from Egyptian captivity, they repeatedly disobeyed when God spoke to them. In these verses God warns us to respond when He speaks and not disobey as Israel did.

The phrase "today, if ye will hear His voice," confirms that God still speaks to men in present times just as He did in times past. The warning to listen confirms that what He has to say is important.

MANY VOICES

The Bible reveals that there are many voices in the world clamoring for attention:

There are, it may be, so many kinds of voices in the world, and none of them is without signification. (I Corinthians 14:10)

What are these voices in the world?

THE VOICE OF MAN:

The voice of man is easy to recognize. It is the audible voice of another human being:
Then Peter and the other apostles answered and said, We ought to obey God rather than men. (Acts 5:29)

Sometimes the voice of man may give wise advice, but anytime the voice of man conflicts with the voice of God, you must obey God.

THE VOICE OF SATAN:

The voice of Satan was first heard by man when he spoke to Eve in the Garden of Eden (Genesis 3:1,4,5). Satan's voice lies, deceives, and always attempts to lead man into sin away from God. You can easily recognize this when you read about the temptation of Jesus by Satan in Matthew 4:1-13. You can study examples of conversations Satan has with God in Job 1:7-12 and 2:1-6.

Evil spirits (demons of Satan) also have voices:

For unclean spirits, crying with loud voice, came out of many that were possessed with them. . . (Acts 8:7)

And in the synagogue there was a man, which had a spirit of an unclean devil, and cried out with a loud voice,

Saying, Let us alone; what have we to do with thee, thou Jesus of Nazareth? art thou come to destroy us? I know thee who thou art; the Holy One of God. (Luke 4:33-34)

Sometimes the voice of Satan is actually audible when demons use the vocal cords of a possessed man or woman. Most often, however, Satan speaks in an inaudible voice. He speaks lies, deceit, and sinful thoughts into your mind.

THE VOICE OF SELF:
The voice of self is man talking to himself. You can read examples of this in Luke 16:3 and 18:4 and in Jonah 4:8 where the prophet wished in himself to die. The Bible warns concerning the voice of self:

O Lord, I know that the way of man is not in himself; it is not in man that walketh to direct his steps. (Jeremiah 10:23)

THE VOICE OF GOD:

Jesus said believers could know God's voice and distinguish it from other voices:

To Him the porter openeth; and the sheep hear His voice; and He calleth His own sheep by name, and leadeth them out.

And when He putteth forth His own sheep, He goeth before them, and the sheep follow Him; for they know His voice.

And a stranger will they not follow, but will flee from Him; for they know not the voice of strangers. (John 10:3-5)

Believers are compared to sheep. It is the characteristic of sheep not to know where they are going. They must be led. Jesus said He was the shepherd or leader of the sheep. He said His sheep would know His voice and follow Him instead of the voices of man, self, or Satan.

HEARING THE VOICE OF GOD

Open your Bible to the book of Genesis and read from chapters 1 - 3. These chapters record the creation of the world and of the first human beings, Adam and Eve. From the time of creation, God communicated His will to mankind. He gave specific instructions to Adam and Eve. They were to name the animals, tend the Garden, have companionship with each other, and reproduce to populate the earth. Most important of all, they were to maintain intimate fellowship with God. This intimate fellowship with God enabled them to know God's voice. When God spoke, He communicated His plan to them:

And the Lord God commanded the man, saying, Of every tree of the garden thou mayest freely eat;

But of the tree of the knowledge of good and evil, thou shalt not eat of it; for in the day that thou eatest thereof thou shalt surely die. (Genesis 2:16-17)

By the voice of God the will of God was revealed to Adam and Eve. They could freely eat of every tree in the garden, with the exception of the tree of the knowledge of good and evil.

Adam and Eve did not follow God's plan. They listened to the voice of Satan and ate of the forbidden tree. When they realized what they had done, they hid themselves from God:

And they heard the voice of the Lord God walking in the garden in the cool of the day; and Adam and his wife hid themselves from the presence of the Lord God amongst the trees of the garden.

And the Lord God called unto Adam, and said unto him, Where art thou? (Genesis 3:8-9)

It is sin which separates man from God. God did not remove His presence from man. Because of sin, man hid himself from the presence of God. Sin results in a hardened heart. The Bible warns:

While it is said, Today if ye will hear His voice, harden not your hearts... (Hebrews 3:15)

God wants to communicate to man, but communication requires relationship. Sin separates man from intimate relationship to God, hardens his heart, and hinders him from knowing the voice of God.

THE VOICE AND THE WILL

Believers often ask, "What is God will for me?" What do we actually mean when we say we want to know the will of God? It means we want to know His general plan for our lives. We want His guidance in specific decisions so we can make wise choices. We desire His direction in the circumstances of life. The question we should be asking is, "How can I know the voice of God?" Knowing God's voice results in finding the will of God.

God wants you to know His will:

Wherefore be ye not unwise, but understanding what the will of the Lord is. (Ephesians 5:17)

If you know His voice then you will understand His will as He speaks it to you. Learning to receive divine guidance is learning to walk in intimate fellowship with God. The Bible says:

Man shall not live by bread alone, but by every word that proceedeth out of the mouth of God. (Matthew 4:4)

The word "proceedeth" speaks of a continuing function. It means something that happened in the past, is happening in the present, and will continue in the future. God speaks to communicate His will to mankind. This is why it is important to know the voice of God.

WHEN GOD SPEAKS

There are two Greek words translated as "word" in the Bible. The Greek words are "logos" and "rhema." "Logos" refers to the written Word of God. "Rhema" refers to the living or life-giving Word of God. It was said of believers in the city of Berea:

These were more noble than those in Thessalonica, in that they received the word (rhema) with all readiness of mind, and searched the Scriptures (logos) daily, whether those things were so. (Acts 17:11)

This verse illustrates the relationship of the "logos" and "rhema" word. The "logos" or written Word always agrees with the "rhema" or spoken, life-giving Word. This is how you can know the voice you hear is from the Lord. A "rhema" Word from God usually applies to a specific situation, meets a personal need, and provides individual guidance. Because you recognize the Word as applying to a specific need or situation in your life, it becomes a life-giving Word to you.

A "rhema" Word may be communicated through a sermon or a verse from the Bible which suddenly strikes you with great meaning. It may be spoken to you by God through the use of spiritual gifts. It may also be spoken in your inner spirit by the Lord. (You will learn more about how God speaks through spiritual gifts and in your spirit in later chapters.)

But remember: The "rhema" Word will always agree with the written Word of God. The written Word of God is complete. Nothing is to be added to it or taken from it (Revelation 22:18-19). When God speaks through the "rhema" Word it will always be in harmony with His written Word.

TYPES OF LISTENERS

The Bible speaks of two main divisions of listeners:

Therefore whosoever heareth these sayings of mine and doeth them,

I will liken him unto a wise man, which built his house upon a rock. . .

And every one that heareth these sayings of mine, and doeth them not shall be likened unto a foolish man, which built his house upon the sand. . .
    (Matthew 7:24,26)

A foolish listener hears the voice of God, but does not act upon it. A wise listener hears and acts upon the message of God. One listener is a "hearer of the Word" only. The other is both a "hearer and a doer."

You must not only come to know the voice of God, you must learn to respond in obedience to that voice:

But be ye doers of the Word, and not hearers only, deceiving your own selves.

For if any be a hearer of the Word, and not a doer, he is like unto a man beholding his natural face in a glass:

For he beholdeth himself, and goeth his way, and straightway forgetteth what manner of man he was.

But whoso looketh into the perfect law of liberty, and continueth therein, he being not a forgetful hearer, but a doer of the work, this man shall be blessed in his deed. (James 1:22-25)

Jesus also told a story about seed sown in several types of soil which illustrates various types of listeners. Read the story in Matthew

13:1-9. Jesus explains the story in Matthew 13:18-23. He compares the different soils to listeners and their response to the Word of God.

SEED BY THE WAYSIDE:

Some seed fell by the wayside and was snatched up by birds before it could take root. This is an example of a man who hears the voice of God but the words do not take root in his heart. Satan snatches away God's Word.

SEED IN STONY PLACES:

Some seed fell in stony places and sprang up quickly. But when the heat of the sun came, the plant withered and died because it had no roots. This is the listener who hears God's Word and receives it with joy, but it does not really take root in his life. When circumstances get tough, he is offended and ceases to respond to God's voice.

SEED AMONG THE THORNS:

Some seed fell among thorns which choked outgrowth of the plants. This is an example of the voice of God being choked out by the cares of the world, materialism, etc.

SEED ON GOOD GROUND:

Some seed fell on good ground and brought forth a rich harvest. This is an example of the listener who receives God's Word, listens to His voice, and roots himself in that revelation. This person will mature spiritually and become a reproducing, fruitful believer.

HOW CAN YOU KNOW GOD'S VOICE?

Do you want to be able to know God's voice? Do you want to know His will for your life? In the next chapter you will learn of requirements which prepare you to hear the voice of God and discover His will for your life.

DR. ABRAHAM PETERS

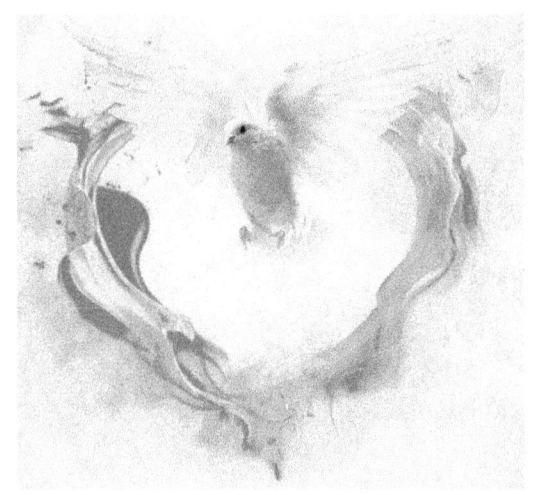

CHAPTER SIXTEEN

"IF ANY MAN WILL DO. . .
HE SHALL KNOW"

I beseech you therefore brethren, by the mercies of God, that you present your bodies a living sacrifice, holy, acceptable unto God, which is your reasonable service.

And be not conformed to this world; but be ye transformed by the renewing of your mind, that ye may prove what is that good, and acceptable, and perfect will of God. (Romans 12:1-2)

There are some necessary prerequisites if you are to come to know the voice of God. A prerequisite is something you must do before you can do something else. It is something required before you are able to reach a certain goal. Your goal in this section is to come to know the voice of God. This chapter explains the prerequisites, those things required before you can achieve this objective. Jesus said:

If any man will do His will, He shall know of the doctrine, whether it be of God, or whether I speak of myself. (John 7:17)

The Key Verses of this chapter, Romans 12:1-2, list some things that are God's will for you to do. If you meet these prerequisites, then you will come to know God's voice and His will for your life.

BORN-AGAIN EXPERIENCE

I beseech you therefore brethren, by the mercies of God, that ye present your bodies a living sacrifice, holy, acceptable unto God, which is your reasonable service. (Romans 12:1)

As you learned in the previous chapter, sin separates you from God's presence. Because of sin, you have difficulty hearing and responding positively to the voice of God. In the natural world you do not recognize the voice of a stranger. You recognize voices of those you know and with whom you have developed a relationship. The same is true in the spiritual world. If you are to come to know God's voice, you must first come to know God and you cannot develop an intimate relationship with Him with sin in your life.

Romans 12:1 requires that YOU make the move towards God by giving your life to Him. God has already spoken through His written Word and revealed it is His will for you to develop such a relationship:

The Lord is not slack concerning His promise, as some men count slackness; but is longsuffering to usward, not willing that any should perish, but that all should come to repentance. (2 Peter 3:9)

God does not want you to spend your life in sin. He wants you to live it according to His plan:

That he no longer should live the rest of his time in the flesh to the lusts of men, but to the will of God. (1 Peter 4:2)

God is pictured standing at the door of your life desiring entrance so He can develop a relationship with you:

Behold, I stand at the door, and knock: if any man hear my voice, and open the door, I will come in to him, and will sup with him, and he with me. (Revelation 3:20)

God's stated purpose from the beginning of the world was to bring all men into the knowledge of Christ Jesus:

Having made known unto us the mystery of His will, according to His good pleasure which He hath purposed in Himself:

That in the dispensation of the fullness of times He might gather together in one all things in Christ, both which are in heaven, and which are on earth; even in Him. (Ephesians 1:9-10)

You are "gathered into Christ" by becoming part of the family of God. Just as you are born into a natural family, you must be "born again" spiritually into this spiritual family.

Read John chapter 3. This chapter explains in detail what it means to be born-again. To experience the new birth you must:

1. Acknowledge you are a sinner:

For all have sinned and come short of the glory of God. (Romans 3:23)

2. Recognize the penalty of sin is death:

God warned Adam and Eve that if they sinned, they would die. This meant both spiritual death (separation from God's presence) and physical death. When Jesus died on the cross He died in your place. He died for your sins so you could have everlasting life:

For the wages of sin is death, but the gift of God eternal life through Jesus Christ our Lord. (Romans 6:23)

If you accept His sacrifice for sin, you are no longer under the penalty of death.

3. Confess your sins, ask forgiveness, and believe that Jesus died for you:

If we say that we have no sin, we deceive ourselves and the truth is not in us.

If we confess our sins, He is faithful and just to forgive us our sins, and to cleanse us from all unrighteousness. (1 John 1:8-9)

For God so loved the world that He gave His only begotten Son that whosoever believeth in Him should not perish but have everlasting life. (John 3:16)

When you present your life to God in this manner, you are "born-again" spiritually:

Therefore, if any man be in Christ He a new creature; old things have passed away; Behold, all things are become new. (2 Corinthians 5:17)

When you are born again you become part of God's spiritual family. You are no longer separated from the presence of God. When you die physically, you will live eternally with Him. You have established a relationship with God through Jesus Christ. You have heard and responded to the truth of the Gospel. You are now in a position to learn how to recognize God's voice:

... Every one that is of the truth heareth my voice. (John 18:37)

INDWELLING OF THE HOLY SPIRIT

There is another prerequisite that will help you come to know God's voice. The Bible speaks of an experience called the Baptism of the Holy Spirit. This experience results in the Holy Spirit dwelling in your life and empowering you to live a holy life which is acceptable to God.

The ministries of the Holy Spirit in the life of the believer I have discussed in great details extensively in the first part of this book. One of the most important ministries of the indwelling Holy Spirit is to guide the believer into God's will:

When He, the Spirit of truth is come (the Holy Spirit), He will guide you into all truth. . . and He will show you things to come and He shall receive of mine (God's will) and show it to you. (John 16:13-14)

The Bible says:

For as many as are led by the Spirit of God, they are the sons of God. (Romans 8:14)

There is a definite relationship between being a child of God (born again) and being led by the Holy Spirit. The natural man (who is not born-again) does not receive and follow guidance of the Holy Spirit. Because he has not become a "spiritual man" through the new birth experience, He does not recognize the voice of God:

But the natural man receiveth not the things of the Spirit of God; for they are foolishness unto him; neither can he know them, because they are spiritually discerned. (1 Corinthians 2:14)

The following examples from the book of Acts demonstrate the leading of the Holy Spirit in the lives of believers:

PHILIP:

A church deacon by the name of Philip was led by the Spirit to join a chariot he saw on a desert road to Gaza:

Then the Spirit said unto Philip, Go near and join thyself to this chariot.
    (Acts 8:29)

Philip obeyed the leading of the Holy Spirit. This resulted in the salvation and water baptism of an Ethiopian man who was riding in the chariot.

PETER:

Peter was told by the Holy Spirit to go with three men who came from Caesarea. Peter said:

And the Spirit bade me go with them, nothing doubting. (Acts 11:12)

Peter recognized the leading of the Holy Spirit. He had no doubts when the Spirit spoke in his inner being and revealed God's will to him. He obeyed and it resulted in the first cross-cultural ministry to the Gentiles.

PAUL:

Paul often changed his evangelistic schedule at the prompting of the Holy Spirit:

After they were come to Mysia, they assayed to go into Bithynia; but the Spirit suffered them not. (Acts 16:7)

Paul planned to go to Mysia, but the Holy Spirit gave him different directions.

These three examples are just a few of many in the Bible which illustrate how the Holy Spirit enables you to hear God's voice. As Jesus promised, the Holy Spirit takes the will of God and reveals it to you.

SPIRITUAL MATURITY

And be not conformed to this world. . . (Romans 12:2)

In the natural world when a baby is born he must attain a certain level of maturity before he begins to recognize the voice of his parents. The same is true in the spiritual world. When you are first born again you may not be able to recognize the voice of God when He speaks to you. When you first receive the Holy Spirit you may not always understand when the Spirit reveals God's will to you. But the Holy Spirit will continue to reveal God's will and guide you. As you mature spiritually, you will come to recognize this voice within your spirit.

The Bible speaks of this parallel between the natural and spiritual:

For every one that useth milk is unskillful in the word of righteousness: For he is a babe. But strong meat belongeth to them that are of full age, even those who by reason of use have their senses exercised to discern both good and evil. (Hebrews 5:13-14)

The "milk" and "meat" mentioned in these verses refer to the written Word of God, the Holy Bible. When you are first born again you start learning some of the simple truths (milk) of the written Word of God. As you mature, you are able to master the deeper truths (meat) of the Word of God. As you continue to study God's written Word, your spiritual senses will mature. You will be able to exercise them to discern good and evil. This means you will be able to distinguish God's will and His way from the wrong ways of life. This is why it is important for you to study God's written Word. As you mature spiritually, you will no longer "conform" to the world. To be conformed means to be fashioned or shaped according to a set standard. Spiritual maturity will conform you to the image of Christ rather than the image of worldly standards.

Spiritual maturity also helps you achieve emotional maturity. If you lack emotional maturity, important decisions may be made in a fit of anger or self-pity. This can have disastrous long-range results. As you mature spiritually you will develop the "Fruit of the Holy Spirit," evidences of spiritual maturity that result in emotional maturity:

But the fruit of the Spirit is love, joy, peace, longsuffering, gentleness, goodness, faith, Meekness, temperance: against such there is no law. (Galatians 5:22-23)

TRANSFORMATION

. . . But be ye transformed by the renewing of your mind. . . (Romans 12:2)

Spiritual maturity leads finally to transformation, another prerequisite that enables you to know the voice of God. What natural man (human nature) desires to do and what God desires for your life is different. This creates a conflict between the flesh (natural man) and the spirit (spiritual man).

Paul wrote of this conflict:

For the flesh lusteth against the Spirit, and the Spirit against the flesh; and these are contrary the one to the other; so that ye cannot do the things ye would. (Galatians 5:17)

Paul recognized there is a continuing struggle of the flesh against the Spirit in matters relating to the fulfilling of God's will. He identified this struggle as taking place in the mind:

But I see another law in my members, warring against the law of my mind, and bringing me into captivity to the law of sin which is in my members. (Romans 7:23)

Because of this he urged:

I beseech you therefore, brethren, by the mercies of God, that ye present your bodies a living sacrifice, holy, acceptable unto God, which is your reasonable service.

DR. ABRAHAM PETERS

And be not conformed to this world; but be ye transformed by the renewing of your mind, that ye may prove what is that good, and acceptable, and perfect will of God. (Romans 12:1-2)

The word "beseech" means to plead, implore, or beg. The phrase "present your bodies a living sacrifice" indicates an unreserved surrender to God.

To offer something for a sacrifice means to give it up completely. In the Old Testament when a sacrifice was made, it was given completely to God to be burned with fire, consumed by the priest, or both, as the law indicated. The giver of the sacrifice had no further claim to it.

So must be our surrender to God. The natural man, the old self nature must die to the world and the flesh. This is what is meant by "transformation." It is being changed into another image patterned after the Lord Jesus Christ:

I am crucified with Christ. (Galatians 2:20)

They that are Christ's have crucified the flesh. (Galatians 5:24)

But I keep under my body, and bring it into subjection; lest that by any means, when I have preached to others, I myself should be a castaway.
    (1 Corinthians 9:27)

Let not sin therefore reign in your mortal body, that ye should obey it in the lusts thereof. (Romans 6:12)

Having therefore these promises, dearly beloved, let us cleanse ourselves from all filthiness of the flesh and spirit, perfecting holiness in the fear of God. (2 Corinthians 7:1)

Likewise reckon ye also yourselves to be dead indeed unto sin. (Romans 6:11)

Actual physical crucifixion, as Jesus experienced, is an unnatural death. There is significance in the fact that the death prescribed for the self-nature is crucifixion. The fleshly nature of man will never die a natural death. It will not die voluntarily. It must be put to death by force just as in actual crucifixion in the natural world.

According to Romans 12:1-2, such surrender precedes the knowledge of God's will. If you want to know God's voice and His will, you must first surrender. We often want to reverse the process. We want to know His will, then decide if we will surrender to it. But Romans 12:1-2 indicates surrender comes first.

The reason we are hesitant about surrender is because we do not understand God's will is always acceptable, good, and perfect. We are afraid to surrender to God totally because we have not grasped this basic concept:

For I know the plans I have for you, says the Lord. They are plans for good and not for evil, to give you a future and a hope. (Jeremiah 29:11 TLB)

RENEWING YOUR MIND

Your mind is naturally conformed to the principles of the world around you. It happens because of your basic sin nature. It also happens through the influence of your culture.

But God says you are not to conform to the world but to be transformed. The word "transform" means to be changed or into a new image. The pattern for that image is the Lord Jesus Christ:

But we all, with open face, beholding as in a glass the glory of the Lord, are changed into the same image from glory to glory, even as by the Spirit of the Lord. (2 Corinthians 3:18)

According to Romans 12:2, transformation comes through renewing your mind. This means you must get rid of worldly standards and principles and conform to the principles revealed in

God's written Word.

Your mind is transformed as you develop the mind of Christ:

Let this mind be in you which was also in Christ Jesus. (Philippians 2:5)

The word "let" indicates that you have to make a choice in order to have the mind of Christ. You must permit the transformation of the mind to happen. You have a responsibility in development of the transformed mind. It is not something done automatically for you by God:

Wherefore (YOU) gird up the loins of your mind. (1 Peter 1:13)

To "gird up" the mind means to clothe or protect your mental powers. To transform or gird up the mind, it is necessary to immerse it in the Word of God. Search the Bible to discover what type of mind was in Christ and discover the necessity of transformation of the mind.

The Scriptures indicate believers are NOT to have minds that are:

Hardened:	Daniel 5:20
Reprobate:	Romans 1:28
Carnal:	Romans 8:6
Doubtful:	Luke 12:29
Blinded:	2 Corinthians 3:14; 4:14
Corrupted:	2 Corinthians 11:3
Fleshly:	Ephesians 2:3; Colossians 2:18
Vain:	Ephesians 4:17
Earthly:	Philippians 3:19
Alienated by wicked works:	Colossians 1:21
Double minded:	James 1:8; 4:8
Defiled:	Titus 1:15

The Bible indicates the transformed mind of believers should be:

Spiritual:	Romans 8:6
Ready:	1 Peter 5:2
Pure:	2 Peter 3:1
Stayed:	Isaiah 26:3
Peaceful:	Philippians 4:7
Renewed:	Ephesians 4:23
Humble:	Colossians 3:12
Sober:	Titus 2:6
Sound:	2 Timothy 1:7

DR. ABRAHAM PETERS

      Loving: Matthew 22:37
      Serving: Romans 7:25
      Fully persuaded: Romans 14:5
      United: 1 Peter 3:8; 4:1; Romans 15:6; 1 Corinthians 1:10
      Honest and willing: 1 Chronicles 28:9
      Disciplined to work: Nehemiah 4:6

Your mind is transformed as God puts His laws into it:

. . . I will put my laws into their mind. (Hebrews 8:10)

Use the power of the mind to cast down and bring into captivity wrong thoughts:

Casting down imaginations, and every high thing that exalteth itself against the knowledge of God, and bringing into captivity every thought to the obedience of Christ. (2 Corinthians 10:5)

You have the responsibility to control your thought life:

Finally, brethren, whatsoever things are true, whatsoever things are honest, whatsoever things are just, whatsoever things are pure, whatsoever things are lovely, whatsoever things are of good report; if there be any virtue, and if there by any praise, think on these things. (Philippians 4:8)

Then you can say with Paul:

But we have the mind of Christ. (1 Corinthians 2:6)

The mind of Christ was set and determined to do the will of God.

PROVING GOD'S WILL

Study the following chart. You will discover that each prerequisite discussed in this chapter is included in Romans 12:1-2:

I beseech you therefore brethren   You come to God through
by the mercies of God...   His mercy extended through the sacrifice of Jesus for your sins.

that you present your bodies a living	Spiritual
maturity is enabled by	
sacrifice, holy, acceptable unto God,	the working of
the Holy Spirit	
which is your reasonable service...	in your life.
And be not conformed to this world but	You are
transformed by the Word,	
be ye transformed by the renewing	your mind is
renewed.	
of your mind.	

The new birth experience, the indwelling of the Holy Spirit, spiritual maturity, and transformation of the mind--how do these relate to knowing God's will? According to Romans 12:1-2 they are prerequisites leading to knowledge of His will:

... that ye may prove what is that good, and acceptable, and perfect will of God. (Romans 12:2)

The word "prove" means to determine, confirm, and be sure of something. These prerequisites lead to assurance of the will of God.

But what exactly is meant by the "will of God"? And what are the "good, perfect, and acceptable" wills of God? Why is it important to "prove" or determine God's will?

We will explore answers to these questions in the following chapters.

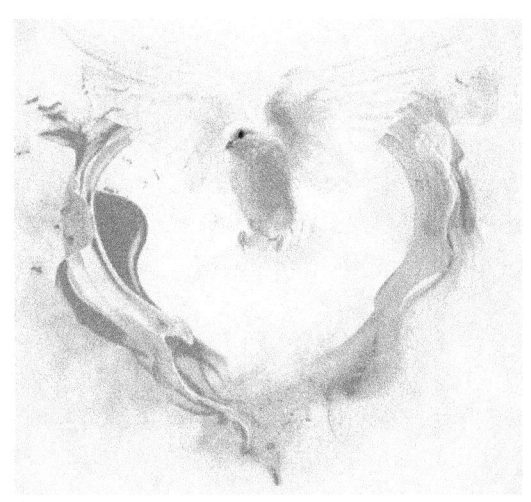

CHAPTER SEVENTEEN

THE WILL OF GOD

The Bible says, 'For I came down from Heaven not to do mine own will, but the will of Him that sent me. (John 6:38)

This chapter identifies three types of will in operation in the world today. It defines the expression "God's will", examines the life of Jesus in relation to that will, and stresses the importance of the will of God.

THE MEANING OF "WILL"

The common meaning of the word "will" is to determine or decide on the basis of the will. The will is the power of choice. There are three types of will operating in the world today:

SELF-WILL:

This is the will of man, the basic selfish nature which desires to walk its own way. When you guide your life by self-will, you make choices on the basis of your will apart from God. The Bible warns about self-will:

O Lord, I know that the way of man is not in himself; it is not in man that walketh to direct his steps. (Jeremiah 10:23)

Self-will is the operation of the fleshly nature of man:

But chiefly them that walk after the flesh in the lust of uncleanness, and despise government. Presumptuous are they, self-willed; they are not afraid to speak evil of dignities. (2 Peter 2:10)

The Bible records the results of self-will:

So I gave them up unto their own hearts' lust: and they walked in their own counsels. (Psalms 81:12)

Sin, suffering, and trouble in the world today are all results of man living in disobedience to the will of God. David speaks of self-will operating in the lives of wicked men:

Deliver me not over unto the will of mine enemies: for false witnesses are risen up against me, and such as breathe out cruelty. (Psalms 27:12)

The Bible states that leaders in the church should not be self-willed:

For the bishop must be blameless as the steward of God: not self willed... (Titus 1:7)

SATAN'S WILL:

Satan has a will. He desires to destroy all that is good in your life. Jesus warned Peter about this:

And the Lord said, Simon, Simon, behold, Satan hath desired to have you, that he may sift you as wheat. (Luke 22:31)

Satan wants to sift all that is good out of your life. Jesus said:

The thief cometh not, but for to steal, and to kill, and to destroy: I am come that they might have life, and that they might have it more abundantly. (John 10:10)

Paul said some believers are taken captive by the will of Satan:

And that they may recover themselves out of the snare of the devil, who are taken captive by him at his will. (2 Timothy 2:26)

GOD'S WILL:

The third will operating in the world is the will of God. This is the subject of our study.

THE MEANING OF GOD'S WILL

The New Testament was originally written in the Greek language. In Greek there are two terms used for the word "will" in reference to the will of God.

One word is "boulema," which refers to God's sovereign will. This is His predetermined plan for everything that happens in the universe. This type of "God's will" is fulfilled regardless of decisions made by man. It is His master plan for the world.

The "boulema" will of God does not require the cooperation of man. In the "boulema" will of God, the outcome is predetermined. The "boulema" will of God is written in His Word and is quite clear. There is no need to seek this will of God because it is revealed in the Bible.

The other word "thelema" refers to God's desire for man to experience and live in His will. It refers to His individual plan or will for each man and women. In order for God to fulfill His "thelema" will, it requires your cooperation. You have the power to choose whether or not you will walk in the "thelema" or individual will of God for your life. It is this "thelema" will, or God's will for you as an individual, to which we refer when we speak of seeking God's will.

One other type of God's will is the "moral" will of God, commandments revealed in the written Word of God which teach how believers should live. The individual and sovereign wills of God for man never conflict with the moral will of God as revealed in His Word. The following chart summarizes the various meanings of the "will of God":

| **Sovereign** | **Individual** | **Moral** |
(Boulema)	**(Thelema)**	
God's predetermined plan for the universe	God's detailed plan for each individual	The moral commands revealed it the written Word of God which teach how we should believe and live
Unaffected by the decisions of man	Affected by the decisions of man	The individual will of God in harmony with His moral will

JESUS AND GOD'S WILL

God's will was the chief concern of Jesus during His earthly ministry. He declared:

For I came down from Heaven, not to do mine own will, but the will of Him that sent me. (John 6:39)

God's will was to bring men and women into right relationship with Him:

And this is the Father's will which hath sent me, that of all which He hath given me I should lose nothing, but should raise it up again at the last day. (John 6:38)

And this is the will of Him that sent me, that every one which seeth the Son, and believeth on Him, may have everlasting life; and I will raise him up at the last day. (John 6:40)

The purpose of Christ's life was to fulfill God's will. Even as a child, Jesus was concerned with doing God's will. When He was in the temple and His parents came looking for Him, Jesus said:

Wist ye not that I must be about my Father's business? (Luke 2:49)

The secret of His spiritual strength was found in doing God's will:

Jesus saith unto them, My meat is to do the will of Him that sent me, and to finish His work. (John 4:34)

This verse reveals His concern with finishing God's work through His life and ministry.

The power evident in Christ's earthly ministry is related to the will of God:

I can of mine own self do nothing; as I hear, I judge; and my judgment is just; because I seek not mine own will, but the will of the Father which hath sent me. (John 5:30)

Christ's words and deeds were not His own. He spoke and acted according to the Father's will:

My doctrine is not mine, but His that sent me. (John 7:16)
The word which ye hear is not mine, but the Father's. (John 14:24)
I do nothing of myself, but as my Father has taught me. (John 8:28)
I seek not my own will, but the will of the Father which hath sent me.
(John 5:30)

Even as He faced death by crucifixion, Jesus prayed:

. . . O my Father, if it be possible let this cup pass from me: nevertheless, not as I will, but as thou wilt. (Matthew 26:39)

Jesus was willing to die if it was God's will for Him to do so. The life of Jesus is a perfect example of absolute conformity to the sovereign, moral, and individual will of God.

THE IMPORTANCE OF GOD'S WILL

God's will is important because...

IT DETERMINES YOUR ETERNAL DESTINY:

Your eternal destiny depends on doing God's will. You must respond positively to God's plan of redemption for your life...

Because straight is the gate and narrow is the way, which leadeth

DR. ABRAHAM PETERS

unto life, and few there be that find it. (Matthew 7:14)

Not every one that saith unto me, Lord, Lord, shall enter into the Kingdom of Heaven; but he that doeth the will of My Father which is in Heaven.
       (Matthew 7:21)

And the world passeth away, and the lust thereof: but he that doeth the will of God abideth forever. (1 John 2:17)

IT IS THE BASIS OF YOUR RELATIONSHIP WITH GOD:

Your relationship to Jesus is based on doing His will:

For whosoever shall do the will of God, the same is my brother, and my sister, and mother. (Mark 3:35 See also Matthew 12:50)

IT PROVIDES DIRECTION:

God's will is important because you are incapable of directing your own way:

O Lord, I know that the way of man is not in himself; it is not in man that walketh to direct his steps. (Jeremiah 10:23)

You lack the ability to guide your own steps. Without God's guidance you go your own way and stray from the plan of God:

All we like sheep have gone astray; we have turned everyone to his own way. (Isaiah 53:6)

IT PROVIDES KNOWLEDGE OF THE FUTURE:

God is the only one with knowledge of the future. He knows the snares of Satan that await you. He knows the future of the economic and political systems. He knows what events await you in the future:

I am God, and there is none like me, declaring the end from the beginning, and from ancient times the things that are not yet done. (Isaiah 46:9-10)

Man is able to function in the present and recall the past. He can also plan for the future. But God is the only one with actual knowledge of the future.

Some people think Satan has foreknowledge of the future. He does not. If he did, he never would have motivated the crucifixion of Jesus. He would have been able to look into the future and see that by this act redemption from sin would become a reality. Satan only knows what God chooses to reveal about the future. For example, Satan knows that his eternal destiny is Hell because God revealed it.

IT IS COMMANDED THAT YOU KNOW IT:

Knowing God's will is also important because you are commanded to know and do it:

Wherefore be ye not unwise, but understanding what the will of the Lord is. (Ephesians 5:17)

As the servant of Christ, doing the will of God from the heart. (Ephesians 6:6)

God desires your obedience to His will more than He desires your sacrifices or praise:

And Samuel said, Hath the Lord as great delight in burnt offerings and sacrifices as in obeying the voice of the Lord? Behold, to obey is better than sacrifice, and to hearken than the fat of rams.

For rebellion is as the sin of witchcraft, and stubbornness as iniquity and idolatry... (1 Samuel 15:22-23)

God wants you to stand perfect and complete in His will:

Epaphras, who is one of you, a servant of Christ, saluteth you, always labouring fervently for you in prayers, that ye may stand perfect and complete in all the will of God. (Colossians 4:12)

IT RESULTS IN DOCTRINAL SOUNDNESS:

Jesus said:

If any man will do His will, he shall know of the doctrine, whether it be of God, or whether I speak of myself. (John 7:17)

If you do God's will as it is revealed to you, then you will develop spiritual maturity in judging sound doctrine. This will prevent you from being deceived by false teaching.

IT RESULTS IN ANSWERED PRAYER:

When you are living in the will of God you can pray with confidence that your requests will be answered:

And whatsoever we ask, we receive of Him because we keep His commandments, and do those things that are pleasing in His sight. (1 John 3:22)

Now we know that God heareth not sinners; but if any man be a worshiper of God, and doeth His will, him He heareth. (John 9:31)

And this is the confidence that we have in Him, that, if we ask anything according to His will, He heareth us. (1 John 5:14)

IT BRINGS SPIRITUAL BLESSINGS:

Spiritual blessings are promised if you do God's will:

For ye have need of patience, that, after ye have done the will of God, ye might receive the promise. (Hebrews 10:36)

Blessings will actually pursue you:

And it shall come to pass, if thou shalt hearken diligently unto the voice of the Lord thy God, to serve and to do all His commandments which I
command thee this day, that the Lord thy God will set thee on high above all nations of the earth;

And all these blessing shall come on thee, and overtake thee, if thou shalt hearken unto the voice of the Lord thy God. (Deuteronomy 28:1-2)

DR. ABRAHAM PETERS

IT HELPS YOU AVOID CHASTISEMENT:

Chastisement means discipline, reproof, and correction. Those who deliberately turn away from God's revealed will are chastised:

But it shall come to pass, if thou wilt not hearken unto the voice of the Lord thy God, to observe to do all His commandments and His statutes which I command thee this day; that all these curses shall come upon thee, and overtake thee. (Deuteronomy 28:15)

And ye have forgotten the exhortation which speaketh unto you as unto children, My son, despise not thou the chastening of the Lord, nor faint when thou art rebuked of Him;

For whom the Lord loveth, He chasteneth and scourgeth every son whom He receiveth.

If ye endure chastening, God dealeth with you as with sons; for what son is he whom the father chasteneth not?

But if ye are without chastisement, whereof all are partakers, then are ye bastards, and not sons.

Furthermore we have had fathers of our flesh which corrected us, and we gave them reverence: shall we not much rather be in subjection unto the Father of spirits, and live? (Hebrews 12:5-9)

Jesus also warned:

And that servant, which knew his lord's will, and prepared not himself, neither did according to his will, shall be beaten with many stripes. (Luke 12:47)

Knowing God's will is a serious matter for those who desire to live the abundant life and avoid chastisement.

IT RESULTS IN SUCCESS:

One of the instructions given to Joshua when he assumed leadership of the nation of Israel was to keep the commandments of God and walk in His ways. If he did this, Joshua had this guarantee:

Then thou shalt make thy way prosperous and then thou shalt have good success. (Joshua 1:8)

Psalms also records that a man walking in God's way will be successful and "whatsoever he doeth shall prosper" (Psalms 1:3). In a world filled with failure and defeat, knowing and doing the will of God is the secret to successful living.

THE PROPER MOTIVATION

You should be motivated to do God's will because you love Him. Love desires to please the object of that love:

If ye love me, keep my commandments. (John 14:15)

He that hath my commandments and keepeth them, he it is that loveth me;

and he that loveth me shall be loved of my Father, and I will love him, and will manifest myself to him. (John 14:21)

Jesus answered and said unto him, If a man love me, he will keep my words: and my Father will love him and we will come unto him, and make our abode with him. (John 14:23)

The chart given in this chapter on "Three Meanings Of The Will Of God" is expanded below with the addition of Biblical references. Study these verses for further understanding of the sovereign, individual, and moral will of God.

THREE MEANINGS OF "THE WILL OF GOD"

Sovereign (Boulema)	Individual (Thelema)	Moral
God's pre-determined plan for the universe	God's detailed plan for each individual written Word of	The moral commands revealed in the God which teach how we should believe and live
Unaffected by the will of decisions of man always in harmony	Affected by the decisions of man	The individual God is with His moral will
Romans 11:33-36 Acts 2:23 Acts 4:27-28	Genesis 24 Proverbs 16:9 Psalms 32:8	Examples: 2 Corinthians 6:14 Romans 2:18

Romans 9:19   Proverbs 3:5-6   1
Thessalonians 5:18
Proverbs 16:33   Ephesians 5:17   1
Thessalonians 4:3
Ephesians 1:11   Ephesians 6:6   (Plus all other
Revelation 4:11   Romans 12:2   commands in
the Proverbs 21:1   Colossians 1:9   written
Word of God)
Daniel 4:35   Colossians 4:12

DR. ABRAHAM PETERS

CHAPTER EIGHTEEN

HEADING THE WRONG DIRECTION

O Lord, I know that the way of man is not in himself: It is not in man that walketh to direct his steps. (Jeremiah 10:23)

It is just as important to know how not to do something as it is to know how to do it.

A great inventor in the United States named Thomas Edison conducted over 1,000 experiments which failed before he perfected the light bulb. When asked if he regretted all that wasted time, he said "No. I discovered over 1,000 ways NOT to do it." In the future, he did not have to waste time using methods which did not work.

In the Bible God warns of ways you should NOT seek guidance for your life. If you heed these warnings, you will not waste time with non-Biblical methods of guidance of which God does not approve. This will prevent you from making bad decisions and heading the wrong direction in life.

In other chapters you will learn how God revealed His will in the past and how He speaks to men in present times. But first, we must eliminate the negatives. These are the ways you should NOT seek guidance.

THE OCCULT

There are numerous Satanic practices grouped under the heading of the occult. Many of these practices are used to determine guidance. Occult practices vary from nation to nation but they include such methods as witches, shamen, sorcerers, magicians, fortune tellers, astrology, horoscopes, the reading of tea leaves, crystals, cards, and the palm of the hand. Occult practices include any form of supernatural involvement which is not of God. Such practices are motivated by Satan.

God warned His people not to deal with occult practices. You can read these warnings in Deuteronomy 18:9-14 and Exodus 22:18.

Witchcraft is the practice of witches including white and black magic, sorcery, astrology, voodoo, use of potions, spells, enchantments, and drugs. It includes all similar Satanic practices and worship. Witchcraft and other such Satanic practices are spiritual rebellion against God:

For rebellion is as the sin of witchcraft... (1 Samuel 15:23)

The Bible records that sorcerers tried to turn people away from the Gospel:

But Elymas the sorcerer . . . withstood them, seeking to turn away the deputy from the faith. (Acts 13:8)

Witchcraft deceives people:

. . . for by thy sorceries were all nations deceived. (Revelation 18:23)

Sorcerers will not enter the Kingdom of Heaven:

For without are... sorcerers... (Revelation 22:15)

The book of Revelation reveals the end of those who use such

Satanic practices:

> But... sorcerers... shall have their part in the lake which burneth with fire and brimstone... (Revelation 21:8)

No true child of God should be involved in any way with occult practices for purposes of guidance or any other reason.

METHODS OF CHANCE

Casting lots was one method of seeking guidance used in the Old Testament. You can read about the use of this method in Leviticus 16:7-10; Numbers 26:55; 27:21; and Joshua 18:10.

The casting of lots was a method of chance. The belief was that God controlled the outcome of the lot which was cast. Casting of lots was similar to the rolling of dice or flipping of a coin today.

This method of seeking guidance from God was acceptable in the Old Testament. The only New Testament use of casting of lots by believers was prior to the coming of the Holy Spirit. The Apostles of Jesus were seeking to fill the vacancy left by Judas who had betrayed Jesus and later committed suicide. Two candidates were nominated for the position:

> And they gave forth their lots; and the lot fell upon Matthias; and he was numbered with the eleven apostles. (Acts 1:26)

Matthias, the man picked to replace Judas, is never again mentioned in the New Testament record. It is the Apostle Paul who actually fills the vacancy among the Apostles. Matthias was man's choice by casting lots. The Apostle Paul was God's choice by the Holy Spirit.

After the coming of the Holy Spirit as recorded in Acts chapter 2, the casting of lots was not used by believers as a means of determining direction. The guidance of the Holy Spirit replaced this Old Testament method. You should not use any method of chance to determine God's will. You must know God's voice and be led by the Holy Spirit.

FLEECES

There is one Old Testament record of the use of something called a "fleece" to determine God's will. You can read the story of Gideon's fleece in Judges 6:36-40.

God spoke to Gideon and revealed His will. To confirm what God said, Gideon put out a fleece of skin on the ground. One day he asked God to let the dew fall all around but not on the fleece. On another day He asked God for dew on the fleece and for the surrounding ground to remain dry.

There is no verse in the Bible that instructs believers to do as Gideon did during this terrible national crisis when great responsibility rested upon him. This event occurred only once in the Bible and, as casting of lots, was used only before the New Testament outpouring of the Holy Spirit.

We are not to seek God's will by putting out a fleece. Modern putting out of a fleece is usually done by saying, "If a certain thing happens, then I will know it is God's will"--but our fleeces are often things that could occur naturally.

In the one case of a "fleece" recorded in the Bible, Gideon already knew God's will. He had heard the voice of God. The fleece was used as confirmation, not for direction. It was also something that could be answered only by supernatural means.

In New Testament days when Zacharias asked for a sign to confirm God's message about the birth of John the Baptism, he was stricken dumb. This was because he did not believe the voice of God and sought a sign (Luke 1:18-20).

Jesus said that "an evil and adulterous generation seeketh after a sign" (Matthew 12:39). A fleece can be a sign of unbelief or unwillingness to do God's revealed will. Fleeces which can be answered through natural means can be deceptive and misleading.

On occasion, God has graciously answered those who have asked for some indication of what they should do by a fleece or sign. This practice, however, has been the exception rather than the rule for seeking guidance in the lives of great saints of God. Remember. . . God wants men of faith, not of fleeces. He wants men and women who know His voice when He speaks and have no need to test it by confirming signs.

FALSE PROPHETS

The Bible records the stories of many prophets of God. It reveals that God sets leaders in the church known as prophets, and explains the spiritual gift of the Holy Spirit known as prophecy (Ephesians 4:11 and 1 Corinthians 12:10).

DR. ABRAHAM PETERS

To "prophesy" is to speak under the special inspiration of God. It is a special ability to receive and communicate an immediate message of God to His people through a divinely-anointed utterance. The words spoken by a prophet under divine inspiration are called prophecies. To prophesy means to declare openly words from God that exhort, edify, and comfort:

But he that prophesieth speaketh unto men to edification and exhortation, and comfort. (1 Corinthians 14:3)

Prophecy never replaces the written Word of God. The Bible says prophecy will cease, but the Word of God abides forever (1 Corinthians 13:8 and 1 Peter 1:25).

In the Old Testament people went to prophets for guidance because the gift of the Holy Spirit infilling was not yet given. It is no longer necessary to be solely dependent by going to seek out a prophet to receive spiritual guidance. This is one of the functions of the Holy Spirit in the life of the believer. Each believer should learn to be led by God's Spirit. Again, I will recommend my book Awakening the Prophet in You. I'm not ruling out the importance of the prophetic ministry and ministers but stressing that you don't need to idolize seeking the prophet when you can hear directly God's voice by the Holy Spirit.

The New Testament gives no record of believers seeking guidance from prophets after the gift of the Holy Spirit was given, but God still uses this gift to confirm the future. You can study such an example in Acts 21:1-14. Agabus gave Paul a personal prophecy, in that it was given specifically to Paul.

Paul already knew what awaited him in Jerusalem. The prophecy only confirmed what would happen there. It was not a prophecy of guidance telling Paul whether or not to go to Jerusalem.

The Bible warns of false prophets in the world (Matthew 24:11, 24: Mark 13:22). Because of this, God has provided ways to identify true prophecies. The Bible states:

Having then gifts differing according to the grace that is given to us, whether prophecy, let us prophesy according to the proportion of faith.(Romans 12:6)

The phrase "in proportion to faith" means in right relation to the faith. The way to recognize true prophecies is by whether or not they are in harmony with the Bible. The Bible states:

Let the prophets speak, two or three, and let the other judge. (1 Corinthians 14:29)

We are told to judge prophecies. The standard for judgment is the Word of God.

God has provided many ways to recognize false prophets. False prophets are known because what they speak does not come to pass:

But the prophet, which shall presume to speak a word in my name, which I have not commanded him to speak, or that shall speak in the name of other gods, even that prophet shall die.

And if thou say in thine heart, How shall we know the word which the Lord hath not spoken?

DR. ABRAHAM PETERS

When a prophet speaketh in the name of the Lord, the thing follow not, nor come to pass, that is the thing which the Lord hath not spoken, but the prophet hath spoken it presumptuously: thou shalt not be afraid of him. (Deuteronomy 18:20-22)

Study the following references in your Bible which explain other ways to recognize false prophets:

-False prophets do not confess the deity of Jesus Christ: 1 John 4:1-3

-False prophets teach false doctrine: 2 Peter 2:1-3

-False prophets lead people away from obedience to God's Word: Deuteronomy 13:1-5

-False prophets deceive people with miraculous signs: Matthew 24:11-24

-False prophets make false claims: Matthew 24:23-24

-Their fruit reveals their error: One of the best ways to distinguish false prophets from true prophets is to observe their lives. The Bible says that by their "fruits"

you will know them. False prophets do not have evidence of spiritual fruit in their lives: Matthew 7:16

Because there are false prophets in the world, you must exercise caution in accepting prophecies. Prophecy often has been misused to direct and control believers. When personal prophecy is given it should be examined in relation to the Scriptures and it should agree with the written Word of God. In regards to guidance, prophecy should be confirming, not directing or controlling. Because of misuse of this spiritual gift some believers reject it totally. They will not accept the miraculous gift of prophetic utterance. But you should not reject the ministry of the Holy Spirit because you witness a few carnal examples in a human vessel.

WRONG COUNSEL

No man can determine God's will for someone else except in matters specifically revealed in the Bible. For example, we know it is God's will that all men come to repentance, for this is taught in Scripture.

Spiritual counseling by Godly leaders has a definite place in the guidance of a believer, but no counselor has the right to control another person or determine God's will for him in matters not dealt with in the Scriptures.

When the Apostle Paul was determined to go to Jerusalem, his friends at Caesarea tried to prevent him from doing so. They warned of the serious trouble which might befall him there. When Paul rejected their counsel and went on to Jerusalem, they accepted his decision stating:

The will of the Lord be done. (Acts 21:14)

They realized that even though it was their personal desire that he should not go, the apostle Paul must determine God's will for himself. It is very important that you come to know God's voice for yourself. You cannot trust others to guide your life because there are evil spirits in the world whose intent is to deceive. We are warned:

Beloved, believe not every spirit, but try the spirits whether they are of God. (1 John 4:1)

When you receive counsel from another person, that guidance should be tested against other methods of determining God's will which will be detailed in a later chapter of this study.

EMULATIONS

Emulation is listed as one of the works of the flesh in Galatians 5:20. The works of the flesh are various sinful conducts which are not pleasing to God.

Emulation is the desire to copy others and to equal or excel them. It stems from a spirit of rivalry and is a form of jealousy. Some believers emulate the successful ministries of others instead of seeking God's plan for their own lives. No two believers have the same work to do. The Holy Spirit calls people into specific ministries:

As they ministered to the Lord, and fasted, the Holy Ghost said, separate me Barnabas and Saul for the work whereunto I have called them. (Acts 13:2)

The Bible states that believers have differing spiritual gifts:

There are diversities of gifts..but all these worketh that one and selfsame Spirit, dividing to every man severally as He will. (1

Corinthians 12:4,11)

Although we are told to "covet earnestly the best gifts" (1 Corinthians 12:31) and to "desire spiritual gifts" (1 Corinthians 14:1), it does not mean we are to imitate others who have significant ministries. When Peter was concerned about John's ministry, Jesus said:

What is that to thee? Follow thou me. (John 21:22)

God gave Noah the plan for an ark. He gave Moses the plan for the tabernacle. He gave Solomon the plan for a great temple of worship. Nehemiah was given the plan to rebuild the walls of Jerusalem. God has not told you to build an ark, construct the temple, or build walls around the city of Jerusalem. But God has a special plan for you! If you fall into the sin of emulations and imitate others, you will miss His plan.

When you pattern your life after the lives of others, you become engulfed by human tradition--and human tradition conceals divine revelation.

The Bible records the stories of great men of God who headed the wrong direction because they did not listen to the voice of God. Read and summarize what you learn about. . .

King Saul who went to a witch for guidance: 1 Samuel 28.

Manasseh who consulted sorcerer: 2 Chronicles 33:16.

An unnamed man of God who listened to a man who claimed to be a prophet instead of obeying what God told him to do: 1 Kings 13.

Balaam who listened to wrong counsel of man: Numbers 22.

THE PATTERN OF GOD'S WILL

Having made known unto us the mystery of His will, according to the good pleasure which He hath purposed in Himself; That in the dispensation of the fullness of times He might gather together in one all things in Christ, both which are in heaven, and which are on earth; even in Him; In whom also we have obtained an inheritance, being predestinated according to the purpose of Him who worketh all things after the counsel of His own will. (Ephesians 1:9-11)

Before you examine the methods God uses to speak to man to reveal His will, you must have some basic knowledge about the will of God. Previous chapters defined what is meant by "the will of God" and identified ways of seeking guidance which are wrong. This chapter presents basic facts about the will of God, explains two major divisions of that will, examines the pattern of God's will, and discusses the believer's development in knowing the voice of God.

FACTS ABOUT GOD'S WILL

Here are some basic facts about God's will:

GOD WANTS YOU TO KNOW HIS WILL:

Faith that it is possible to know God's voice rests on two foundational facts:

First: The belief that God has a plan for you.

Second: The ability of God to communicate to you.

The following chapters explain methods by which God communicates with man. As mentioned in a previous chapter, God wants to communicate to man so much that He actually used a donkey to speak to a prophet on one occasion (Numbers 22).

The Bible commands:

Wherefore be ye not unwise, but understanding what the will of the Lord is. (Ephesians 5:17)

Paul wrote the Colossians:

For this cause we also, since the day we heard it, do not cease to pray for you, and to desire that ye might be filled with the knowledge of His will in all wisdom and spiritual understanding. (Colossians 1:9)

In Acts Paul spoke to one man and said:

. . . The God of our fathers hath chosen thee, that thou shouldest know His will, and see that Just one, and shouldest hear the voice of His mouth.
    (Acts 22:14)

In addition to these verses, God has given many promises of guidance in His written Word. (You will study some of these later). On the basis of these Scriptures it can be concluded that God wants you to know His will.

DR. ABRAHAM PETERS

GOD'S WILL IS PLANNED:

God is working in this world to bring to pass all things on the basis of His plan:

In whom also we have obtained an inheritance, being predestinated according to the purpose of Him who worketh all things after the counsel of His own will. (Ephesians 1:11)

God has an overall plan for the universe which He is working out. We call this His master plan. He also has an individual plan for each person. Those plans fall within this sovereign plan and His moral will.

GOD'S PLAN IS INDIVIDUAL AND PERSONAL:

God's will for each individual includes His sovereign plan of redemption:

The Lord is not slack concerning His promise, as some men count slackness; but is longsuffering to usward, not willing that any should perish, but that all should come to repentance. (2 Peter 3:9)

But God's plan goes beyond the revelation of His sovereign and moral wills. God has an individual plan for each person which He seeks to communicate. The Bible confirms this by many stories of God at work in the lives of individuals. He placed men in specific situations at exact times for special purposes. Each of the life stories recorded in the Bible is unique.

God told the Prophet Jeremiah:

Before I formed thee in the belly I knew thee; and before thou camest out of the womb, I sanctified thee and ordained thee. (Jeremiah 1:5)

What greater witness is there to the personal plan of God for an individual?

When the Apostle Peter was overly concerned about what ministry John was to have, Jesus said to him. . .

. . . If I will that he tarry till I come, what is that to thee? follow thou me. (John 21:22)

Jesus had different plans for the lives of Peter and John.

Everywhere we look in the universe intelligent planning is apparent. The arrangement of planets, the stars, and the individual designs of each snowflake and flower reflect this planning. Given this evidence, we must conclude that the divine Creator also has an individual plan for man, the highest of His created beings.

God promised:

I will instruct thee and teach thee in the way which thou shalt go: I will guide thee with mine eye. (Psalms 32:8)

An individual pathway is indicated in this verse.

Psalms 37 states that every step of a righteous man is ordered by the Lord:

The steps of a good man are ordered by the Lord: and he delighteth in his way. (Psalms 37:23)

The same word used here for "ordered" is used in Psalms 8:3 in relation to the moon and stars which God created. The science of astronomy has recorded the amazing precision of the movement of heavenly bodies.

The same precision that has scheduled the movement of the planets orders the steps of believers. He promised:

Thine ear shall hear a word behind thee, saying This is the way, walk ye in it, when ye turn to the right hand and when ye turn to the left. (Isaiah 30:21)

God orders not just the big events of life, but each step.

GOD'S WILL IS NOT MAN'S WAY:

God's will is often contrary to the ways of man:

For my thoughts are not your thoughts, neither are your ways my ways, saith the Lord. For as the heavens are higher than the earth, so are my ways higher than your ways, and my thoughts than your thoughts. (Isaiah 55:8-9)

God's will is not always the path you would naturally select. This is why it is important to recognize the voice of God. But this does not mean the will of God is something which will bring unhappiness, as the next point reveals.

GOD'S WILL IS GOOD:

The Bible teaches that God's will is always good. Although His way may not be the one you would select, God knows what is best. Psalms 37:23 states you will delight in the way ordered by the Lord.

Paul confirms God's will is good:

And be not conformed to this world; but be ye transformed by the renewing of your mind that ye may prove what is that good, and acceptable, and perfect will of God. (Romans 12:2)

GOD'S PLAN IS PROGRESSIVE:

Ephesians 2:10 states "we are His workmanship." The word "are" is the present tense. God is constantly working in your life. It is a continuing, progressive process of revealing His will.

For it is God which worketh in you both to will and to do of His good pleasure. (Philippians 2:13)

Paul wrote to the Hebrew believers that it was God's desire to. . .

Make you perfect in every good work to do His will, working in you that which is well pleasing in His sight, through Jesus Christ: to whom be glory for ever and ever. (Hebrews 13:21)

"Working" is in the present tense. God is continually guiding, developing, and speaking to you regarding His plan. You are promised continual guidance:

DR. ABRAHAM PETERS

The Lord shall guide thee continually. (Isaiah 58:11)

TWO DIVISIONS OF GOD'S WILL

When we speak of knowing God's voice, we must understand there are two basic divisions of the will of God. Each division is in harmony with the other:

FIRST: THAT REVEALED IN HIS WRITTEN WORD:

The first division of the will of God is that which is specifically revealed in the Bible.
In a previous chapter we discussed the three meanings of "the will of God." We learned there is a sovereign, individual, and moral will of God. These are shown on the following
diagram.

God's Sovereign Will

God's Moral Will

God's Individual Will

As the diagram shows, the will of God for each individual always falls within His sovereign and moral will as revealed in His written Word. The written Word of God includes the complete revelation of God's moral will. This includes all the commandments as to how you should live. As you can see on the diagram, God's sovereign will includes His moral will. It is His sovereign will that each man and woman live within the moral standards of His written Word. The written Word of God includes portions of His sovereign will

Fellowship With The Holy Spirit

which He has chosen to reveal to us and includes the general outline of His master plan for the world and man in general.

The best summary of this plan is the Key Verses for this chapter:

Having made known unto us the mystery of His will, according to the good pleasure which He hath purposed in Himself; That in the dispensation of the fullness of times He might gather together in one all things in Christ, both which are in heaven, and which are on earth; even in Him; In whom also we have obtained an inheritance, being predestinated according to the purpose of Him who worketh all things after the counsel of His own will. (Ephesians 1:9-11)

I have listed specific references which are examples of God's will as revealed in His written Word. These are general principles and examples in God's written Word through which He communicates His will to man. There are also specific instructions in God's written Word which reveal His will in many matters. These include all the promises and commandments of the Bible. In some verses, God is so specific He actually states "This is my will for you. . . " These references are listed for you to study. You can add to this list from your own study of God's Word.

What are some of the things God has revealed as His will for you? Study the following references:

HIS PLAN FOR YOU:

And this is the will of Him that sent me, that every one which seeth the Son, and believeth on Him, may have everlasting life; and I will raise him up at the last day. (John 6:40)

DR. ABRAHAM PETERS

And this is the Father's will which hath sent me, that of all which He hath given me I should lose nothing, but should raise it up again at the last day. (John 6:39)

All that the Father giveth me shall come to me; and Him that cometh to me I will in no wise cast out. (John 6:37)

Who gave Himself for our sins, that He might deliver us from this present evil world, according to the will of God and our Father. (Galatians 1:4)

Having predestinated us unto the adoption of children by Jesus Christ to Himself, according to the good pleasure of His will. . .

Having made known unto us the mystery of His will, according to His good pleasure which He hath purposed in Himself:

That in the dispensation of the fullness of times, He might gather together in one all things in Christ, both which are in Heaven, and which are on earth; even in Him;

In whom also we have obtained an inheritance, being predestinated according to the purpose of Him who worketh all things after the counsel of His own will. (Ephesians 1, 5, 9-11)

Of His own will begat He us with the word of truth, that we should be a kind of firstfruits of His creatures. (James 1:18)

HIS WILL FOR YOUR LOVED ONES:

The Lord is not slack concerning His promise, as some men count slackness; but is longsuffering to usward, not willing that any should perish, but that all should come to repentance. (2 Peter 3:9)

HIS WILL CONCERNING YOUR SANCTIFICATION:

For this is the will of God, even your sanctification, that ye should abstain from fornication. (1 Thessalonians 4:3)

HIS WILL REGARDING PRAYER AND THANKSGIVING:

Pray without ceasing. In everything give thanks for this is the will of God in Christ Jesus concerning you. (1 Thessalonians 5:17-18)

And I will give unto thee the keys of the Kingdom of Heaven; and whatsoever thou shalt bind on earth shall be bound in heaven: and whatsoever thou shalt loose on earth shall be loosed in Heaven. (Matthew 16:19)

HIS WILL REGARDING YOUR LIFESTYLE:

For so is the will of God, that with well doing ye may put to silence the ignorance of foolish men. (1 Peter 2:15)

HIS WILL FOR YOU REGARDING THE HOLY SPIRIT:

And it shall come to pass in the last days, saith God, I will pour out of my Spirit upon all flesh and your sons and your daughters shall prophesy, and your young men shall see visions, and your old men shall dream dreams:

An on my servants and on my handmaidens I will pour out in those days of my Spirit: and they shall prophesy. (Acts 2:17-18)

HIS WILL REGARDING YOUR CHRISTIAN WITNESS:

And Jesus said unto them, Come ye after me, and I will make you fishers of men. (Mark 1:17)
But ye shall receive power after that the Holy Ghost is come upon you: and ye shall be witnesses unto me both in Jerusalem, and in all Judaea, and in Samaria, and unto the uttermost part of the earth. (Acts 1:8)

HIS WILL REGARDING CHILDREN AND BABES IN CHRIST:

Even so, it is not the will of your Father which is in Heaven, that one of these little ones should perish. (Matthew 18:14)

HIS WILL REGARDING SUFFERING:

Let them that suffer according to the will of God commit the keeping of their souls to Him in well doing as unto a faithful creator. (1 Peter 4:19)

HIS WILL REGARDING MATERIAL POSSESSIONS:

But seek ye first the Kingdom of God and His righteousness, and all these things shall be added unto you. (Matthew 6:33)

Give and it shall be given unto you. . . (Luke 6:38)

HIS WILL REGARDING YOUR ETERNAL DESTINY:

Father I will that they also, whom thou hast given me, be with me where I am; that they may behold my glory, which thou hast given me: for thou lovedst me before the foundation the world. (John 17:24)

SECOND: THAT NOT REVEALED IN HIS WORD:

The second division of God's will is that which is not revealed in His Word. This includes the individual life plan for each believer. God's Word does not reveal your specific life ministry or occupation, what church you are to attend, who you are to marry, where you are to live, etc. Yet each of these decisions are important. It is for decisions like these that you must seek God's will and be able to hear His voice when He speaks to you.

THE TWO COMPARED:

When desiring to know God's will in regards to a certain life situation, first study the Scriptures to see if specific guidance is given in the written Word of God. There is no need to "seek God's will" or ask for confirmation of His will when He has already spoken in His written Word. Examine the Scriptures carefully for specific guidance already given. Accept the written Word as God's voice speaking to you. If you refuse the guidance God has given in His written Word, you open yourself up to deception.

In many situations the Bible provides general principles, which when understood and applied, will lead to a decision consistent with God's will. These principles apply to a variety of specific situations.

For example, Paul warns:

Be ye not unequally yoked together with unbelievers: for what fellowship hath righteousness with unrighteousness? and what communion hath light with darkness? And what concord hath Christ with Belial (Satan)? or what part hath he that believeth with an infidel? (2 Corinthians 6:14-15)

Here the Bible gives a general principle that believers and unbelievers should not be yoked together. This principle can be applied to many life situations: Being married to an unbeliever, going into business partnership with an unbeliever, making unbelievers your closest friends, etc.

Search the Scriptures for biographical examples which apply to your situation. Study the lives of Biblical characters to see what decisions they made in similar situations and if such decisions were in harmony with the will of God.

In matters where guidance is not given in the written Word of God, the Lord has other methods by which He speaks to man. We will examine these in the following two chapters. But remember: Guidance for individual life situations always will agree with the written Word of God. God's voice leads within the limits of the written Word. The following chart summarizes the two divisions of God's will just discussed:

TWO DIVISIONS OF GOD'S WILL

That Revealed   **That Not Revealed**
(Written Word)

Moral and sovereign will revealed The individual life plan for each believer in His written Word.

Includes His general will for all mankind Includes specific decisions such as life work, and His master plan for the world. ministry, residence, education, marriage, and guidance in other specific situations.

Includes specific commandments and promises to govern living.

Includes general principles upon Some individual decisions can be made upon which specific decisions the basis of general principles, examples, and can be based specific commands revealed in God's Word.

THE PATTERN OF GOD'S WILL

The first chapter of this course focused on Romans 12:1-2:

I beseech you therefore, brethren, by the mercies of God, that ye present your bodies a living sacrifice, holy, acceptable unto God which is your reasonable service. And be not conformed to this world: but be ye transformed by the renewing of your mind, that ye may prove what is that good, and acceptable, and perfect will of God. (Romans 12:1-2)

We asked the question, "What is meant by the good, acceptable, and perfect will of God?" We will now deal with that question, and in doing so discover the pattern of God's will.

DR. ABRAHAM PETERS

THE PERFECT WILL OF GOD:

The perfect will of God is accomplished when a believer is in harmony with the moral, sovereign, and individual wills of God for his life.

The believer has accepted the sovereign plan of God for his salvation through the new birth experience. He is in harmony with the moral commandments of God's written Word. He also has determined God's specific guidance for his individual life plan.

THE GOOD WILL OF GOD:

In the good will of God, the believer is not in the perfect plan for his life but he is within God's sovereign will and moral will. He is not disobedient to God's revealed will, and he is still seeking to find that perfect individual plan of God for His life.

THE ACCEPTABLE WILL OF GOD:

This believer is missing the perfect will of God for his life but is still in an acceptable area. He is living in the permissive will of God. He may not even be concerned about God's perfect will for His life. God is permitting him to live in this area, although it is not God's perfect will for him.

OUTSIDE THE WILL OF GOD:

The believer in this realm is in direct disobedience to God's revealed will.

AN EXAMPLE FROM SCRIPTURE

The story of Balaam in Numbers chapter 22 illustrates these realms of God's will. Read the story before you continue with this lesson. Some men from Moab asked a prophet of God named Balaam to go with them and prophesy against God's people, Israel. God spoke to Balaam and told him not to go:

And God said unto Balaam, Thou shalt not go with them; thou shalt not curse the people: for they are blessed. (Numbers 22:12)

It was the perfect will of God for Balaam NOT to go with the men of Moab. But Balaam disobeyed God's voice and went with the men. When he did, he was functioning in disobedience outside the revealed will of God.

God desired so much for Balaam to know His will that He used a donkey to speak to him and convict him of his sin. After this God permitted Balaam to continue on with the men of Moab with orders that he was to bless rather than curse the Israelites. Balaam was now functioning in the permissive will of God.

The journey resulted in a series of trying encounters with a man named Balak. These could have been avoided if Balaam had obeyed the voice of God and never gone in the first place.

Now compare this story to the diagram of the "Pattern Of God's Will." The perfect will of God was that Balaam not go with the men of Moab. Balaam disobeyed and moved outside of the will of God. He was not in the good will of God where the believer is missing the perfect will but seeking it. He was in complete disobedience to the voice of God. The acceptable or permissive will of God permitted Balaam to continue on the journey even though it was not God's perfect will for him.

WALKING IN THE WILL

Following the born-again experience and motivated by love for God, the goal of the believer is to walk in harmony with the will of God. God's will is represented by a straight unbroken line. The walk of man in relation to that will is represented by arrows. Before the born-again experience man walks in His own way which is exactly opposite of the will of God. After the new birth experience, a believer often anticipates walking in complete harmony with God's will. Since he is a new creature in Christ, he expects to be able to conform exactly to God's will. But in the reality of daily life, his pattern of conformity looks more like this:

Instead of exact conformity to God's will, the believer has an "up and down" experience. Sometimes he hears God's voice and does His will. Other times he does not. He becomes greatly discouraged when he makes mistakes and misses God's will. Some even give up in their quest to hear God's voice. While it is true that sometimes the believer misses God's will, note that the overall direction representing his life walk is upward. Although he may fall short of the will of God at times, the overall pattern is one of progress. This shows how he strays from the will of God, realizes it, learns from the experience, and comes back into conformity to God's plan. Through failure as well as success, the believer is learning to hear God's voice. Through both positive and negative experiences he is continuing his growth in understanding the principles of a God-directed life.

When the will of God is perceived in this manner, it becomes a liberating relationship with Him in which you are privileged to live. The will of God ceases to become just restrictions or commandments. It becomes a challenge of learning to align your life with His plan.

A BIBLICAL EXAMPLE

Consider the example of King David. When David first became king, he walked in conformity to the will of God. To the extent that God even called David a man after His own heart (1 Samuel 13:14 & Acts 13:22) But then David sinned with another man's wife who gave birth to an illegitimate child. This was in direct disobedience to God's written Word. David came before the Lord in repentance, was forgiven, and came back in line with God's will. As we examine further the ways God speaks to us always keep in mind it is the repentance and obedience overall pattern of your conformity to God's will that is important. Through every experience of learning to know God's voice, both positive and negative, you can continue to advance in your ability to discern God's perfect will. Continue to strive for conformity despite occasional failures. Don't ever give up!

DR. ABRAHAM PETERS

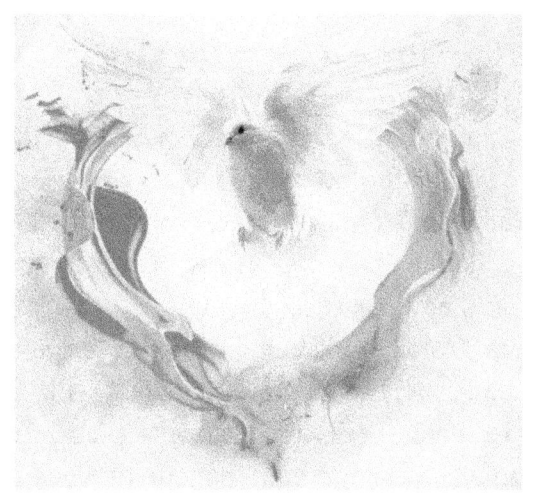

CHAPTER NINETEEN

HOW GOD SPEAKS TO MAN

The bible says, Be ye not unwise, but understanding what the will of the Lord is.
(Ephesians 5:17)

The Bible is a history of methods by which God communicated to man and the response of mankind to the voice of God. This chapter examines the Biblical record to discover the methods by which God communicates to man.

THE WRITTEN WORD

As God speaks to man through His written Word. God does not need to speak to you concerning things already revealed in the Scriptures. When God uses other methods to communicate, they will never conflict with His written Word.

PRAYER

There are many Biblical examples of God speaking as a result of prayer. Prayer is not a monologue but a dialogue where you speak to God and you listen in expectation the He will answer and speak back to you that's where the communication and communion takes place. For further study in-depth on prayer, I recommend my book titled: PRAYER: Communicating With GOD, Connecting With Heaven And Changing The World. Prayer and fasting doing without food for spiritual reasons resulted in God speaking to Paul and Barnabas:

And as they ministered to the Lord and fasted, the Holy Ghost said, Separate unto me Barnabas and Saul for the work whereunto I have called them. And when they had fasted and prayed, and laid their hands on them, they sent them away.(Acts 13:2-3)

Prayer is to include the request for the fulfillment of God's will on earth. Jesus taught His followers to pray:

Thy Kingdom come, Thy will be done in earth, as it is in Heaven.(Matthew 6:10)

Jesus prayed for direction from God prior to the selection of His disciples:

And it came to pass in those days that He went out into a mountain to pray and continued all night in prayer to God. And when it was day, He called unto Him His disciples; and of them He chose twelve, whom also He named apostles.(Luke 6:12-13)

Jesus prayed for God's will prior to His death:

. . . Saying, Father, if thou be willing, remove this cup from me: nevertheless, not my will, but thine be done. (Luke 22:42)

COUNSELORS

God communicates His will through Christian counselors. There are many Biblical examples of people seeking guidance from men of God.

The Bible states:

Where no counsel is, the people fall; but in the multitude of counselors there is safety. (Proverbs 11:14)

The way of a fool is right in his own eyes: but he that hearkeneth unto counsel is wise. (Proverbs 12:15)

CIRCUMSTANCES

God communicates His plan through circumstances. One excellent Old Testament example of this is the life of Joseph recorded in Genesis 37-50.

Joseph's brothers sold him into slavery in Egypt but he viewed this as the direction of God:

Now therefore be not grieved, nor angry with yourselves that ye sold me hither; for God did send me before you to preserve life. . . And God sent me before you to preserve you a posterity in the earth and to save your lives by a great deliverance. So now it was not you that sent me hither, but God.
        (Genesis 45:5-8)

Through circumstances over which Joseph had no personal control, he was used of God to save the lives of thousands of people in a time of severe famine.

Paul wrote some interesting words in I Thessalonians 2:18. He told believers at Thessalonica he was prevented from visiting them because Satan hindered. Since he could not go to them, he wrote to the church at Thessalonica. Satan's hindering resulted in the book of 1 Thessalonians and the important message Paul shared had greater impact than would have resulted from a visit. It has been passed down through the centuries for the benefit of all believers.

Nothing occurs apart from God's knowledge. Even when circumstances block what you might perceive to be God's will, God is still in control. God can take any deed, whether of Satan or man, and use it for His own purposes. We have a wonderful promise from God regarding circumstances:

And we know that all things work together for good to them that love God, to them who are the called according to His purpose. (Romans 8:28)

One word of warning: Caution must be used in considering circumstances alone to determine God's will. For example, God told a prophet named Jonah to go to Ninevah to preach. When he came to the waterfront, there was a boat leaving for Tarsus. He took this boat instead of going to Ninevah. He might have said, "There is a cabin open on this boat going the opposite direction, so it must be God's will that I go."

Circumstances of life must be viewed in relation to what God reveals through other methods. God had already communicated His will to Jonah. Jonah manipulated circumstances to fulfill his own wishes.

OPEN AND CLOSED DOORS

Circumstances of life result in what has come to be called "open and closed doors." Paul wrote to the Corinthians:

But I will tarry at Ephesus until Pentecost. For a great door and effectual is opened unto me, and there are many adversaries.(1 Corinthians 16:8-9)

Paul decided to stay at Ephesus because through circumstances arranged by God, there was a great opportunity for Christian service open to him. He called this an open door. On another occasion Paul records his desire to minister in certain areas, but the doors there were closed:

Now when they had gone throughout Phrgia and the region of Galatia and were forbidden of the Holy Ghost to preach the word in Asia, After they were come to Mysia, they assayed to go into Bithynia: but the Spirit suffered them not. (Acts 16:6-7)

A closed door does not mean you have missed God's will. It does not mean it is not His will to do something. Paul later evangelized Asia. God is directing you by closing a door. He leads through closed as well as open doors. Sometimes a door is closed because it is not the right timing in the plan of God. Later, that same door may open to you.

ANGELS

Lot was given direction by angels who appeared at his home in Sodom. He was told to leave Sodom because the judgment of God was going to fall on the city (Genesis 19). An angel spoke to Philip and told him to go to Samaria (Acts 8:26). The births of John the Baptist and Jesus were announced by angels (Luke 1). There are numerous Biblical records of angels appearing to communicate the will of God to man. You can find other examples in your own study of Scriptures.

DR. ABRAHAM PETERS

MIRACLES

A miracle is a supernatural event which is beyond the power of man to perform. God spoke through a miracle in the event recorded in 1 Kings chapter 18. The prophet Elijah was told to prepare an altar before the Lord. Elijah prepared the altar and cried:

. . . Lord God of Abraham, Isaac, and of Israel, let it be known this day that thou art God in Israel, and that I am thy servant, and that I have done all these things at thy word. . .

Then the fire of the Lord fell and consumed the burnt sacrifice, and the wood, and the stones, and the dust, and licked up the water that was in the trench.

And when all the people saw it, they fell on their faces: and they said, The Lord, He is God; the Lord He is God. (I Kings 18:36,38,39)

God used this miracle to speak to men who worshiped idols and reveal Himself as the true and living God.

God has also revealed His will through miracles in nature. A pillar of fire and a cloud in the sky gave direction to the nation of Israel by night and day as they traveled through the desert:

And the Lord went before them by day in a pillar of a cloud to lead them in the way; and by night in a pillar of fire, to give them light; to go by day and night.

He took not away the pillar of the cloud by day, nor the pillar of fire by night, from before the people. (Exodus 13:21-22)

You can find many other Biblical examples of God communicating to men through miracles. Watch for these in your own personal Bible study.

DREAMS

God desires so much to communicate with us that He even speaks while we sleep! God speaks in dreams. These are not the normal dreams experienced by everyone. They are supernatural dreams given by God. They are detailed, specific, and reveal His will.

The following are a few of many Biblical examples:

-God warned Abimelech in a dream about his sin of taking Abraham's wife, Sarah. Genesis 20:3

-An angel spoke to Jacob in a dream to remind him of his vow to God. Genesis 31:11-13

-God used dreams to reveal His will to Joseph. Genesis 37.

-God appeared to Solomon in a dream and gave him the opportunity to ask for whatever he desired. 1 Kings 3:5

-A dream was used to direct wise men to return to their country by a different route because of an evil king. Matthew 2:12-13

These are just a few of the many examples of how God communicates through dreams. You can find other examples as you continue to study this method of guidance in God's Word.

VISIONS

A vision is similar to a dream but differs because you are awake. It is like having a dream without being asleep. Visions may be seen with spiritual eyes as well as the physical eyes. This means you might not actually see it with your natural eye, but God gives you a picture of something in your spirit.

The following are a few of many Biblical examples where visions were used by God to communicate with man:

-God appeared to Abraham in a vision and made him a great promise. Genesis 15

-The book of Daniel is filled with visions (as well as dreams). God used these to reveal many things about the future of the world. He spoke to many other Old Testament prophets through visions.

-God gave Peter a vision concerning the need to take the Gospel to the Gentile nations. Acts 10

-God called Paul to Macedonia through a vision. Acts 16:9

-God spoke to Paul in the night through a vision. Acts 18:9-10

-The final book in the Bible, Revelation, is based on a vision seen by the Apostle John.

AN AUDIBLE VOICE

God spoke to Paul in an audible voice during a journey along the Damascus road. You can read the story in Acts chapter 9:

And he fell to the earth and head a voice saying unto him, Saul, Saul, why persecutest thou me? And he said, Who art thou Lord? And the Lord said, I am Jesus whom thou persecutest; it is hard for thee to kick against the pricks. (Acts 9:4-5)

God also spoke to Samuel in an audible voice:

And the Lord came, and stood and called as at other times, Samuel, Samuel. The Samuel answered, Speak: for thy servant heareth.(1 Samuel 3:10)

The Bible is full of the declaration "and God said" or references to the fact that God "spoke" or "commanded." Often this was an audible voice. But there is another voice through which

God speaks. . .

THE INNER VOICE OF THE HOLY SPIRIT

More often than an audible voice, God uses the inner voice of the Holy Spirit to speak to man. This is called being "led by the Spirit":

For as many as are led by the Spirit of God, they are the sons of God.(Romans 8:14)

To be "led by the Spirit" assumes a spiritual life in those being led. A soul dead in sin, with no spiritual life, cannot be led by the Holy

Spirit. Being led of the Spirit also assumes an inability to lead yourself. You have learned in previous chapters that this is true.

When you experience the new birth of salvation, God gives you a new spirit which is receptive to His communications:

A new heart also will I give you, and a new spirit will I put within you: and I will take away the stony heart out of your flesh, and I will give you an heart of flesh. And I will put my spirit within you. . . (Ezekiel 36:26-27)

When you are led by the Spirit, the will of God is revealed to your spirit by the Holy Spirit. One of the ministries of the Holy Spirit is guidance:

Howbeit when He, the Spirit of truth, is come, He will guide you into all truth: for He shall not speak of Himself, but whatsoever He shall hear, that shall He speak: and He will shew you things to come. (John 16:13)

The spirit of man is that "hidden man of the heart" mentioned by Peter (I Peter 3:4). When God speaks to the inner man He is speaking to your spirit. The writer of Proverbs said the spirit of man is the candle, or lamp, of the Lord:

The spirit of man is the candle of the Lord. . . (Proverbs 20:27)

In the natural world, a candle enables you to see in darkness. In the spiritual world, God uses the candle of your spirit to direct your steps to His will. He enlightens and guides through your spirit.

Fellowship With The Holy Spirit

Once during a journey by ship the Apostle Paul warned the captain of the vessel:

Sir, I perceive that this voyage will be with hurt and much damage, not only of the lading and ship, but also of our lives. (Acts 27:10)

Paul did not say "I had a vision." He did not claim to have a dream or that God had audibly spoken to him. His spirit had a witness from God and that witness proved to be correct.

You must train your spirit to be sensitive to God. Much time is spent on intellectual development through education. Much time is spent on physical development through exercise and athletics. But often, little time is spent on spiritual development. Your spirit can be educated just as your mind. Your spirit can develop in spiritual strength just as your body can be built and trained. You train your spirit by meditating on the Word of God:

This book of the law shall not depart out of thy mouth; but thou shalt meditate therein day and night, that thou mayest observe to do according to all that is written therein: for then thou shalt make thy way prosperous, and then thou shalt have good success. (Joshua 1:8)

God also uses the inward voice of the Holy Spirit to convict your conscience. The conscience is an inward awareness of right and wrong given by God.

Feeling is the voice of the body. God does not use how you feel to direct you. The flesh is an enemy of the spirit, so feelings can deceive you.

DR. ABRAHAM PETERS

Reason is the voice of the mind. God's ways are often beyond human reason. His thought processes are much higher than yours.

Conscience is the voice of the spirit of man, convicting and directing you to the perfect will of God. The Holy Spirit speaks to your spirit. The spirit convicts the conscience. Through this you are brought into conformity to the will of God. When the Holy Spirit speaks to your spirit, the conscience is convicted, but if you continue to ignore it, your conscience can become "seared." This means it becomes hardened to the conviction of the Holy Spirit:

. . . having their conscience seared with a hot iron. . . (1 Timothy 4:2)

The book of Proverbs contains many verses that indicate God controls inner thoughts and the conscience of man to guide him into His will:

The preparations of the heart in man, and the answer of the tongue, is from the Lord. (Proverbs 16:1)

A man's heart deviseth his way: but the Lord directeth his steps.(Proverbs 16:9)

The king's heart is in the hand of the Lord as the rivers of water: He turneth it whithersoever He will. (Proverbs 21:1)

GIFTS OF THE HOLY SPIRIT

Spiritual gifts are also used by God to speak to man. Spiritual gifts are special abilities given by the Holy Spirit. Several of these gifts enable you to receive communication from God. There is a gift of tongues through which God speaks to man in a language he does not know. Interpretation from God follows to translate the message. The prayer language of the Holy Spirit (other tongues) is also used by the Spirit to guide you to the will of God. When you do not know how to pray regarding God's will, pray in other tongues and. . .

. . . He that searcheth the hearts knoweth what is in the mind of the Spirit, because He maketh intercession for the saints according to the will of God. (Romans 8:27)

There is also the gift of prophecy which brings an immediate message from God to His people. There is a gift called discernment through which God communicates regarding the spirits operating in others. God also communicates through the gifts of wisdom and knowledge. These gifts provide divine insight about people and circumstances beyond what is known by the natural mind.

MISCELLANEOUS METHODS

Two other methods of Biblical guidance are casting of lots and the use of fleeces. We discussed both of these in previous chapters. As we learned, the casting of lots was a method of chance. It was used only prior to the giving of the Holy Spirit in a new dimension. Its use is never again recorded after the guiding ministry of the Holy Spirit became available (Acts 2). We learned that a fleece is only mentioned once in the Bible. It was used by Gideon at a time of great national crisis. It was a miraculous sign used for confirmation, not direction.

DR. ABRAHAM PETERS

GOD IS NOT LIMITED

God does not always speak in the same way. We try to limit God to a set pattern. Because God has spoken in a certain way one time, we believe He will always direct in the same way. But as we have learned in this chapter, God has many methods of communicating with man. God is not limited by a set pattern. Consider these examples:

MOSES:

When Moses was leading the nation of Israel across the dessert to the land God promised them, providing water for two million people was a major challenge. On one occasion God told Moses to strike a rock with his rod. When he did, water poured out of the rock. On another occasion when the Israelites were thirsty God wanted Moses to speak to the rock. Instead, Moses struck the rock as he had done previously. This was displeasing to God, and Moses was punished. This story illustrates the importance of waiting for guidance from God even when facing a familiar situation. God is not limited to any previous pattern which you have experienced.

You might think God was unjust to punish Moses for such a little thing as striking the rock instead of speaking to it. The rock held symbolic meaning. It represented the Lord Jesus Christ and the living water of redemption which would burst forth through His death. Jesus was stricken once and for all. There was no need for another striking. It was the importance of this symbolism that made the offense of Moses so great.

ELIJAH:

God used many supernatural methods to communicate to the Prophet Elijah. Once Elijah had a unique experience which illustrated the importance of knowing God's voice. Elijah was told to go and stand on a certain mountain and wait for God to speak to him. This is what happened:

And behold, the Lord passed by, and a great and strong wind rent the mountains, and brake in pieces the rocks before the Lord; but the Lord was not in the wind: and after the wind an earthquake; but the Lord was not in the earthquake: And after the earthquake a fire: but the Lord was not in the fire: and after the fire a still small voice. (1 Kings 19:11-12)

There were several supernatural events in this account. There was a wind, an earthquake, and fire. These were methods by which God had previously communicated with Elijah. But this time, God did not speak in all the glorious events that occurred. He spoke in a still small voice. This could have been either an audible voice or a silent voice in Elijah's spirit.

PAUL:

God used many ways to direct the Apostle Paul during his missionary ministry:

-On the Damascus road Paul was directed by a bright light and a voice from Heaven. Acts 9:1-8
-When a plot was formed to murder Paul, he was warned by believers who were used of God to help him escape. Acts 9:20-25

-Barnabas was used by God to establish relationships between Paul and the other disciples. Acts 9:20-28
-Believers were used of God to help Paul escape the angry Grecians. Acts 9:29-30
-When Paul met an occultist, God gave him discernment to bring deliverance. Acts 13:6-12
-Prayer and the Holy Spirit guided Paul into a special missionary ministry. Acts 13:2-4
-Personal prophecy by Agabus confirmed the experience that awaited Paul in Jerusalem. Acts 21:10-14
-God spoke to Paul through dreams and visions. Acts 22:18; 26:19; 27:23-24
-An effectual door of service for the Lord caused Paul to change his personal plans. 1 Corinthians 16:8-10

PHILIP:

And the angel of the Lord spake unto Philip, saying, Arise and go toward the south unto the way that goeth down from Jerusalem unto Gaza, which is desert. And he arose and went; and behold, a man of Ethiopia, an unich of great authority under Candace, queen of the Ethiopians, who had the charge of all her treasure, and had come to Jerusalem for to worship, was returning and sitting in his chariot reading Essaias the prophet. Then the spirit said unto Philip, Go near, and join thyself to this chariot. (Acts 8:26-29)

God spoke to Philip the first time through an angel. The second time He spoke through the Holy Spirit and Philip responded immediately. He did not wait for confirmation from an angel the second time God spoke just because that method had been used previously.

DAVID:

When David was a young man, he battled an enemy of God's people named Goliath. Although Goliath was a giant and well armed, God told David not to use traditional weapons of warfare. Instead, David used a sling shot. In a glorious victory, David brought down the enemy with one well-directed shot which struck him in the forehead. In later years David could have been slain by a giant named Isbibenob if his nephew Abishai had not come to his aid. Are we to conclude that God was with David when he met Goliath, but not when he confronted the second giant? No. God simply used a different method. The first time God used David's skill with a sling. The second time He used Abishai's military skill.

When God does not choose to speak to you as He has in the past, do not become frustrated. If His will for you in a similar situation is not identical to what it was previously, do not become confused. God is not restricted to certain communication patterns. The great Creator is also a great Communicator. His methods are unlimited.

1. Study the following Prayers for guidance:

   Psalms 25:4
   Colossians 1:9
   Psalms 86:11
   Colossians 4:12
   Ephesians 6:18-20

2. God communicates His will to man, but sometimes man is too hasty in making decisions. Study the following examples of men who acted too hastily, not allowing God opportunity

to communicate His will to them:

Moses slaying the Egyptian: Exodus 2

Joshua's league with the Gibeonites: Joshua 9

Abraham and Ishmael: Abraham did not wait for the promised heir: Genesis 16

3. Read the book of Acts. Make a list of the different ways God communicated with men in the early church.

CHAPTER TWENTY

THE BUSH STILL BURNS

Trust in the Lord with all thine heart; and lean not to thine own understanding. In all thy ways acknowledge Him and He shall direct thy paths. (Proverbs 3:5-6)

In the previous chapter we examined the Biblical record of God's communication with man in the past. But the question is, does God still speak to men today? The Apostle Paul summarized:

God, who at sundry times and in divers manners spake in time past unto the fathers by the prophets. Hath in these last days spoken unto us by His Son, who He hath appointed heir of all things, by whom also He made the worlds. (Hebrews 1:1-2)

God spoke in various ways in times past. He continued to speak to men in the time of Paul. Paul said the greatest message God ever communicated was through His Son, Jesus Christ.

TIMES PAST: THE BURNING BUSH

God communicated His message in Biblical times by many methods. One method He used is recorded in Exodus chapter 3:

Now Moses kept the flock of Jethro his father in law the priest of Midian: and he led the flock to the backside of the desert, and came to the mountain of God, even to Horeb. And the angel of the Lord appeared unto him in a flame of fire out of the midst of a bush: and he looked, and behold, the bush burned with fire and the bush was not consumed. And Moses said, I will now turn aside, and see this great sight, why the bush is not burnt. And when the Lord saw that he turned aside to see, God called unto him out of the midst of the bush and said, Moses, Moses. (Exodus 3:1-4)

From a burning bush which was not consumed, God to Moses called Moses to deliver the nation of Israel from Egyptian bondage. Yes, God definitely spoke to men in times past!

THE PRESENT TIME: THE BUSH STILL BURNS

But does God still speak to men today in such miraculous ways? Were these forms of communication limited to Old Testament times before the infilling of the Holy Spirit was given?

The bush still burns! You may not actually experience this specific form of guidance given Moses, but God still speaks to men in miraculous ways just as He did in Old Testament times.

In Hebrews 1:1-2 Paul pointed out that God continues to speak to the world through Jesus Christ. Not only does God speak through the written Word which records the life and teachings of Jesus, but Jesus promised:

Howbeit, when He, the Spirit of truth is come, He will guide you into all truth: for He shall not speak of Himself, but whatsoever He shall hear, that shall He speak: and He will shew you things to come. (John 16:13)

The Holy Spirit continues to speak by Jesus communicating God's message to man.

After the coming of the Holy Spirit in Acts 2, special revelations from God continued just as in Old Testament times. People dreamed dreams, saw visions, talked with angels, heard the audible voice of

God, and experienced other miraculous revelations from God.

Miraculous communication from God did not cease with the coming of the Holy Spirit. The Holy Spirit just added a new dimension of guidance. That dimension included inward direction, intercession according to the will God through the prayer language of other tongues, and special spiritual gifts through which God speaks.

The final book of the Bible, Revelation, is an extended record of a vision God gave to the Apostle John. Right up to the end of His written Word, God is speaking to man in miraculous ways.

God continues to speak to man through these methods. Modern church history contains many well documented instances of miraculous communications from God to man because. . .

Jesus Christ the same yesterday, and to day, and for ever. (Hebrews 13:8)

WHAT IF THERE IS NO BUSH?

But what happens if God does not choose to speak to you through a miraculous method. What if you do not experience a dream, vision or miracle? What if He does not speak to you through an audible voice or through supernatural gifts of prophecy, tongues, or interpretation? What if there is no burning bush?

Some people wait all their lives for a supernatural revelation from God. Multitudes of believers waste their lives, immobile and ineffective, waiting for some unusual or dramatic message from God.

The early church did not do this. They rejoiced when God chose to lead through miraculous methods, but in the many decisions of everyday life they were not guided by angels, dreams, and visions. Yet they moved ahead as a mighty force for God.

So, what do you do if there is no burning bush? Here are seven steps to finding God's will:

1. PRAY:

Pray for God's direction in your life. Jesus taught His followers that part of the regular pattern of prayer was to be for the will of God to be done:

Thy Kingdom come, Thy will be done in earth, as it is in Heaven. (Matthew 6:10)

When you pray, express your desire for God to reveal His will to you. Moses did this:

Now therefore, I pray thee, if I have found grace in thy sight, shew me now thy way, that I may know thee, that I may find grace in thy sight: and consider that this nation is thy people. (Exodus 33:13)

David did this:

Shew me thy ways, O Lord; teach me thy paths. (Psalms 25:4)

Ask for wisdom to make the right choices:

If any of you lack wisdom (in determining the will of God) let him ask of God, that giveth to all men liberally and upbraideth not; and it shall be given him. But let him ask in faith, nothing wavering. For he that wavereth is like a wave of the sea driven with the wind and tossed. For let not that man think that he shall receive anything of the Lord. (James 1:5-7)

Request the prayers of other believers. God often reveals His will through spiritual gifts exercised in group prayer meetings. Paul and Barnabas received confirmation of their calling to missionary service in such a gathering.

2. STUDY THE SCRIPTURES:

Earnestly search God's written Word to determine if specific guidance is given for your situation. Determine if there are general Biblical principles or biographical examples which apply.

Searching the Scriptures does not mean letting the Bible fall open and taking the first verse your eyes fall on as your answer. Searching the Scriptures is a detailed examination of the Word and application of its principles to the decisions you must make. Every open door, every opportunity, every other leading you think might be from the Lord should first be tested by the written Word of God. Jesus used this principle. When He was tempted by Satan to act apart from God's will he answered repeatedly "It is written. . ." (Matthew 4). He analyzed everything on the basis of God's written Word.

As you search the Scriptures, be sure to study the many promises for direction. We have listed some of these in the "For Further Study" section of this chapter. As you study these passages it will increase your faith that God does speak and that you can know His voice.

3.   LISTEN TO THE INNER VOICE OF THE HOLY SPIRIT:

Through prayer and study of the Scriptures, God speaks His will into your spirit by the inner voice of the Holy Spirit. We discussed this at length in the last chapter. Part of the "voice of the Holy Spirit" is the prayer language of other tongues. When you are not certain of God's will in a matter, pray in the prayer language of the Holy Spirit.

The Holy Spirit knows the perfect will of God and will pray through you in harmony with that will:

. . .He that searcheth the hearts knoweth what is in the mind of the spirit, because He maketh intercession for the saints according to the will of God. (Romans 8:27)

Remember--Jesus said that the Holy Spirit would "shew you things to come." This means He reveals God's plan to you. He guides you according to the will of God.

4.   SEEK CHRISTIAN COUNSEL:

As we mentioned in the last chapter, God uses Christian counselors to assist believers in the decision making process. The Bible states:

Where there is no counsel, the people fall; but in the multitude of counselors there is a safety. (Proverbs 11:14)

The way of a fool is right in his own eyes: but he that hearkeneth unto counsel is wise. (Proverbs 12:15)

It is important that believers seek counsel only from mature Christians. Never seek counsel from secular psychologists or psychiatrists. They will give worldly counsel. They are "blind leaders of the blind":

Woe unto you, ye blind guides. . . (Matthew 23:16)

Blessed is the man that walketh not in the counsel of the ungodly. . . (Psalms 1:1)

Never seek counsel from new Christians, as they lack experience and spiritual maturity.

Some people only go to a counselor hoping to get them to agree with their own opinions. You will receive little benefit from counseling if this is your attitude. Some believers consult many counselors comparing the counsel they receive. They appear to be taking a poll as to how many are in favor of one course of action as opposed to another. This is not the purpose of counseling. Most important, always remember that all counsel of man must agree with the written Word of God.

5.   ANALYZE THE CIRCUMSTANCES:

Analyze the circumstances relating to the decision you need to make. These should be considered in relation to the guidance God gives through prayer, study of the Word, the inner voice of the Spirit, and Christian counsel.

Circumstances should not be used alone to determine God's will, but they do define the context of the decision which is to be made. Sometimes circumstances limit choices or provide opportunity for new direction in life.

6.   USE THE BIBLICAL KEYS TO DIRECTION:

In the natural world, keys open doors. In the spiritual world, God has provided keys to open the door to His will. The keys are found in the book of Proverbs:

Trust in the Lord with all thine heart; and lean not unto thine own understanding. In all thy ways acknowledge Him, and He shall direct thy paths. (Proverbs 3:5-6)

The First Key: Trust.

Do not fear what God may ask of you. Know that His plan for you is best. Certainly, men should be able to trust one who would give His only Son to die for them. Your trust must be in the Lord and not in man:

Thus saith the Lord, Cursed by be the man that trusteth in man and maketh flesh his arm, and whose heart departeth from the Lord. (Jeremiah 17:5)

The Second Key: Lean Not To Your Own Understanding.

Do not depend on your own human reasoning. This does not mean there is no place for intelligent judgment. The book of Proverbs is filled with commands to use understanding and common sense. God is not saying you should abandon sound judgment. He is simply saying do not depend solely on human reasoning when you are seeking the will of God.

When David was returning the ark to Jerusalem, He did not ask God for direction. He leaned on his own understanding and started to move the ark in the most practical way possible.(2 Samuel 6:1-7). But this was not God's way and judgment fell. It was God's will to bring the ark back to Jerusalem, but David had not aligned God's will with His way. This is an important principle of guidance.

The Third Key: In All Thy Ways Acknowledge Him.

To acknowledge God in all ways is to honor Him in thought, word, and deed. Give Him first place in your life:

That in all things He might have the preeminence. (Colossians 1:18)

Joshua made a serious mistake when "he asked not counsel of the mouth of the Lord" concerning a treaty with the Gibeonites (Joshua 9). His decision resulted in an alliance with an ungodly nation, something which was forbidden by God.

The three keys. . .

-Trust in the Lord with all thine heart. . .
    -Lean not to thine own understanding. . .
    -In all thy ways acknowledge Him. . ..

These keys open the door. . ..And He shall direct thy paths.

7.   CHOOSE THE WAY OF WISDOM:

In decisions specifically dealt with in the written Word of God, you must always make a decision consistent with the revealed Word. In other decisions, after prayer, study of the Word, listening to the voice of the Spirit, seeking counsel, and analyzing the circumstances, you can make a choice according to "the way of wisdom." (Remember, you prayed for wisdom from God. Now you make a choice on the basis of that wisdom.)

The way of wisdom is the option in any decision which offers the greatest opportunity for spiritual advancement in every area of life. It is the option in harmony with what God has revealed through prayer, the written Word, the inner voice of the Holy Spirit, and Christian counsel.

Ability to recognize the way of wisdom increases through spiritual maturity:

For when for the time ye ought to be teachers, ye have need that one teach you again which be the first principles of the oracles of God: and are become such as have need of milk and not of strong meat. For every one that useth milk is unskillful in the word of righteousness; for he is a babe. But strong meat belongeth to them that are of full age, even those who by reason of use have their senses exercised to discern both good and evil. (Hebrews 5:12-14)

Spiritual maturity comes from relationship with God, prayer, and meditation in His written Word.

ASSURANCE OF THE WILL OF GOD

DR. ABRAHAM PETERS

And let the peace (soul harmony which comes) from the Christ rule (act as umpire continually) in your hearts-deciding and settling with finality all questions that arise in your minds- (in that peaceful state) to which (as members of Christ's) one body you were also called (to live). . .
(Colossians 3:15 The Amplified Version)

An umpire is a person responsible for reviewing a sports event to determine if the game is being playing according to the rules.

In the spiritual world, the peace of God is the umpire of the will of God. Your actions and decisions are reviewed. When they are in harmony with God's will, you will have peace in your spirit. When you are confused or frustrated, do not act. Wait until you receive peace concerning the decision you are making. Lack of peace is a signal from the umpire that something is wrong:

For God is not the author of confusion, but of peace. . . (1 Corinthians 14:33)

A STEP AT A TIME

One final important principle in the matter of God's will is to recognize God reveals His plan a step at a time. This means He does not reveal the entire plan for your life, with all the details, at one time. God does not just speak once in a lifetime to you. You cannot develop a relationship with someone on the basis of one conversation. Relationship is a continuing process of communication. God continues to speak, and you increase in your ability to recognize His voice.

God has reasons for revealing His will a step at a time. Often, you are not ready to know the whole plan because it might overwhelm you or cause feelings of inadequacy for the task ahead.
Jesus once said to His disciples:

I have many things to say unto you, but ye cannot bear them now. (John 16:12)

God told Israel that he would defeat their enemies in Canaan "little by little" as they were ready and able to assume responsibility for the new land He was giving them.

God also does not reveal His entire plan because we tend to worry over the future. The Bible warns:

Take therefore no thought for the morrow; for the morrow shall take thought for the things of itself. (Matthew 6:34)

Do not worry about the future. Make only the decisions necessary for today. The future is controlled by God. This does not mean you should not do wise planning for the future. But you are not to worry about it. What is important is to live in the revealed will of God for this day. Learn to hear His voice in your daily Christian walk. A daily walk in His will results in a life- long walk in His will.

God does not reveal His total plan because He wants you to learn to live by faith. It is easier to take the first step if one knows where the path is headed. It is not as easy to make a step of faith into the unknown.

The Bible states regarding Abraham:

DR. ABRAHAM PETERS

By faith, Abraham, when he was called to go out into a place which he should after receive for an inheritance obeyed; and he went out, not knowing whither he went. (Hebrews 11:8)

Nothing can build faith in God better that walking a step at a time. Taking a step at a time as God reveals it means you cannot move too hastily. Moses moved too quickly and killed an Egyptian. Abraham moved ahead of God's plan and tried to substitute Ishmael for the chosen heir.

The book of Esther stresses the importance of waiting on God. The people of God were in danger of being destroyed by an evil man named Haaman. He had asked the King to destroy all Jews.

Queen Esther was aware of the plot. She knew it was not God's will for the Jewish people to be destroyed, but she did not act in haste. She waited until God gave her a plan and then she waited an extra day before talking to the King. During that waiting period an important thing happened. The King discovered that Mordeacai, a Jew, had saved his life from a plot to murder him.

When this was made known, then Esther revealed Haaman's plot against the Jews. The king acted against Haaman's plan, the Jews were saved, and Haaman was punished for his evil, all because Esther waited one more day before acting.

THE BUSH STILL BURNS

In a spiritual sense, the bush still burns. God still guides us and desires to speak to us:

Call unto me, and I will answer thee, and shew thee great and mighty things, which thou knowest not. (Jeremiah 33:3)

God wants to reveal His will and communicate His plans. He continues to guide and direct. God is a still God who speaks if you will only listen. One of the greatest examples of guidance was God's leading the nation of Israel from Egypt to the promised land. You can read about this in the following passages:

>   Exodus 13:17, 18, 21: 15:13
>   Deuteronomy 8:2, 15; 29:5; 32:10;
>   1 Chronicles 11:2
>   2 Chronicles 25:11
>   2 Samuel 5:2
>   Nehemiah 9:12
>   Psalms 77:20; 78:14, 53; 80:1; 106:9; 107:7; 136:16
>   Isaiah 48:21; 63:12-14
>   Jeremiah 2:6, 17
>   Hebrews 8:9

Here is a simple pattern to follow when making a decision:
    Contradiction: Make sure there is no contradiction to God's Word in the decision you are making.
    Control: Control your emotions. Do not make decisions in anger, despondency, fear, etc. based on your mood at the moment.
    Counsel: Seek Godly counsel regarding the decision.

Circumstances: Analyze both positive and negative situations that relate to the decision. God often uses circumstances to direct your life.

Compulsion: Analyze your passions. Sometimes, God gives you a compelling desire to do something in order to direct you to His will. If it is from Him, it will always be in harmony with His Word.

Conscience: Check your inner warning system, your conscience, which is a God-given alarm that lets you know if you are heading the right direction.

Contentment: Be sure that you have the peace of the Holy Spirit which results when you make right decisions.

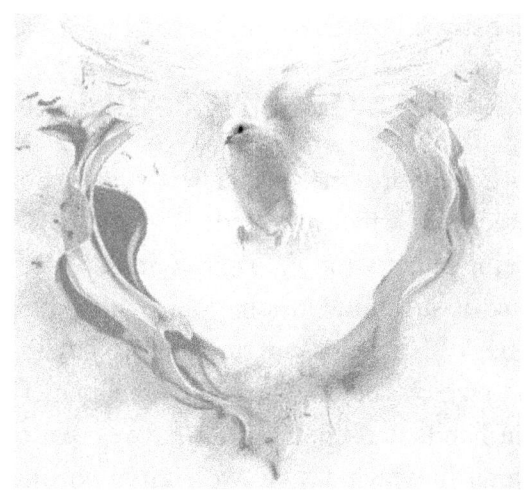

CHAPTER TWENTY ONE

AVOIDING QUESTIONABLE PRACTICES

Whether therefore ye eat, or drink, or whatsoever ye do, do all to the glory of God. (1 Corinthians 10:31)

This chapter concerns decision making about questionable practices. The term is defined and discussion includes guidelines for dealing with questionable practices, dealing with weaker brethren, handling disagreements between believers, and resolving offenses.

WHAT ARE SOME QUESTIONABLE PRACTICES

In every culture there are certain practices which are questionable. These are practices which are not specifically mentioned in Scripture as being either wrong or right for a follower of Jesus. You can easily think of such practices in your own culture. They might include activities of leisure or entertainment. They may be clubs or organizations to which you could choose to belong. These practices include certain habits and choices of what you eat or drink. They may be questions on which days to worship or holy days.

How do you determine the will of God regarding questionable practices when specific guidance on such matters is not given in the Bible? Ask yourself these questions:

DOES IT GLORIFY GOD?

Perhaps the most important principle by which to judge a questionable practice is to ask the question, "Does it glorify God?"

The Bible indicates all you do should glorify the Lord:

Whether therefore ye eat, or drink, or whatsoever ye do, do all to the glory of God. (1 Corinthians 10:31)

And whatsoever ye do in word or deed, do all in the name of the Lord Jesus, giving thanks to God and the Father by Him. (Colossians 3:17)

And whatsoever ye do, do it heartily, as to the Lord, and not unto men; Knowing that of the Lord ye shall receive the reward of the inheritance: for ye serve the Lord Christ. (Colossians 3:23-24)

WHAT IS YOUR MOTIVATION?

Why do you want to engage in this practice? What is your reason or motive for doing it? Even a good activity can be done with a wrong motive. For example, James gives an illustration of a wrong motive for prayer:

Ye ask, and receive not, because ye ask amiss, that ye may consume it upon your lusts. (James 4:3)

Praying is certainly not wrong but the motives for some requests are improper. The motivation described in this verse is the wish to fulfill lustful desires.

IS IT NECESSARY?

Paul states that while some things may be considered lawful (not in violation of God's written Word), you should consider whether they are really necessary. He states:

All things are lawful unto me, but all things are not expedient. . .

DR. ABRAHAM PETERS

(1 Corinthians 6:12)

WILL IT PROMOTE SPIRITUAL GROWTH?

Many activities can hinder spiritual growth. Other activities can become so time consuming that they choke out spiritual growth:

And these are they which are sown among thorns; such as hear the word.

And the cares of this world, and the deceitfulness of riches, and the lusts of other things entering in, choke the word, and it becometh unfruitful.
    (Mark 4:18-19)

And that which fell among thorns are they, which when they have heard, go forth, and are choked with cares and riches and pleasures of this life, and bring no fruit to perfection. (Luke 8:14)

Ask yourself: "Will this activity hinder or promote my spiritual development?"

Activities that hinder spiritual development become weights which interfere with the spiritual race God has set before you:

Wherefore seeing we also are compassed about with so great a cloud of witnesses, let us lay aside every weight and the sin which doth so easily beset us, and let us run with patience the race that is set before us. (Hebrews 12:1)

IS IT AN ENSLAVING HABIT?

When considering a questionable practice, ask yourself "Will this practice enslave me to a habit?" An enslaving habit is one which controls you. You feel you cannot get along without it and you have difficulty giving it up.

Paul comments regarding enslaving habits:

...All things are lawful unto me, but I will not be brought under the power of any. (1 Corinthians 6:12)

Any activity which is enslaving physically, mentally, spiritually, or habitually demands valuable time should be avoided.

IS IT A COMPROMISE?

Paul asks in 2 Corinthians 6:14, "... what communion hath light with darkness?"

Will the questionable practice you are considering be a spiritual compromise? Will you be engaging in activities of the world or accepting its standards by doing this thing? The Bible commands:

Wherefore come out from among them, and be ye separate, saith the Lord, and touch not the unclean thing; and I will receive you. (2 Corinthians 6:17)

WILL IT LEAD TO TEMPTATION?

Jesus taught us to pray "lead us not into temptation." It is useless to pray this prayer and then by means of a questionable activity deliberately place yourself in a place of temptation. The Bible warns:

Let no man say when he is tempted, I am tempted of God, for God cannot be tempted with evil, neither tempteth He any man; But every man is tempted when he is drawn away of his own lust and enticed. Then when lust hath conceived, it bringeth forth sin; and sin, when it is finished, bringeth forth death. (James 1:13-15)

Temptation is different from a trial of faith. A trial of faith occurs when a believer faces a difficult situation through no fault of his own. The situation tries his faith in God. God permits trials to strengthen your faith and bring spiritual maturity. But God does not tempt man. Temptation is the desire to do wrong. Temptation comes when you do not control your thoughts and actions properly or when Satan entices you to do evil. Some questionable practices may put you in situations of temptation. If you yield to the temptation, lust results in sin, and sin results in spiritual death.

DOES IT GIVE THE APPEARANCE OF EVIL?

Does the practice you are considering give an appearance of evil to others? The Bible commands:

Abstain from all appearance of evil. (1 Thessalonians 5:22)

DOES IT VIOLATE YOUR CONSCIENCE?

When making a decision regarding questionable practices, you should be fully persuaded the choice you make is right. In New

Testament times believers disagreed over whether or not it was right to eat meat since meat had been used for sacrifices under the Old Testament law. These sacrifices were used as atonement for man's sin before Jesus gave His life as the final and complete sacrifice for sin. Because meat was used for sacrifices there were laws against eating certain meats. Paul wrote regarding this question:

And he that doubteth is damned if he eat, because he eateth not of faith: for whatsoever is not of faith is sin. (Romans 14:23)

The principle is that you must be fully persuaded in questionable matters that what you are doing is right. If you have doubts, then it becomes sin for you to engage in such practices.

HOW WILL IT AFFECT OTHERS?

This leads to the final guideline in regards to questionable practices. How will engaging in this activity affect others? Will it edify others? To edify means to instruct, build up, or improve spiritually. The Bible states:

Let us therefore follow after the things which make for peace and things wherewith one may edify another. (Romans 14:19)

Does this activity contribute in a positive way to the spiritual development of others? Paul writes:

All things are not lawful for me, but all things are not expedient: all things are lawful for me, but all things edify not. (1 Corinthians 10:23)

DR. ABRAHAM PETERS

Some practices in which you might engage may cause other believers to be hindered in their spiritual walk. Again, speaking on the question of eating meat, Paul wrote:

Wherefore, if meat make my brother to offend, I will eat no flesh while the world standeth lest I make my brother to offend. (1 Corinthians 8:13)

Paul did not consider it wrong to eat meat. But he would not eat it if it hindered a weaker brother in the Lord. A weaker brother is a believer who, because of weakness of faith, knowledge, or conscience can be affected by the example of a stronger brother. He can be influenced to sin against his conscience and his spiritual progress can be hindered.

A stronger believer is one who, because of his understanding of freedom in certain areas and the strength of his conviction, exercises liberty with good conscience. He is not influenced by the differing opinions of others.

Any action by a stronger brother which ordinarily would be permissible is wrong if it influences a weaker brother to sin against his conscience or hinders his spiritual progress. Paul wrote:

It is good neither to eat flesh nor to drink wine nor any thing whereby thy brother stumbleth, or is offended, or is made weak. (Romans 14:21)

SUMMARY: DECISION MAKING ON QUESTIONABLE PRACTICES

The following chart summarizes Biblical guidelines for decision making on questionable practices:

Ask Yourself...	Biblical Reference
Does it glorify God?	1 Corinthians 10:31; Colossians 3:17,23
What is your motivation?	James 4:3
Is it necessary?	1 Corinthians 6:12
Will it promote spiritual growth?	Mark 4:18,19; Luke 8:14; Hebrews 12:1
Is it an enslaving habit?	1 Corinthians 6:12
Is it a compromise?	2 Corinthians 6:17
Will it lead to temptation?	James 1:13-15
Does it give the appearance of evil?	1 Thessalonians 5:22
Does it violate your conscience?	Romans 14:23
How will it affect others?	Romans 14:19,21; 1 Corinthians 8:13; 10:23

WHEN BELIEVERS DIFFER

Study Romans 14:1 through 15:2. These verses reveal believers will sometimes have differences in opinion. Such differences often arise over questionable practices not specifically dealt with in God's Word as being either right or wrong.

This passage explains that such differences will not result in harm if we love one another and continue to search the Scriptures. Romans

14 gives the following guidelines for dealing with disagreements between believers in matters not specifically covered in the written Word of God:

DISTINGUISH BETWEEN MATTERS OF COMMAND AND FREEDOM:

Romans 14:14 indicates that when believers differ it is important to distinguish between matters of command and freedom. Concerning matters of freedom not specifically dealt with in God's Word, Paul writes:

I know, and am persuaded by the Lord Jesus, that there is nothing unclean of itself: but to him that esteemeth any thing to be unclean, to him it is unclean. (Romans 14:14)

In matters of command recorded in the written Word of God, we should all conform to the same pattern. In other matters, freedom of choice may be exercised.

CULTIVATE YOUR OWN CONVICTIONS:

You must cultivate your own convictions regarding questionable practices. In regards to observing holy days Paul wrote:

One man esteemeth one day above another; another esteemeth every day alike. Let every man be fully persuaded in his own mind. (Romans 14:5)

Use the guidelines given in the previous section of this chapter to help you determine your own convictions on questionable matters.

ALLOW OTHERS FREEDOM TO DETERMINE THEIR CONVICTIONS:

Even if others differ from you, allow them freedom to determine their own convictions on questionable matters:

But why dost thou judge thy brother? Or why dost thou set at nought thy brother. . .Let us not therefore judge one another any more. . .(Romans 14:10 and 13)

LIMIT LIBERTY BY LOVE:

The basic message of Romans 14:13-15:2 is that Christian liberty should be limited by love:

Let every one of us please his neighbor for his good to edification.(Romans 15:2)

You should care for other believers so much that you limit your own behavior by love for them. You should love them so much that you will not do anything that would cause them to stumble spiritually:

. . .but judge this rather, that no man put a stumbling block or an occasion to fall in his brother's way. (Romans 14:13)

RESOLVE ALL OFFENSES:

When a brother has been offended by another believer, Matthew 18:15-17 provides the Biblical
formula for resolving such offenses:

DR. ABRAHAM PETERS

Moreover if thy brother shall trespass against thee, go and tell him his fault between thee and him alone: If he shall hear thee, thou hast gained thy brother. But if he will not hear thee, then take with thee one or two more, that in the mouth of two or three witnesses every word may be established. And if he shall neglect to hear them, tell it unto the church; but if he neglect to hear the church, let him be unto thee as an heathen man and a publican. (Matthew 18:15-17)

The steps to follow when a brother has offended you are:

1. Go to him privately to resolve the matter. Do not talk about the offense to others. Go directly to the one who offended you and try to resolve the matter. Pray and search God's written Word together.

2. If he will not listen to you, take one or two witnesses and try again. The witnesses should be impartial believers. Elders or leaders in the church would be a good choice. Take the witnesses and go to your brother and again attempt to discuss, pray, and search the Scriptures together regarding the problem.

3. Take the matter before the entire church body. If, after going to your brother with a witness he still refuses to resolve the matter, take the issue before the entire church body. This should be done at the proper time. It should not be done during a regular worship service or when unbelievers are present. After hearing the matter, the decision of the church should be abided by and the problem should be resolved. If not, then the offending party is acting like the heathen and

unbelievers.

SUMMARY: WHEN BELIEVERS DIFFER

The following chart summarizes Scriptural guidelines to follow when believers differ in regards to questionable practices:

When Believers Differ
Romans 14-15:2 and Matthew 18:15-17

Distinguish between matters of command and freedom.
Cultivate your own convictions.
Allow others freedom to determine their own convictions.
Limit liberty by love.
Resolve all offenses.

Prayerfully examine your own life. Make a list of questionable practices in which you are currently engaging or considering.

Examine each of these in terms of the Biblical guidelines given in this chapter which are summarized on the following chart:

DECISION MAKING ON QUESTIONABLE PRACTICES

Ask Yourself...	Biblical Reference
Does it glorify God?	1 Corinthians 10:31; Colossians 3:17,23
What is your motivation?	James 4:3
Is it necessary?	1 Corinthians 6:12
Will it promote spiritual growth?	Mark 4:18,19; Luke

DR. ABRAHAM PETERS

8:14; Hebrews 12:1	
Is it an enslaving habit?	1 Corinthians 6:12
Is it a compromise?	2 Corinthians 6:17
Will it lead to temptation?	James 1:13-15
Does it give the appearance of evil?	1 Thessalonians 5:22
Does it violate your conscience?	Romans 14:23
How will it affect others?	Romans 14:19,21; 1

CHAPTER TWENTY TWO

A BIBLICAL MODEL FOR DECISION MAKING

DR. ABRAHAM PETERS

A man's heart deviseth his way; but the Lord directeth his steps.(Proverbs 16:9)

This chapter presents a Biblical model for decision making. A model is an example of something. Its purpose is to provide an example for you to follow. A decision is a choice. You must determine an answer for a real life situation and choose what action you will take. This is called decision making. A model for decision making provides an example to follow when making decisions. Life is an endless succession of choices and decisions. Making choices is a responsibility. Constantly refusing to make a decision is in itself a decision.

The Biblical model presented in this chapter will help you make wise choices within the will of God:

A man's heart deviseth his way; but the Lord directeth his steps.(Proverbs 16:9)

THE MODEL

Study the Biblical model for decision making on the following page. The chart summarizes what you have learned in previous chapters. Then proceed on to discussion of the model in the remainder of this chapter.

Identify the problem, question, or life situation for which guidance is sought.

Is it dealt with in Scripture by specific command, general principle or example?

The first step in the decision making model is to identify the problem, question, or life situation for which guidance is sought. Next, search the written Word of God to see if the problem is dealt with by commandment, example, or general principle.

YES:

If the answer is "Yes, it is dealt with in the written Word of God," then make the decision based upon this written revelation. Make sure your decision is in harmony with the Scriptures.

NO:

If the answer is "no," then proceed on with the decision making model. Here you will find two choices for situations not dealt with in the Bible. You must determine whether the decision to be made involves a questionable practice or a real life situation.

QUESTIONABLE PRACTICES:

A questionable practice is something not dealt with in Scripture as either right or wrong. It can involve a choice of entertainment or leisure activities, a habit, permissible food or drinks, style of dress, or day on which to worship.

If the decision with which you are faced involves a questionable practice, ask yourself the questions. These are Biblical principles for guidance in questionable situations. Answer each of these questions and pray, then make your decision on the basis of your answers to the questions on the model.

DR. ABRAHAM PETERS

LIFE SITUATIONS:

A life situation can include, but is not limited to, decisions regarding marriage, ministry, occupation, residence, choice of churches, etc. It is a choice which can affect your future life in a major way.

For decisions on life issues, First pray about the decision. Ask God for His will to be accomplished in your life. Ask Him for wisdom to make the right decision. Praise Him for guidance to make the right decision. Ask others to pray with you. Study the Scriptures and as you study claim the promises for direction given in the written Word of God.

Listen to the inner voice of the Holy Spirit as He speaks God's will into your heart. Acknowledge supernatural revelation, should God choose to send it. These might include dreams, visions, angels, an audible voice from God, or other special forms of guidance in harmony with God's Word.

Seek Christian counsel. Analyze the circumstances affecting the decision. Use the Biblical keys for direction you learned in the last chapter. (These are found in Proverbs 3:5-6). On the basis of agreement of these methods, make a decision.

THE UMPIRE OF PEACE

On decisions not specifically dealt with by Biblical command, principle, or example, the umpire of peace is your guide. When you make a decision on a questionable practice or life situation and you do not have peace in your spirit, continue to seek the Lord using the steps on the model. Do not make a final decision until you have the peace of God confirming your choice.

Never be in a hurry:

Wait on the Lord; be of good courage, and He shall strengthen thine heart: wait, I say, on the Lord. (Psalms 27:14)

My soul, wait thou only upon God; for my expectation is from him. (Psalms 62:5)

Rest in the Lord, and wait patiently for Him . . . (Psalms 37:7)

But they that wait upon the Lord shall renew their strength; they shall mount up with wings as eagles; they shall run, and not be weary; and they shall walk, and not faint. (Isaiah 40:31)

Saul was in a hurry and made a decision which cost him the kingdom. You can read about it in 1 Samuel 13. Nehemiah waited for direction from God and the right timing, and he became part of the rebuilding of a kingdom. You can read his story in the book of Nehemiah. Use the Biblical model presented in this chapter to help you make a decision about a problem, question, or life situation for which you need guidance.

TRIED AND FAILED?

Oh, that my people had hearkened unto me and Israel had walked in my ways. (Psalms 81:13)

In this book you learned many ways God speaks to man to

communicate His will. But what happens when you fail to discern the will of God? Perhaps you deliberately disobey His voice. Perhaps you miss His direction through error or misunderstanding of Biblical principles. Maybe you act too quickly without His guidance. What should you do when you have tried and failed?

FAILURES WHO WERE SUCCESSES

The Bible contains many examples of great leaders who at some point in their lives failed to listen to the voice of God and missed His will. Yet, these men who failed became great successes:

Abraham: He lied about Sarah being his wife for fear he would be killed and his wife taken from him. Yet he is called a man of faith and the friend of God.

Moses: He struck the rock and called forth water instead of speaking to it as God directed. Yet the Bible states there has never been another prophet as great as Moses.

David: He committed adultery with another man's wife, then had the man killed to try to cover his sin. Yet he was a great king and is called a man after God's own heart.

Jonah: This preacher went the opposite direction when God called him to preach in Ninevah. Later he preached the greatest revival in history. The whole city repented.

Peter: He denied Jesus, but later became a great leader in the early church.

FAILURES WHO WERE FAILURES

The Bible also contains many examples of men who missed the will of God and their lives ended in failure and defeat:

Samson: He was an important judge in the nation of Israel and had great physical strength given him from God. He began to deliver Israel from the Philistine enemy. But through involvement with a heathen woman, Samson was taken captive and died while yet a prisoner of the enemy.

Uziah: This king originally did what was right in the sight of the Lord and God made him prosper. But Uziah sinned by entering the temple and performing duties which only the priests were permitted to do. He was stricken with leprosy and died.

Saul: The first king of Israel, Saul was a man adored by the people and upon whom the Spirit of God rested. Because of disobedience, Saul was rejected by God and another king was selected to complete his task. Saul's life ended in failure, disgrace, and suicide.

Eli: Originally a great priest in the house of the Lord, Eli and his sons died in disgrace because of disobedience.

Judas: Judas was a disciple of Jesus during His earthly ministry. He witnessed the great miracles of Jesus and heard His teachings. Yet he betrayed Jesus and ended his own life by suicide.

WHAT MADE THE DIFFERENCE?

I have listed several Biblical examples of men who at some point in their lives failed to discern God's will. Some of these men recovered from failure and went on to be great men of God. Others never reversed their direction. Their lives ended in failure. What made the difference?

To answer this question, let us examine in more detail the lives of two kings of Israel, David and Saul. First, read the story of David's departure from God's will in 2 Samuel chapters 11-12. Then read the story of Saul's failure in I Samuel chapter 15. David's failure appears so much greater than that of Saul. Saul simply brought back some oxen as spoil from battle when God had told him not to do so.

David committed adultery with another man's wife. When she became pregnant he had her husband killed to try to cover the sin. Saul was rejected by God as king, yet David remained on the throne and was called a man after God's own heart. Why did one man's life end in failure while the other went on to future successes?

When the prophet Samuel confronted Saul with his sin, Saul said. . .

. . .I have sinned: for I have transgressed the commandment of the Lord, and thy words: because I feared the people, and obeyed their voice.

Then he said, I have sinned; yet honor me now, I pray thee, before the elders of my people and before Israel, and turn again with me, that I worship the Lord thy God. (1 Samuel 15:24 and 30)

Saul was caught in his sin and he admitted it. He was sorry, but only for being caught. Being sorry for sin is not enough. Sorrow must lead to repentance:

For godly sorrow worketh repentance to salvation not to be repented of: but the sorrow of the world worketh death. (2 Corinthians 7:10)

Saul admitted he failed, but he blamed his failure on other people. He wanted Samuel to honor him before the leaders so he would not be disgraced. He wanted Samuel to worship God with him to show people he was still a spiritual man.

Saul never confessed his sin to God, repented, and asked forgiveness. He refused to accept personal responsibility for his actions. He offered God worship when God wanted repentance. Saul was more concerned about his reputation among the people than his relationship to God. Because of this, Samuel told Saul:

...The Lord hath rent the kingdom of Israel from thee this day, and hath given it to a neighbor of thine, that is better than thou. (1 Samuel 15:28)

The kingdom was taken from Saul and given to David.

When the prophet Nathan confronted David about his sin, David immediately acknowledged:

I have sinned against the Lord. (2 Samuel 12:13)

He did not try to blame others. He did not blame Bathsheba. He admitted his failure and humbly repented before God. David's great prayer of repentance is recorded in Psalms 51.Read this entire Psalm in your Bible. David acknowledged his sin and asked forgiveness:

For I acknowledge my transgressions: and my sin is ever before me.

Against thee, thee only have I sinned and done this evil in thy sight. . .

Create in me a clean heart O God; and renew a right spirit within me. (Portions of Psalms 51)

Both Saul and David made wrong choices. When confronted with his error, David repented and changed direction. Saul did not. He strayed farther from the will of God and his life ended in failure, defeat, and suicide.

TRIED AND FAILED?

When you have missed the will of God, there are Biblical guidelines which will enable you to return to the will of the Lord. To illustrate these guidelines we will use the example of Jonah. Read the book of Jonah in your Bible before proceeding with this lesson.

Jonah was commanded by the Lord to go and preach repentance to the sinful nation of Ninevah. Instead of obeying God, he headed the opposite direction. Jonah took the following steps to return to the will of God. These are steps to take when you experience failure:

REALIZE YOUR FAILURE:

It took a great storm at sea to convince Jonah he was out of the will of God. (Jonah 1:2) Be assured: God has ways of letting you know when you have missed His will!

As long as you fail to realize you have missed the will of God, you can never get back into His will. Do not let any excuse prevent you from admitting failure. Here are some common ones:

> "People will lose confidence in me."
> "If I admit failure it is admitting I was wrong."
> "I already failed. I might as well give up."
> "It is too late."
> "I am a bad example, so I should just quit."
> "I am too far out of the will of God to ever get things right."
> "I don't know if I can even find the will of God again."

REPENT OF YOUR SIN:

Jonah's great prayer of repentance is recorded in Jonah chapter 2. Jonah acknowledged his sin before God, repented, and asked forgiveness. When you miss the will of God, come before the Lord in repentance and ask God to forgive you. Be sure to forgive yourself, too! It is not necessary to repent publicly unless it has affected the lives of others and you need to ask their forgiveness. It is necessary to repent before God.

RECOGNIZE THE DEPARTURE POINT:

Through prayer, the written Word of God, and the guidance of the Holy Spirit, determine the point at which you missed God's will. In the case of Jonah, he recognized his departure from the will of God began when he went the opposite direction from Ninevah.

DR. ABRAHAM PETERS

RETURN TO CORRECT THE ERROR:

Return to the point of departure and correct the error, if possible. When Jonah recognized his failure began by heading the opposite direction from Ninevah, he reversed directions. He went to Ninevah. He corrected his error (Jonah 3:3).

Sometimes you can do nothing to correct an error except repent. In the example of David which we discussed, he could do nothing about his sin with Bathsheba after it was committed. The mistake was already made. There was nothing he could do to correct it except repent. In situations where you can take corrective action, however, it should be done.

REVELATION. . .SEEK GOD FOR AND ACT UPON NEW DIRECTION:

After you admit your failure, ask forgiveness, determine the point of departure, and correct any errors possible, seek the Lord for new direction. Remove any hindrances to hearing the voice of God. These might include sins of rebellion, self-will, and wrong attitudes. Continue to train your spiritual ear to hear God's voice by praying and studying His written Word. As Jonah sought God for new direction, the Lord spoke unto him a second time and said, "Arise, and go to Ninevah" (Jonah 3:1-2). This time, Jonah obeyed the voice of the Lord. He went to Ninevah and preached the message of God. He experienced the greatest revival in history. The whole city repented (Jonah chapter 3).

The Bible contains many stories of men like Jonah. These men failed but admitted their failure and asked forgiveness. When they did, God always forgave them and provided new direction. He will do the same for you! God is not looking at your past record. He is not looking at you as you are. He is seeing the man or woman you can be if you walk in obedience to the voice of God.

The following chart summarizes Biblical guidelines to follow when you miss the will of God:

WHEN YOU MISS GOD'S WILL

Recognize Your Failure

Repent Of Your Sin

Recognize The Departure Point

Return To Correct The Error

Revelation: Seek God For And Act Upon New Direction

In Luke 15:11-32 Jesus told the story of a young man who left his father and went to live in a strange country. Study this story carefully, especially the portion which tells of the son's return to the house of his father. You will discover he followed the guidelines for correcting failure which were discussed in this chapter.

Study the following examples of men who at some point in their lives missed the will of God.

DR. ABRAHAM PETERS

Which ones corrected their failures? How did they turn their failures into success? Which ones did not correct their failures? What was the result?

Abraham:	Genesis 20-21
Moses:	Exodus; see also Acts 7:20-44
Balaam:	Numbers 22
Uziah:	2 Chronicles 26
Samson:	Judges 13-16
David:	2 Samuel 11-12; Psalms 51.
Saul:	1 Samuel 8-15
Jonah:	The book of Jonah
Peter:	Matthew, Mark, Luke, John, Acts
John Mark:	Acts 12:12, 25; 15:39; 2 Timothy 4:11

You can add other examples to this list from your own study of God's Word.

Jesus told two important parables about the will of God. Study Luke 12:42-48 and Matthew 21:28-32 and summarize what you learn.

CHAPTER TWENTY THREE

GOD'S WILL AND SUFFERING

DR. ABRAHAM PETERS

Wherefore let them that suffer according to the will of God, commit the keeping of their souls to Him in well doing as unto a faithful creator. (1 Peter 4:19)

You heard the voice of God. You sought guidance, it was given, and you set off along the road of life which God seemed to indicate. But as a result of this decision you are experiencing problems which would not have arisen apart from this new path of "God's will" on which you travel. Did you really hear the voice of God or have you made a mistake? Are these difficult experiences a sign from God that you are not living in His will? Does God permit suffering to come to someone who is living righteously within the will of God?

When Jesus was here on earth and spoke of the suffering He was to face on the cross, many of His followers deserted Him (John 6:55-66). They expected the Messiah to reign in power and glory. Instead, He spoke of suffering. They could not understand, so they turned away. If you do not understand suffering as it relates to the will of God, then you too may turn from following Jesus when you face difficult circumstances. God did not create suffering. It originally entered the world through man's sin (Genesis 3).But God can take that which is intended for evil and use it for good to accomplish His purposes.

THE REASONS FOR SUFFERING

The Bible has much to say concerning suffering, problems, and afflictions. In summarizing its teaching, we discover five ways suffering can come into the life of a believer:

OTHERS AROUND YOU:

Suffering may come through others around you. Joseph is an example of this type of suffering. Through no fault of his own, Joseph was sold into Egypt by his brothers, imprisoned falsely by Potiphar's wife, and forgotten by those he helped in prison.

But listen to his response. Joseph said...

Now therefore be not grieved, nor angry with yourselves, that ye sold me hither; for God did send me before you to preserve life...so now it was not you that sent me hither but God. (Genesis 45:5,7)

CIRCUMSTANCES OF LIFE:

The second way suffering comes is through the circumstances of life. This is illustrated by the example of Naomi, recorded in the book of Ruth in the Bible, who experienced the death of her husband and sons. Until Jesus returns and the final enemy of death is conquered, death is part of life. Death entered through the original sin of man and it is a natural circumstance which we all will face, because "it is appointed unto man once to die" (Hebrews 9:27).

YOUR MINISTRY:

The third reason for suffering is because of your ministry for the Lord. The New Testament speaks of suffering for His name's sake (Acts 9:16), in behalf of Christ, (Philippians 1:29) for the Kingdom of God (2 Thessalonians 1:5), for the Gospel (2 Timothy 1:11-12), for well-doing (1 Peter 2:19-20; 3:17), for righteousness sake (1 Peter 3:14), as a Christian (1 Peter 4:15-16), and according to the will of God (1 Peter 4:19).

The Apostle Paul is an example of suffering resulting from ministry. Some people view suffering as a sign of failure or lack of faith. If this is true, then the Apostle Paul had no faith and was the greatest failure in the history of the church. Paul said that while in Asia he was so utterly crushed that he despaired of life itself (2 Corinthians 1:8). He presents a different image than that of the cheerful evangelist who promises believers nothing but peace and prosperity. When Paul was first called of God to ministry he was told of "great things" he would suffer for the sake of the Lord.(Acts 9:16).

Paul's response to suffering was to endure "the loss of all things to win some for Christ." He wrote to believers "to you it is given not only to believe, but to suffer for Him" (Philippians 1:29).

Paul was not alone in suffering for the ministry. The whole church suffered in New Testament times (Acts 8). Hebrews chapter 11 records the stories some of the cruel persecutions they endured. Many of these men and women of faith were delivered by the power of God. Prison doors were opened and they walked out. They were sentenced to death in fiery furnaces but emerged unaffected by the flames. But some of these believers, who are also called men and women of faith, did not receive deliverance. They were imprisoned, afflicted, tormented, and even martyred because of their testimony of the Gospel (Hebrews 11:36-40). We focus on living faith but God also reveals His power in dying faith. This is a faith that stands true in the bad times, not just in good times when mighty deliverances are manifested.

DIRECT SATANIC ACTIVITY:

Suffering can also enter your life as a result of direct Satanic activity. This is evident in the story of Job. This book wrestles with the question, "Why do the righteous suffer?" God's testimony of Job was that he was a righteous man (Job 1-2). Job did not suffer because he sinned, as his friends claimed. They believed if Job repented, his circumstances would change. These friends tried to make a universal application based on individual experience. It would be similar to saying that because God delivered Peter from prison He will do the same for you. This is not true. Many have been martyred in prison despite their great faith and sinless lives.

We must be careful when we view the suffering of others that we do not accuse them of sin, faithlessness, or unbelief. The Bible does teach that a sinful man reaps a bitter harvest because of sowing in fleshly corruption (Galatians 6:8). But sowing and reaping cannot be used to explain the suffering of the innocent.

Job did not suffer because of anything he did. He was a righteous man. This was God's testimony of Job, Job's testimony of himself, and his reputation before man. Behind the scenes in the spiritual world was the true cause of Job's suffering. There was a spiritual battle going on over the heart, mind, and allegiance of Job.

There is warfare going on in the spiritual world over you. That warfare is manifested in the difficult circumstances you experience in the natural world. An important truth evident in Job's suffering is that nothing can enter the life of a believer without the knowledge of God. God does not cause your suffering. It is inflicted by Satan, but its limits are set by God.

DR. ABRAHAM PETERS

YOUR OWN SIN:

The fifth way suffering enters your life is because of your own sin. Jonah is an example of such suffering. In disobedience to God, Jonah headed the opposite direction from Ninevah where he was told to go and preach repentance. He experienced a terrible storm at sea and ended up in the belly of a great fish because of his own sin (Jonah 1-2).

Trouble should always be treated as a call to consider your ways and examine your heart before God. Like Jonah, you may be suffering because of your own sin. The Bible reveals that God chastises those who live in disobedience to His Word. Chastise means to discipline, reprove, and correct:

Now no chastening for the present seemeth to be joyous, but grievous: nevertheless afterward it yieldeth the peaceable fruit of righteousness unto them which are exercised thereby. (Hebrews 12:11)

God uses suffering to correct you and bring you back to His will for your life:

Before I was afflicted I went astray; but now have I kept thy Word.
. .

It is good for me that I have been afflicted; that I might learn thy statutes.

I know, O Lord, that thy judgments are right, and that THOU in faithfulness hast afflicted me. (Psalms 119:67,71,75)

THE PROPER ATTITUDE TOWARDS SUFFERING

But trouble is not necessarily a sign of being out of God's will. The Bible declares that "many are the afflictions of the righteous" (Psalms 34:19). When you suffer innocently and not because of your own sin, you should maintain a proper attitude towards suffering. The real test of your spirituality is how you respond in the day of distress:

If thou faint in the day of adversity, thy strength is small. (Proverbs 24:10)

The Bible describes the attitude you should have when you suffer as a believer within the will of God. You should not be ashamed:

If any man suffer as a Christian let him not be ashamed, but let him glorify God on this behalf. . .(1 Peter 4:16)

You should commit your soul (your suffering) to God, knowing He works all things for your good:

Wherefore let them that suffer according to the will of God commit the keeping of their souls to Him in well doing as unto a faithful Creator.
(1 Peter 4:19)

You should be happy when you suffer according to the will of God:

DR. ABRAHAM PETERS

And they departed from the presence of the council, rejoicing that they were counted worthy to suffer shame for His name. (Acts 5:41)

Paul says you should be:

Rejoicing in hope; patient in tribulation; continuing instant in prayer. (Romans 12:12)

...being reviled, we bless; being persecuted, we suffer it... (1 Corinthians 4:12)

...in all things approving ourselves as the ministers of God, in much patience, in afflictions, in necessities, in distresses... (2 Corinthians 6:4)

... be thou partaker of the afflictions of the gospel according to the power of God. (2 Timothy 1:8)

That no man should be moved by these afflictions: for yourselves know that we are appointed thereunto. (1 Thessalonians 3:3)

But watch thou in all things, endure afflictions, do the work of an evangelist, make full proof of thy ministry. (2 Timothy 4:5)

You should not think it strange when you experience suffering:

Beloved, think it not strange concerning the fiery trial which is to try you, as though some strange thing happened unto you; but rejoice, inasmuch as ye are partaker of Christ's sufferings; that when His glory shall be revealed ye may be glad with exceeding joy. (1 Peter 4:12-13)

You are to endure hardness like a soldier:

Thou therefore endure hardness as a good soldier of Jesus Christ. (2 Timothy 2:3)

Paul summarizes the proper attitude toward suffering in 2 Corinthians 4:9:

...though our outward man perish, yet the inward man is renewed day by day.

For our light affliction, which is but for a moment, worketh for us a far more exceeding and eternal weight of glory:

While we look not at the things which are seen, but at the things which are not seen: for the things which are seen are temporal; but the things which are not seen are eternal... (2 Corinthians 4:16-18)

Paul viewed suffering as a servant. He said it works for us when we keep our eyes on its eternal benefits instead of the problem.

POSITIVE BENEFITS OF SUFFERING

Here are some positive benefits of suffering according to God's will:

YOUR FAITH IS TESTED:

Everything in the spiritual world is based on faith. This is why the strength of your faith must be tested:

DR. ABRAHAM PETERS

That the trial of your faith being much more precious than of gold that perisheth though it be tried with fire, might be found unto praise and honour and glory at the appearing of Jesus Christ. (1 Peter 1:7)

It is a trial of faith when you pray as Jesus did, for God to let the cup of bitterness pass, and yet it does not pass. Instead, you are forced to drink deeply of its suffering. But faith will learn that our prayers are not unanswered just because they are not answered the way we want.

YOU ARE ABLE TO COMFORT OTHERS:

Blessed be God, even the Father of our Lord Jesus Christ, the Father of mercies, and the God of all comfort;

Who comforteth us in all our tribulation that we may be able to comfort them which are in any trouble, by the comfort wherewith we ourselves are comforted of God. (2 Corinthians 1:3-4)

When you share God's comfort with others you. . .

. . . Lift up the hands which hang down, and the feeble knees;

And make straight paths for your feet, lest that which is lame be turned out of the way; but let it rather be healed. (Hebrews 12:12-13)

YOU LEARN NOT TO TRUST YOUR OWN SELF:

Paul spoke of the purpose of his sufferings in Asia:

Fellowship With The Holy Spirit

. . .In Asia we were pressed out of measure, above strength, insomuch that we despaired even of life;

But we had the sentence of death in ourselves, that we should not trust in ourselves but in God which raiseth the dead. (2 Corinthians 1:8-9)

You will come to recognize that. . .

. . . We have this treasure in earthen vessels, that the excellency of the power may be of God, and not of us. (2 Corinthians 4:7)

POSITIVE QUALITIES ARE DEVELOPED:

We glory in tribulations, knowing that tribulation worketh patience, and patience experience, and experience hope, (resulting in the love of God being shed abroad in our hearts). (Romans 5:3-4)

. . . after ye have suffered awhile, make you perfect, stablish, strengthen, settle you. (1 Peter 5:10)

These qualities conform you to the image of Jesus, which is God's plan for you (Romans 8:28-29; Hebrews 2:10,18).

THE WORKS OF GOD ARE MANIFESTED:

When the disciples saw a man who had been blind from birth, they asked who was responsible for his condition. Was it the sin of his parents or of the man himself? Jesus answered:

Neither this man sinned nor His parents; but that the works of God should be made manifest in Him. (John 9:3)

THE POWER OF GOD IS PERFECTED:

And He said unto me, My grace is sufficient for thee; for my strength is made perfect in weakness. Most gladly therefore will I rather glory in my infirmities, that the power of Christ may rest upon me. (2 Corinthians 12:9)

THAT WHICH IS UNSTABLE IS REMOVED:

Suffering results in all that is unstable being shaken out of your life. You cease to depend on people, programs, or material things because these all fail in your time of need.

God permits this. . .

. . .removing of those things that are shaken as of things that are made, that those things which cannot be shaken may remain.(Hebrews 12:26-27)

During the storms of life, everything crumbles that is not built upon God and His Word (Psalm 119:89 and Matthew 7:24-27).

YOUR FOCUS IS CHANGED:

When you experience suffering you often focus your attention on cause and effect. You are concerned with what caused the difficult circumstances and the terrible effect it is having in your life. God wants to change your focus from the temporal to the eternal:

For our light affliction, which is but for a moment, worketh for us a far more exceeding and eternal weight of glory; While we look not at the things which are seen, but at the things which are not seen; for the things which are seen are temporal; but the things which are not seen are eternal.(2 Corin 4:17-18)

Beloved, think it not strange concerning the fiery trial which is to try you, as though some strange thing happened unto you: But rejoice, inasmuch as ye are partakers of Christ's sufferings; that, when His glory shall be revealed, ye may be glad also with exceeding joy.(1 Peter 4:12-13)

If we suffer, we shall also reign with Him. . . (2 Timothy 2:12)

THE OLD SELF-NATURE IS CHANGED:

God said of the nation of Moab:

Moab hath been at ease from his youth, and he hath settled on his lees, and hath not been emptied from vessel to vessel, neither hath he gone into captivity; therefore his taste remained in him, and his scent is not changed.(Jeremiah 48:11)

Because Moab had not experienced the troublesome pouring out and stirring similar to that necessary to develop good wine, the nation did not change. Because Moab was at ease and settled in prosperity the nation did not develop and mature spiritually. Therefore there was no change. His own scent remained in him.

Suffering rids you of the old self-nature. As you are stirred, troubled, and poured out, your spiritual scent changes from carnal to spiritual.

GOD PREPARES YOU FOR MINISTRY:

You want to be used by God. You desire to be more like Jesus and be a chosen vessel for His use. God answers your prayer through suffering:

Behold I have refined thee, but not with silver; I have chosen thee in the furnace of affliction. (Isaiah 48:10)

It is through affliction that you move beyond the calling as a child of God to become chosen of God. Affliction according to the will of God refines you for His use just as metals are refined in a furnace in the natural world.

YOU ARE PREPARED TO REIGN WITH CHRIST:

If we suffer, we shall also reign with Him. . .(2 Timothy 2:12)

SUFFERING BRINGS SPIRITUAL BLESSING:

Jesus said:

Blessed are they which are persecuted for righteousness sake; for theirs is the Kingdom of Heaven. Blessed are ye, when men shall revile you, and persecute you, and shall say all manner of evil against you falsely, for my sake. Rejoice, and be exceeding glad: for great is your reward in heaven: for so persecuted they the prophets which were before you.(Matthew 5:10-12)

YOU LEARN OBEDIENCE THROUGH SUFFERING:

Though He were a Son, yet learned He obedience by the things which He suffered... (Hebrews 5:8)

SUFFERING TESTS THE WORD OF GOD WITHIN YOU:

The words of the Lord are pure words: as silver tried in a furnace of earth, purified seven times. (Psalms 12:6)

SUFFERING HUMBLES YOU:

Who led thee through that great and terrible wilderness, wherein were fiery serpents, and scorpions, and drought, where there was no water; who brought thee forth water out of the rock of flint; Who fed thee in the wilderness with manna, which thy fathers knew not, that He might humble thee, and that He might prove thee, to do thee good at thy latter end... (Deuteronomy 8:15-16)

SUFFERING ENLARGES YOU:

This means you grow spiritually:

Thou has enlarged me when I was under pressure.(Psalms 4:1 Revised Standard Version)

YOU COME TO KNOW GOD INTIMATELY:

You come to know God on a more intimate basis through suffering. Job, who suffered much, learned this truth and said...

DR. ABRAHAM PETERS

I have heard of thee by the hearing of the ear: but now mine eye seeth thee.

Wherefore I abhor myself and repent in dust and ashes. (Job 42:5-6)

So many know God only second handedly. When you are experiencing the blessings of life, God is often a luxury instead of a necessity. But when you have a real need, God becomes a necessity. Job came to know God more intimately through suffering. Before he suffered, Job knew God through theology. Afterwards, he knew Him by experience.

Paul expressed a similar desire when he said:

That I may know Him, and the power of His resurrection and the fellowship of His sufferings, being made conformable unto His death.(Philippians 3:10)

You can only come to know God in resurrection power through the intimate fellowship of suffering. Throughout his trial, Job questioned God as to the cause of his suffering. It is not wrong to question God. Jesus knew the purpose for which He had come into the world was to die for the sins of all mankind. Yet in His hour of suffering He cried out, "My God, My God, WHY hast thou forsaken me?" It is what follows the questioning that is important. Jesus's next words were, "Into thy hands I commit my spirit."

Despite the questions, Job's response was. . .

Though He slay me, yet will I trust in Him. . .(Job 13:15)

For I know that my Redeemer liveth, and that He shall stand at the latter day upon the earth:

And though after my skin worms destroy this body, yet in my flesh shall I see God. (Job 19:25-26)

After all the questioning is finished, the emphasis must change from "me" to "Thee." You must commit your suffering, with all its unanswered questions, into the hands of God.

Trust in the Lord with all thine heart; and lean not unto thine own understanding. (Proverbs 3:5)

God may reveal some of the purposes in your suffering, but it is possible you will never fully understand it:

It is the glory of God to conceal a thing. . .(Proverbs 25:2)

The secret things belong unto the Lord our God; but those things which are revealed belong unto us. . . (Deuteronomy 29:29)

There are some secret things that belong only to the Lord. As Job, you may never understand all the purposes of your suffering:

Since the Lord is directing our steps, why try to understand everything that happens along the way? (Proverbs 20:24, The Living Bible)

When God finally talked with Job, He used several examples from nature which Job could not explain. God stressed that if Job could not understand what he saw in the natural world, he certainly could not understand that which he could not see in the spiritual world. When Job faced God, it no longer mattered that he did not get an answer to his questions about suffering. He was no longer controlled and tormented by human reasoning. He replaced questions, not with answers, but with faith.

When you come to know God intimately through suffering, you see yourself as you really are. You no longer know God second-handedly. That face-to-face encounter with God does what arguments and discussions cannot do. When Job stood before God, he had no new answers. He was given no new facts about his suffering. But he replaced questions with faith. Job had been in the direct presence of God, and that experience left no room for questions or doubts.

THE STORMS OF LIFE

Suffering is sometimes compared to a natural storm. When you suffer, you experience a storm spiritually speaking. This storm may affect you spiritually, mentally, physically, materially, or emotionally.

The Bible tells of a storm which the disciples of Jesus experienced. Read the story in your Bible in Mark 4:35-41. This storm was an attack of Satan. Jesus had told the disciples to go to the other side. Jesus was with them in the boat. Satan was trying to prevent them from reaching the shore because of the miraculous works that were to be done in the country of the Gadarenes (Mark 5). Jesus took authority over the storm. He rebuked the powers of the enemy. Calm returned to the sea and they continued their journey unhindered.

A storm of Satan is anything that tries to hinder you from fulfilling the will of God for your life. It is not suffering resulting from your disobedience. Neither is this kind of suffering according to the will of God. God does not want anything to hinder His plan for you. When you face this type of storm, exercise authority over the enemy. Jesus has given you power over every power of Satan.

There are two other stories of natural storms recorded in the Bible which illustrate suffering by chastisement for sin and suffering according to the will of God. Read the story of Jonah and the storm in Jonah chapter 1 and the story of Paul and the storm in Acts 27. Then study the following chart:

Jonah	**Paul**
Jonah put himself in the storm	Paul was in it through no fault of his own
He paid the fare to sail	He tried to prevent them from sailing
He was the cause of the storm	He was the remedy, not the cause
Jonah slept during the storm	Paul fasted and prayed
God's blessing was not with Jonah	God's blessing was with Paul
The crew was fearful	The crew was of good cheer

DR. ABRAHAM PETERS

To be saved:	To be saved:
Jonah must be cast out of the ship	All must abide in the ship

There are differences between going through a storm of life within God's will and experiencing a storm out of the will of God. When you go through a storm out of the will of God, it is a situation which you create. For example, a believer who marries an unsaved person will experience trouble because they have violated a Scriptural principle.

When you cause a storm, it is because you violate God's will and are disobedient to His commands. Often you are not even aware of the seriousness of your situation. You sleep spiritually while the storm increases its fury around you. God's blessing is not on you, and those around you grow fearful. This storm is not an attack of Satan. It is chastisement from God who loves you and desires to bring you back into conformity to His will. You can confess promises of "power over the enemy" but it will not change the situation.

When you recognize a storm of suffering as one resulting from disobeying God's voice, there is only one remedy: Ask forgiveness from God! But when you suffer according to the will of God, the situation is different. You suffer through no fault or sin of your own. You can be a remedy to the problems around you instead of a cause. Like Paul, you can assume spiritual leadership because God's blessing is on you. You can bring encouragement to others because you are a solution to the storm instead of the cause. You should not bail out of the ship or run from the trouble. You must abide in the "ship" of this type of suffering for it is the will of God.

SUFFERING IS TO BE EXPECTED

When you suffer according to the will of God, you should realize you are not alone:

. . . Knowing that the same afflictions are accomplished in your brethren that are in the world. (1 Peter 5:9)

Storms of life are inevitable and uncontrollable, as illustrated by the parable of the two houses in Matthew 7:24-27. Storms will come to those who have built their lives upon God's Word as well as those who have not done so. The foundation of a man's life is what will determine the outcome of the storm.

Suffering is to be expected as part of the will of God:

Yea, and all that will live godly in Christ Jesus shall suffer persecution. (2 Timothy 3:12)

For unto you it is given in the behalf of Christ, not only to believe on Him, but also to suffer for His sake. (Philippians 1:29)

. . .that ye may be counted worthy of the Kingdom of God, for which ye also suffer. . . (2 Thessalonians 1:5)

For verily, when we were with you, we told you before that we should suffer tribulation; even as it came to pass and ye know. (1 Thessalonians 3:4)

Then shall they deliver you up to be afflicted, and shall kill you: and ye shall be hated of all nations for my name's sake. (Matthew 24:9)

. . . They shall lay their hands on you, and persecute you, delivering you up to the synagogues, and into prisons, being brought before kings and rulers for my names sake. (Luke 21:12)

Remember the word that I said unto you, The servant is not greater than his lord. If they have persecuted me, they will also persecute you. . .
(John 15:20)

Part of the follow up plan in establishing early churches was to teach believers that they would experience suffering. This is missing in many churches today:

. . .They returned. . .confirming the souls of the disciples, and exhorting them to continue in the faith, and that we must through much tribulation enter the kingdom of God. (Acts 14:22)

The call of Jesus to followers is one of denial and suffering:

And he that taketh not his cross, and followeth after me, is not worthy of me. (Matthew 10:38)

Then said Jesus unto his disciples, If any man will come after me, let him deny himself and take up his cross and follow me. (Matthew 16:24)

. . . Whosoever will come after me, let him deny himself and take up his cross, and follow me. (Mark 8:34)

. . . Come, take up the cross, and follow me. (Mark 10:21)

If any man will come after me, let him deny himself, and take up his cross daily, and follow me. (Luke 9:23)

And whosoever doth not bear his cross, and come after me, cannot be my disciple. (Luke 14:27)

WHEN THE BROOK RUNS DRY

There is an interesting Old Testament story of a man who experienced suffering within the will of God. That is the story of Elijah. Elijah experienced all types of suffering as he prophesied God's message of Israel. But the particular story we want to focus on is found in 1 Kings 17. Read this story in your Bible before continuing with the lesson.

When God first directed Elijah to the Brook Cherith, He provided for him miraculously. Ravens came to feed him, and the brook provided fresh water in a time when the nation was experiencing drought and famine. But eventually, the brook dried up. Why would God send Elijah to a brook He knew would dry up?

The will of God sometimes involves dry brooks. But when we experience such difficulties it does not mean we missed God's will. Elijah had not missed the will of God. The Lord led Elijah to Cherith. He enjoyed its waters. His needs were provided. He was blessed of God. But when it was time to move on, God allowed the brook to dry up. This got Elijah's attention.

Perhaps God has directed you to a "Brook Cherith" in life. You know you heard His voice of direction. He blessed you at your brook. Your needs were met and you rejoiced in God's blessings. But then the brook ran dry. Maybe you no longer experienced the flow of God's power. Perhaps people turned against you. Perhaps leadership above you dammed up the brook and stopped the flow. For whatever reason, your beautiful brook ran dry.

When the brook runs dry you can do one of two things:

1. You can sit on the bank spiritually speaking and complain about your fate. You can spend the rest of your life wondering why it happened and weeping over the dry creek bed. You can question the leading of God. Did He even bring you here in the first place? If He knew the brook was going to run dry, why would He have brought you here? Did you miss God's will? Or. . .

2. You can realize that as surely as God brought you to this brook, He is now ready to move you on to a new dimension of His will. He is gaining your attention through the dry brook.

If brooks never dried up. . .if God never let difficult times come. . .He would never get our attention. Like Elijah, we would settle right where we are and never move on to new things. We would never stray beyond the banks of security of our brook. Drying brooks lead to greater things. Before the experience at Cherith Elijah had ministered only to individuals. After this faith-building encounter, Elijah ministered to multitudes. He stood on Mt. Carmel and proclaimed before a nation of idolaters that God was the true and living God.

Fellowship With The Holy Spirit

When you face drying brooks, your faith must not fail. You are on the banks of receiving new revelation from God. Do not question dry creek beds. Move on to the next dimension of God's plan.

2. Study the following references about suffering:

HARDNESS:

2 Timothy 2:3

TRIBULATION:

Acts 14:20; Romans 5:3; 12:12; 1 Thessalonians 3:4, 2 Thessalonians 1:4

PERSECUTION:

Matthew 5:10-12, 44; 13:21; Mark 4:17; Luke 11:49; 21:12; John 15:20; 1 Corinthians 4:12; 2 Corinthians 4:9; Acts 8:1; 11:19; 13:50; 2 Timothy 3:12; Romans 8:35; Galatians 6:12

SUFFERING:

1 Peter 5:10; Philippians 1:29; 3:8; 4:12; 2 Corinthians 1:6; 2 Timothy 2:12; 3:12; Galatians 5:11; 6:12; Acts 9:16; 1 Thessalonians 3:4; 2 Thessalonians 1:5

AFFLICTION:

Psalms 34:19; 119:67,71,75; Matthew 24:9; Acts 20:23; 2 Corinthians 2:4; 4:17; 6:4; 1 Thessalonians 3:3; 2 Timothy 1:8;

DR. ABRAHAM PETERS

3:11; 4:5; 2 Corinthians 1:6; James 5:10; Hebrews 10:32-33 and chapter 11

CHAPTER TWENTY FOUR

THE STAGES OF REVELATION

DR. ABRAHAM PETERS

And thine ears shall hear a word behind thee, saying, this is the way, walk ye in it, when ye turn to the right hand and when ye turn to the left.(Isaiah 30:21)

In this book you have learned much about knowing God's voice. You learned prerequisites for knowing God's voice. You learned the meaning and pattern of God's will and ways in which God communicates with man. You were warned of non-Biblical ways of seeking guidance and received guidelines for making decisions regarding questionable practices. You studied a Biblical model for decision making and learned what to do when you fail. You also studied about suffering as it is related to God's will.

This final chapter presents the six stages through which you will pass in the revelation of a plan of God. You will experience these stages as you learn to walk in the will of God.

REVELATION KNOWLEDGE

In a confused and misdirected world, God promises revelation knowledge to His followers. This means He will reveal divine plans, wisdom, and knowledge in the circumstances of life:

And thine ears shall hear a word behind thee, saying, this is the way, walk ye in it, when ye turn to the right hand and when ye turn to the left.(Isaiah 30:21)

When God reveals a plan, there are six stages through which you pass in the development of that revelation. These stages are evident in Luke 1:26-47. Read this passage before continuing with the remainder of this lesson. These Scriptures record the revelation of

God given to Mary that she was to become the mother of the Messiah, Jesus Christ.

In this story there are six stages through which Mary passes as God's plan is revealed to her. These stages may be observed in the revelation of any plan of God to man. They are stages through which you will pass as you receive revelation knowledge of His plan for your life.

STAGE ONE: DIRECTION

And the angel came in unto her. . .and when she saw him, she was troubled at his saying and cast in her mind what manner of salutation this should be. (Luke 1:28-29)

When the angel first appeared to Mary, she was troubled or vexed in her spirit. Whenever God wants to give new direction guidance, you often experience vexation. He permits you to be troubled by the circumstances of life in order to gain your attention. Perhaps you are questioning perplexing circumstances around you. You have been troubled and not understood why certain things were happening to upset your life. God is trying to gain your attention. If you are happy and content in present circumstances you will not seek Him for new direction. This is why He allows you to be troubled in this first stage of revelation.

STAGE TWO: REVELATION

And the angel said unto her, Fear not, Mary; for thou hast found favor with God. And behold, thou shalt conceive in thy womb and bring forth a son and shalt call His name Jesus. (Luke 1:30-31)

When God gains your attention through vexation, He will reveal His plan to you. This is the second stage of revelation:

Call upon me and I will answer thee, and shew thee great and mighty things which thou knowest not. (Jeremiah 33:3)

A troubled spirit caused Mary to focus her attention on God then He revealed His plan. She was to be the mother of the Messiah, Jesus Christ.

STAGE THREE: HESITATION

Then said Mary unto the angel, How shall this be, seeing I know not a man? (Luke 1:34)

Mary hesitates to accept this great revelation. She questions, "How can this be?"

When God reveals new direction for your life you are often overwhelmed. You may feel unqualified. You may feel it is too great a step of faith to take. You will think of rational reasons why the plan cannot work. You will hesitate and question God.

Two things happen in the stage of hesitation:

- You present your questions, reasons, and excuses.
- God answers these with details of His plan.

Some people hesitate longer than others. Some people spend years in the hesitation stage thinking up excuses and reasons why they cannot accept the revelation God has given. But if you do not eventually move on from hesitation you will never see the fulfillment of God's revelation.

STAGE FOUR: RESIGNATION

And Mary said, Behold the handmaid of the Lord; be it unto me according to thy word... (Luke 1:38)

Mary moves quickly from hesitation to resignation to the plan of God. This means she resigns her will to God's plan. She gives up her own plans and desires and accepts God's new direction for her life.

STAGE FIVE: VERIFICATION

And blessed is she that believed; for there shall be a performance of those things which were told her from the Lord. (Luke 1:45)

In the verification stage, God verifies or confirms His plan. Mary becomes pregnant and the revelation is verified in her own body. If you resign your will to the revelation of God's plan, it will not be long until you receive verification of that plan.

STAGE SIX: EXALTATION

And Mary said, My soul doth magnify the Lord. (Luke 1:46)

Mary rejoices in the plan of God! Read her complete exaltation of God in Luke 1:46-55. When you accept the plan of God for your life it will always bring happiness and result in exaltation of God.

As you learned in this course, following God's plan does not mean you will be without problems. In the natural world, Mary had a real problem. She was pregnant without being married. But the plan of God is greater than any temporary suffering which it involves. In the end, it always brings joy and exaltation of the Lord Jesus Christ.

A FINAL WORD--LISTEN FOR HIS VOICE

In this course you have received guidelines for knowing the voice of God. As you listen for this voice, remember His promise:

. . .I know the thoughts and plans that I have for you, says the Lord, thoughts and plans for welfare and peace, and not for evil, to give you hope in your final outcome. (Jeremiah 29:11, The Amplified Version)

God will continue to guide you until death:

For this God is our God for ever and ever: He will be our guide even unto death. (Psalms 48:14)

His guidance will continue in the new heaven and earth:

For the Lamb which is in the midst of the throne, shall feed them, and shall lead them unto living fountains of waters; and God shall wipe away all tears from their eyes. (Revelation 7:17)

God is not silent. If you listen, His voice can be heard above the noise and confusion of all the voices of earth. God speaks and you can know His voice:

Now the God of peace, that brought again from the dead our Lord Jesus, that great shepherd of the sheep, through the blood of the everlasting covenant,

Make you perfect in every good work TO DO HIS WILL, working in you that which is well pleasing in His sight, through Jesus Christ; to whom be glory forever and ever. Amen. (Hebrews 13:20-21)

Study the pattern of the six stages of revelation in the lives of Moses and Gideon:

Moses:	Exodus 1-15	
Direction:	Experienced in Egypt (killed an Egyptian)	
Revelation:	Burning bush	
Hesitation:	Man of slow speech	
Resignation:	Decides to go	
Verification:	Miracles before Pharaoh	
Exaltation:	Joy after crossing Red Sea	
Gideon:	Judges 6	
Direction:	Threshing wheat; pours out vexation in verse 13	
Revelation:	Angel appeared in verse 12 and 14	
Hesitation:	"Family poor, I am the least" verse 15	
Resignation:	Verse 17	
Verification:	"Shew me a sign" verses 17 through 23	
Exaltation:	Verse 24. Builds an altar and praises God.	

You can find other examples of this pattern in God's Word

DR. ABRAHAM PETERS

One of the greatest benefits of our salvation has to be that of hearing God speak to us personally. There can be no intimate relationship nor fellowship with our heavenly Father without it. But, as easy as it is for us to speak to Him, the average Christian has a hard time hearing His voice. This is not the way the Lord intended it to be. Learning to clearly distinguish God's voice is invaluable. Instead of going through life blindly, we can have the wisdom of God guide and protect us. There isn't a single person reading this book who couldn't have their life radically transformed by hearing the voice of the Lord better. The worst marital problem is one word from the Lord away from a total turnaround. If you have sickness or disease, one living word from the Lord will instantly heal you. If you are in financial crisis, the Lord knows exactly how to turn your situation around. It's just a matter of hearing His voice and obeying whatever he tells you to do.

The Bible says, "His mother said to the servants, "Do whatever he tells you." John 2:5 New International Version

"But be doers of the word, and not hearers only, deceiving yourselves. 23 For if anyone is a hearer of the word and not a doer, he is like a man observing his natural face in a mirror; 24 for he observes himself, goes away, and immediately forgets what kind of man he was. 25 But he who looks into the perfect law of liberty and continues in it, and is not a forgetful hearer but a doer of the work, this one will be blessed in what he does. James 1:22-25 New King James Version

The Lord constantly speaks to us and gives us His direction by instruction. It's never the Lord who is not speaking, but it's us who are not hearing. Jesus made some radical statements about hearing

Fellowship With The Holy Spirit

His voice in John 10:3-5. He was speaking about Himself as the Shepherd of the sheep and the only way to enter the sheepfold.

"To him the porter openeth; and the sheep hear his voice; and he calleth his own sheep by name, and leadeth them out. And when he putteth forth his own sheep, he goeth before them, and the sheep follow him: for they know his voice. And a stranger will they not follow, but will flee from him: for they know not the voice of strangers."

Notice that He said in verse 3, His sheep hear His voice. He didn't say His sheep CAN hear His voice or SHOULD hear His voice. He made the emphatic statement that His sheep DO hear His voice. Most Christians would question the accuracy of that statement since their experiences don't line up. But it's not what Jesus said that is wrong; all true believers can and do hear the voice of God; they just don't recognize what they are hearing as being God's voice.

Radio and television stations transmit twenty-four hours a day, seven days a week; but we only hear them when we turn the receiver on and tune it in. Failure to hear the signal doesn't mean the station isn't transmitting. Likewise, God is constantly transmitting His voice to His sheep, but few are turned on and tuned in. Most Christians are busy pleading with God in prayer to transmit when the problem is with their receivers.

The first thing we need to do is fix our receivers, believe that God is already speaking and start listening. However, that takes time, effort, and focus. The average Christian's lifestyle is so busy, it isn't conducive to hearing God's voice. For instance, what is your typical answer to the question, "How are you?" Many of you probably answer something about being very busy. I often say, "I'm busier than a one-arm paper hanger." All of us seem to be busier than ever, and that's one of the BIG reasons we don't hear the voice of the Lord better. We're just too busy. Psalm 46:10 says, "Be still, and know that I am God." It's in stillness, not busyness, that we tune our spiritual ears to hear the voice of God. The Lord always speaks to us in that "STILL, small voice" (1 Kings 19:12, emphasis mine), but often it's drowned out amid all the turmoil of our daily lives.

Second, and this is very important, most often we mistake the voice of the Lord for our own thoughts. That's right. I said the voice of the Lord comes to us in our own thoughts.
John 4:24 says, "God is a Spirit: and they that worship him must worship him in spirit and in truth." This is saying that communication with God is Spirit to spirit, not brain to brain or mouth to ear, the way we communicate in the physical realm. The Lord speaks to our spirits, not always by words, but in thoughts and impressions. Then our spirits speak to us in words like, "I think the Lord wants me to do this or that." Sometimes The Lord doesn't typically say "You do this or that," but He will impress your spirit to do something, and then your spirit says, "I think I should do . . ." Therefore, we often miss the leading of the Lord, thinking it's our own thoughts. Every one of us has done something stupid and afterwards said, "I knew that was the wrong thing to do." We didn't feel right about our decision, but we followed logic or pressure only to find that our impression was actually the Lord speaking to us, some of us has had to learned this the hard way.

Psalm 37:4 says, "Delight thyself also in the LORD; and he shall give thee the desires of thine heart." This verse has often been interpreted to mean that the Lord will give you whatever you want and has been used to justify selfishness and greed. But it doesn't mean that the Lord will give you whatever you want; it means that when you are seeking the Lord, He will put His wants or desires into your heart. He will make His desires become your desires. The Lord changes your "want to." That is the dominant way the Lord speaks to us, and we often miss that kind of communication.

I am convinced that our gracious heavenly Father speaks to every one of His children constantly, giving us all the information and guidance we need to be total overcomers. There isn't a problem with His transmitter; it's our receiver that needs help. Most people are imploring God to speak, when it's our hearing that needs to be adjusted. Taking this faith-stance that God is speaking and then learning to listen and obey will transform your relationship with the Lord.

God wants to fellowship and communicate with us. That's two-way communication. Why? Because you can't really have a relationship unless there is true dialogue. How do we get to know a person? By communicating with them. By talking and listening. It's the same with our relationship with God. He talks, we listen. We talk, He listens. God loves us so much that He sent Jesus to take our place and to die for us. He did this so that we could once again have fellowship with Him. In the book of Hebrews we see that we can have access to God's very presence, "...having boldness to enter the Holiest by the blood of Jesus, by a new and living way..." (Hebrews 10:19-20a).

He also wants us to be fulfilled, blessed and successful in the plan that He has established for our lives, so that we can be a reflection of His love and blessing in the Earth. In Jeremiah 29:11 the Lord makes clear His intentions for you and I, "For I know the thoughts that I think toward you, says the Lord, thoughts of peace and not of evil, to give you a future and a hope." We see in Genesis 3:8a, "...they heard the sound of the Lord God walking in the garden in the cool of the day..." This is how God wants to relate to us today as well. It is God's desire to walk with and to communicate with His children. He wants to talk to us. And He wants us to listen and talk to Him, too.

There is more good news, we can hear His voice. The Bible, God's love letter to mankind, makes it clear that we were created to have two-way communication with Him. Jesus tells us in John 10:27, "My sheep hear My voice, and I know them, and they follow Me." As a child of God we don't have to walk blind. We can have confidence that we will hear His voice. The Apostle Paul writes in Romans 8:14, "For as many as are led by the Spirit of God, these are sons of God." Conversely, this scripture implies that if we are God's children, if we are born-again, we will be led by His Spirit.

We have further assurance of this promise in Psalm 37:23 and 24, "The steps of a good (righteous, born-again) person are ordered by the Lord, And He delights in his way. Though he fall, he shall not be utterly cast down; For the Lord upholds him with His hand." God will order our steps, and even when we blow it, if we are truly trying to do His will, He will lift us up and give us a second chance. Jeremiah 29:12-13 says, "Then you will call upon Me and go and pray to Me, and I will listen to you. And you will seek Me and find Me, when you search for Me with all your heart." We can't make demands on Almighty God. We can't shake our fist at the sky and say, 'all right God, let me hear you.' But we can ask, seek, and knock, and the Bible promises that God will open the door. God will reveal Himself to those who humbly seek Him.

The writer of Proverbs describes the way that our thoughts and intentions line up with God's will when we submit ourselves fully to the Lord. "Roll your works upon the Lord [commit and trust them wholly to Him; He will cause your thoughts to become agreeable to His will, and] so shall your plans be established and succeed" (Proverbs 16:3 Amplified Bible). The Lord manifests Himself to us and through us as we humbly seek Him. The familiar passage in Proverbs 3 makes it even more plain. "Trust in the Lord with all your heart, and lean not on your own understanding; In all your ways acknowledge Him, And He shall direct your paths" (Proverbs 3:5-6). Now that we know we can hear God's voice, we need to be alerted to the fact that there are other voices whispering into our ears as well. In fact, there are three voices that we can hear -- the voice of God, the voice of our own fleshly desires, and the voice of the Devil. But Jesus tells us in John 10:4b and 5, "...and the sheep follow Him, for they know His voice. Yet they will by no means follow a stranger, but will flee from him, for they do not know the voice of strangers."

The writer of Hebrews tells us that we can train our ear to recognize the voice of God above all the noise. "But solid food belongs to those who are of full age, that is, those who by reason of use have their senses exercised to discern both good and evil" (Hebrews 5:14). It is by practicing, by reason of use, that we are able to discern whether what we hear is of God, our flesh, or the Devil.

Isaiah 30:21 says, "Your ears shall hear a word behind you, saying, "This is the way, walk in it," Whenever you turn to the right hand or whenever you turn to the left." So God will speak, and you can hear

His voice, but you must be careful, especially when you are a young Christian, that you objectively confirm that you are following the Holy Spirit and not another voice. Our own flesh can scream pretty loud, especially when we are under pressure, or we want something very badly. And the Devil is the father of lies, he is the great deceiver. So how can we know whether we're hearing the voice of God? The Bible gives us seven basic keys or filters through which every possible leading should be judged. We are to carefully examine the thoughts and intentions of our hearts and the words of godly people who may have influence on us by their words and actions through the use of these keys:

The Scripture: "All Scripture is given by inspiration of God, and is profitable for doctrine, for reproof, for correction, for instruction in righteousness, that the man of God may be complete, thoroughly equipped for every good work" (2 Timothy 3:16-17).

The Holy Spirit speaking to our heart: "For this is the covenant that I will make with the house of Israel after those days, says the Lord: I will put my laws into their minds, and I will write them on their hearts. and I will be their God, and they shall be my people. And they shall not teach everyone his fellow citizen, and everyone his brother, saying, 'know the Lord,' for all will know Me, from the least to the greatest of them" (Hebrews 8:10-11).

The Prophetic (word of knowledge, word of wisdom, personal prophecy): "Do not quench the Spirit; do not despise prophetic utterances. But examine everything carefully; hold fast to that which is good" (1 Thessalonians 5:19-21).

Dreams and Visions: God not only opens our ears, but also seals instruction through our dreams so that we are notified of our faults, counseled to avoid going in the wrong direction and given instruction on best ways to move forward from these circumstances. The Bible tells us, "In a dream, in a vision of the night, when deep sleep falls on people as they slumber in their beds, He may speak in their ears and terrify them with warnings" (Job 33:15 - 16). God instructs through dreams, imprints upon the soul and through lasting impressions in a similar way that a seal is used to make an imprint in wax on a document. We can learn a lot through these instructions. We just have to be open to listening to what He is saying.(Acts 16:6-15 Paul's Vision of the Man of Macedonia).

Godly Counsel: "Where no counsel is, the people fall: but in the multitude of counselors there is safety" (Proverbs 11:14).

Confirmation: "By the mouth of two or three witnesses every fact may be confirmed" (Matthew 18:16).

Angelic Visitations: The word angel is a transliteration of the Greek word "angolos," which means "Messager." An angel is one of God's messengers, or one who God sends with his message. We know from scripture that God uses His angels to deliver messages to His people. Angels appearance do have another role as well, defined in Psalm 91. That role is to watch over and protect God's people. Verses 11-12 say, "For He shall give His angels charge over you, to keep you in all your ways. In their hands they shall bear you up, lest you dash your foot against a stone." This verse to recognize the role of angels in guarding or protecting God's people.

DR. ABRAHAM PETERS

People have been known to see and hear angels in visions. It is also possible to have a real physical visit from an angel. When this occurs, you are not having a vision "in the spirit," you are having a direct encounter with one of God's messengers. They come to where you are physically and they manifest to you and they interact with you. There is often a sense of God's glory or of His holiness in their visitation. But there are also times when God causes the sense of His presence to be masked and you may not realize that an angel is appearing to you. Hebrews 13:2 says, "Do not forget to entertain strangers, for by so doing some people have entertained angels without knowing it." Most of the time, you will know it if you are visited by an angel.

The Peace of God: "Let the peace of Christ rule in your hearts, to which indeed you were called in one body; and be thankful" (Colossians 3:15).

Circumstances and Timing: "After these things he (Paul) left Athens and went to Corinth. And he found a certain Jew named Aquila, a native of Pontus, having recently come from Italy with his wife Priscilla, because Claudius had commanded all the Jews to leave Rome. He came to them, and because he was of the same trade, he stayed with them and they were working; for by trade they were tent-makers" (Acts 18:1-3 -- this relationship between Paul, Aquila and Priscilla which happened as a result of circumstances became one of the most important strategic partnerships in the book of Acts).

Many times the Lord will confirm His direction to us through three, four or more of these keys especially when we are in the process of making an important, life-changing decision. The bottom line, is that big decisions take big prayer. In other words, as we humble ourselves before the Lord, seek His guidance in our lives, the Good Shepherd will be faithful to lead us, "...in paths of righteousness for His name's sake" (Psalm 23:3). God has given us His Word to help us discern whether what we are sensing is of God, our flesh or the Devil. Because God loves us and wants us to relate to Him, He has given us these clear principles in the Bible to guide us. The New Testament talks of the early disciples people like Paul, Aquila and Priscilla as people who heard the voice of God. "These who have turned the world upside down have come here too" (Acts 17:6b). Yes, my friend, you can hear and know the voice of God. And because of this the world is changing, more than perhaps you've heard.

In the new testament from time of Christ's ascension and fulfillment of the promise by the Father on the day of Pentecost at the upper room that marks the birthing of the Church, the Holy Spirit started the working of great transformation in the lives of every Christian; therefore we can call the book of acts of the apostles also as the acts of the Holy Spirit since He is the one doing the miracle, signs and wonders through the lives of the believers. Fellowship with the Holy Spirit gives you the boldness to come to God, the boldness with people and the boldness against satan.

Here's a summary theme of the workings of the Holy Spirit in each 28 chapters of the book of Acts of the Apostles.

1. The Holy Spirit will change the way you hear.
2. The Holy Spirit will change the way you speak.
3. The Holy Spirit will change your appearance.
4. The Holy Spirit will change your behavior.
5. The Holy Spirit will change your experience with God.

6. The Holy Spirit will change your position.
7. The Holy Spirit will change your vision.
8. The Holy Spirit will change your discernment.
9. The Holy Spirit will change your attitude.
10. The Holy Spirit will change your tradition.
11. The Holy Spirit will change your outlook.
12. The Holy Spirit will change your prayer life.
13. The Holy Spirit will change your calling.
14. The Holy Spirit will change your authority.
15. The Holy Spirit will be your partner in decision making.
16. The Holy Spirit will change your direction.
17. The Holy Spirit will change your world.
18. The Holy Spirit will change your understanding.
19. The Holy Spirit will change you as His presence lingers upon you.
20. The Holy Spirit will change your leadership.
21. The Holy Spirit will change your insight.
22. The Holy Spirit will change your commission.
23. The Holy Spirit will change your influence.
24. The Holy Spirit will establish your eternal hope.
25. The Holy Spirit will give you great confidence.
26. The Holy Spirit will change your witness.
27. The Holy Spirit will change your chaos into peace.
28. The Holy Spirit will change your conflict into victory.

APPENDIX

DR. ABRAHAM PETERS

HOLY SPIRIT THEME IN EACH BOOK OF THE HOLY BIBLE

The Spirit of Creation - Genesis 1:2

The Name Changer - Genesis 17:5

The Spirit of the Dreamer - Genesis 41:38

The Fire of Evangelism - Exodus 3:2

The Precious Oil - Exodus 30:22-25

The Expert Spirit - Exodus 31:1-6

The Sovereign Fire - Leviticus 9:24

The Pure Oil - Leviticus 24:2

The Spirit of Impartation - Numbers 11:17

The Different Spirit - Numbers 14:24

The Spirit in Joshua - Numbers 27:18

The Fire by Night and the Cloud by Day - Deuteronomy 1:33

The Spirit/Oil of Prosperity - Deuteronomy 33:24

The Spirit of Breakthrough - Joshua 6:3-5

The spirit of discernment - Joshua 7:16-19

The Spirit of Leadership - Judges 3:10

The Fire from the Rock - Judges 6:21

The Spirit of Conquest - Judges 11:29

The Fire of Heaven - Judges 13:20

The Spirit of Supernatural Strength - Judges 14:6

The Gentle Spirit - Judges 16:20

The Kind Spirit of Adoption - Ruth 2:21

The Appointing Spirit - 1 Samuel 10:1; 16:1, 13

The Spirit Who Speaks Through You - 2 Samuel 23:2

The Still Small Voice - 1 Kings 19:12

The Pervasive Oil - 2 Kings 4:1-7

The Heavenly Wind - 2 Kings 2:11

A Kindred Spirit - 1 Chronicles 12:18

The Fortifying Spirit - 2 Chronicles 15:1 - 4

DR. ABRAHAM PETERS

The Convicting Spirit - Ezra 10:1

The Comforter - Hebrew Meaning of "Nehemiah" The Good Spirit - Nehemiah 2:4 - 5

The Good Spirit - Nehemiah 9:20

The Voice of Destiny - Esther 4:13-14

The Life-Giving Spirit - Job 33:4

The Spirit of Worship - Psalm 51: 11

The Oil of Honor - Psalm 23:5

The Oil of Joy - Psalm 45:7

The Oil of Favor - Psalm 84:9

The Spirit of Wisdom - Proverbs 1:20-23

The Spirit of Purpose - Ecclesiastes 3:11

The Hidden Dove - Song of Solomon 2:14

The Seven Spirit of God - Isaiah 11: 1-2

The Generational Spirit - Isaiah 44:3

The Spirit upon Jesus - Isaiah 61:1

The Fire in your Bones - Jeremiah 20:9

The One Who Grieves over Sin - Lamentation 2:11

Life of the Heavenly Beings - Ezekiel 1:20-21

The Fiery Being - Ezekiel 8:1-4

The Giver of Spiritual Visions - Ezekiel 11:24

The Spirit of Oneness - Ezekiel 36:25-27

The Excellent Spirit - Daniel 5:12

The Patient Spirit - Hosea 2:14

The Promise of the Father - Joel 2:28-31

The Consuming Fire - Amos 5:4-6

The Vindicating Fire - Obadiah 1:18

The Protector of the Call - Jonah 1:4

The Unchanging Spirit - Micah 2:7

The Spirit of Warning - Nahum 1:6

The Spirit of Indignation - Habakkuk 1:13

The Spirit of Hope - Zephaniah 3:14-15

DR. ABRAHAM PETERS

The Enemy of Fear - Haggai 2:5

A Wall of Protection - Zechariah 2:5

The Spirit of Grace - Zechariah 12:10

The Refiner's Fire - Malachi 3:1-2

The Spirit of Incarnation - Matthew 1:18

The Spirit of The Father - Matthew 10: 20

The Spirit of Deliverance - Matthew 10: 28

The Beloved Spirit - Mark 3: 29

The Omni Spirit (Omnipotent, Omniscient and Omnipresent) - Luke 1:35, 2 Corinthians 2:10 and Psalm 139:7

The Threshing Wind - Luke 3:16-17

The Spirit of Salvation - John 3:3-8

The Rivers of Living Water - John 7:38-39

The Power of Greater Works - John 14:12

Our Helper - John 14:16-17

The Trusted Spirit - John 16:7

Fellowship With The Holy Spirit

The Spirit of Power - Acts 2:1-4

The Spirit of Boldness - Acts 2: 38

The Sender - Acts 13:4

The One Who Loves Jesus - Romans 5:5

The One Who Leads God's Children - Romans 8:9, 14

The Resurrection Spirit - Romans 8:11

The Mighty Intercessor - Romans 8:26-27

The Giver of Signs and Wonder - Romans 15:19

The Spirit of God - 1 Corinthians 2:10-12

The Spirit of Good Judgment - 1 Corinthians 2:15

The Mind of Christ - 1 Corinthians 2: 16

The Transcending Spirit - 1 Corinthians 5: 3

The Indwelling Spirit - 1 Corinthians 6:19

The Gift Giver - 1 Corinthians 12:11

The Transforming Spirit - 2 Corinthians 3:18

DR. ABRAHAM PETERS

The Spirit of Faith - 2 Corinthians 4:13

The Christ-Like Spirit - Galatians 5: 22-24

The Miracle-Working Spirit - Galatians 3:5

The Sustaining Power - Ephesians 5:18

The Spiritual Armour Bearer - Ephesians 6:17

The Personal Spirit - Philippians 2:1-2

The Spirit of Love - Colossians 1:8

The Delicate Fire - 1 Thessalonians 5:19

The Restrainer - 2 Thessalonians 2:7-8

The Prophetic Spirit - 1Timothy 4:1

The Spirit of Peace - 2 Timothy 1: 7

The Giver of New Life - Titus 3: 5-7

The Spirit of Forgiveness - Philemon 1: 25

The Holy Spirit is God - Hebrews 9: 14

The Jealous Spirit - James 4:5

The Oil of Healing - James 5: 14-15

Fellowship With The Holy Spirit

The Spirit of Jesus - 1 Peter 1:11

The Glorious Spirit - 1 Peter 4:14

The Breath of The Scriptures - 2 Peter 1: 20 - 21

The Witness of The Incarnation - 1 John 4: 1 - 2

The Masterful Teacher - 2 John 1 - 3

The Spirit of Unity - 3 John 1: 1 - 3

The Spirit of Prayer - Jude 1: 20

The Revealer of Christ - Revelation 1: 10 - 11

The Sevenfold Spirit - Revelation 3:1

DR. ABRAHAM PETERS

Biblical References to the Holy Spirit

Genesis

1:2 – The Spirit hovered over the waters. 6:3 – My Spirit will not always strive with man.

41:38 – Joseph, a man in whom the Spirit of the Lord is.

Exodus

31:3 & 31 – Bezaleel, a man filled with the Spirit of God in wisdom, in understanding, in knowledge and in all manner of workmanship.

Numbers

11:25-26, 29 – The Spirit of God on Moses was shared with the 70 elders. When they received it they prophesied. 24:2 – The Spirit of God came upon Balaam and he prophesied.

27:18 – Joshua, a man in whom is the Spirit. Moses laid his hand on him, but he already had the Spirit.

Judges

3:10 – The Spirit of the Lord came upon Othniel, the younger brother of Caleb.

6:34 – Upon Gideon.

11:29 – Upon Jephthah.

13:25 – Upon Samson from birth.

14:6 – Upon Samson for strength.

14:19 – Upon Samson.

15:14 – Upon Samson.

1 Samuel

10:6 – You will be turned into another man.

10:10 – Upon Saul.

11:6 – Upon Saul, who prophesied.

16:13 – Upon David.

16:14 – Departed from Saul. 19:20 – Upon messengers of Saul, who prophesied.

19:23 – Upon Saul, who prophesied.

2 Samuel

23:2 – The Spirit of the Lord spoke by David.

1 Kings

18:12 – Obadiah was afraid the Spirit would carry Elijah away.

2 Kings

2:9 – A double portion of the Spirit on Elisha. 2:16 – The Spirit took Elijah up.

2 Chronicles

15:1 – Upon Azariah for prophecy.

20:14 – Upon Jahaziel for prophecy. 24:20 – Upon Zechariah.

Job

33:4 – The Spirit of God has made me.

Psalm

51:11 – Do not cast me away from Your presence, and do not take Your Holy Spirit from me.

104:30 – You send for Your Spirit, they are created.

106:33 – Israel rebelled against the Spirit.

139:7 – Where can I go from Your Spirit?

Proverbs

1:23 – I will pour out My Spirit on you.

Isaiah

63:10 – They rebelled and grieved His Holy Spirit.

63:11 – Put His Holy Spirit with them (Israel).

63:14 – The Spirit caused the beast to rest.

Ezekiel

2:2 – The Spirit entered Ezekiel when God spoke.

3:12 – The Spirit lifted Ezekiel up. 3:14 – The Spirit lifted him up and took him away.

3:24 – The Spirit entered, and spoke words to Ezekiel.

8:3 – The Spirit took Ezekiel in vision to Jerusalem.

11:1 – The Spirit took Ezekiel again.

11:5 – The Spirit fell upon Ezekiel and said,

"Speak."

11:19 – A new spirit can be received.

11:24 – The Spirit took Ezekiel to Chaldea.

18:31 – A new heart and a new spirit. 36:26 – A new heart and new spirit are from the Holy Spirit.

37:1 – The Spirit took Ezekiel to a valley of dry bones.

37:14 – The Spirit makes dry bones live.

39:29 – The Spirit makes us to know God. 43:5 – The Spirit carried away Ezekiel to God's temple.

Daniel

4:8, 9, 18 & 5:11, 14 – The knew Daniel was full of the Spirit of God.

Joel

2:28 – The Spirit brings dreams and visions in the last days.

Micah

2:7 – The Spirit of the Lord is not restricted. 3:8 – Micah knew he was full of power by the Spirit.

Haggai

2:5 – The Spirit was with Zerubbabel, but he needed assurance.

Zechariah

4:6 – Not by might, nor power, but by the Spirit.

7:12 – The Spirit came by former prophets. 12:10 – He will pour out the Spirit of Grace and supplication and we will look on Him whom we have pierced.

Matthew

1:18 – Mary was with child of the Holy Spirit.

1:20 – The child was conceived of the Holy Spirit.

3:11 – He will baptize you with the Holy Spirit and fire.

3:12 – They saw the Spirit descend like a dove.

4:1 – Jesus was led by the Spirit into the wilderness.

10:20 – The Spirit will speak through us in our hour of trial.

12:18 – The Spirit was given to Jesus to declare justice.

12:31 – Blasphemy against the Spirit will not be forgiven men.

12:32 – Whoever speaks against the Holy Spirit will not be forgiven. 22:43 – David in the Spirit spoke concerning Jesus.

28:19 – Baptize them in the name of the Father, the Son and the Holy Spirit.

Mark

1:8 – He will baptize you with the Holy Spirit.

1:10 – The Spirit descended like a dove. 3:29 – He who blasphemes against the Holy Spirit never has forgiveness.

12:36 – David spoke by the Holy Spirit. 13:11 – When arrested the Holy Spirit will give you what to speak.

Luke

1:15 – John the Baptist was filled with the Holy Spirit from the womb. 1:17 – The Spirit turns the hearts of family to one another.

1:35 – The Holy Spirit upon Mary – the power of the Highest to overshadow. 1:41 – Elizabeth was filled with the Spirit and prophesied.

1:67 – Zacharias was filled with the Holy Spirit and prophesied.

1:80 – Jesus grew and was strong in the Spirit.

2:26 – The Holy Spirit revealed to him that he would not die until the Messiah. 2:27 – He came by the Spirit into the temple. 2:40 – Jesus filled with the Spirit, wisdom, and grace upon Him. 3:16 – He will baptize you with the Holy Spirit and fire.

3:22 – The Holy Spirit descended in bodily form like a dove.

4:1 – Jesus was filled with the Holy Spirit and led by the Spirit.

4:14 – Jesus returned to Galilee in the power of the Spirit.

4:18 – The Spirit of the Lord is upon Me. 11:13 – The Holy

Spirit is given to them that ask Him.

12:10 – To him who blasphemes against the Holy Spirit, it will not be forgiven. 12:11 – When arrested the Holy Spirit will teach you in that very hour.

John

1:32 – The Spirit descended like a dove.

1:33 – Jesus baptizes with the Holy Spirit. 3:5 – Unless we are born of water and the Spirit we will not see the kingdom.

3:6 – That which is born of the Spirit is Spirit. 3:8 – Those born of the Spirit are like the wind, coming and going as it wishes and you don't know where. 3:34 – God does not give the Spirit by measure.

4:23 – True worshipers worship in Spirit and truth. 4:24 – God is Spirit.

6:63 – The Spirit gives life. The words of Jesus are Spirit.

7:39 – The Spirit brings rivers of living water when Jesus is glorified. 7:38-39 – He who believes in Jesus will receive the Holy Spirit. 11:33 – Jesus groaned in the Spirit. 14:16-17 – The Spirit is the Helper, the Spirit of Truth whom the world cannot receive. 14:26 – The Helper, the Holy Spirit will teach us all things and bring them to our remembrance.

15:26 – The spirit of Truth proceeds from the Father and He will testify of Jesus. 16:7-11 – The Spirit convicts of sin, judgment and righteousness.

16:13-14 – The of truth will guide us into all truth and glorify Jesus. 20:22 – Jesus breathed on them and they received the Holy Spirit.

Acts

1:2 – Jesus gave commandments through the Holy Spirit.

1:5 – John baptized with water but they were to be baptized in the Holy Spirit. 1:8 – You shall receive power when the Holy Spirit has come upon you.

1:16 – David spoke by the Holy Spirit. 2:4 – They were filled with the Holy Spirit and spoke with tongues. 2:17-18 – Pentecost fulfilled Joel's promise of the Spirit.

2:33 – Jesus received the promise of the Holy Spirit and poured it out on His disciples. 2:38 – Repent and be baptized and you shall receive the gift of the Holy Spirit. 4:8 – Peter was filled and spoke by the Holy Spirit.

4:31 – They prayed and the place was shaken. They were filled with the Holy Spirit and they spoke with boldness.

5:3-4 – Ananias lied to the Holy Spirit, to God.

5:9 – Ananias and Sapphira tempted the Spirit.

5:32 – The Holy Spirit is a Witness given to those who obey God.

6:3 – Seek out men full of the Holy Spirit. 7:51 – The Pharisees always resisted the Holy Spirit.

7:55 – Stephen was full of the Holy Spirit and saw the glory of God.

8:15 – The apostles prayed for them that they might receive the Holy Spirit. They had already been baptized in water.

8:29 – The Spirit spoke words to Phillip. 8:39 – The Spirit caught Phillip away. 9:17 – Ananias laid hands on Paul and he received the Holy Spirit. 9:31 – The churches had the comfort of the Holy Spirit.

10:19 – The Spirit spoke to Peter. 10:38 – God anointed Jesus with the Holy Spirit.

10:44 – While Peter was preaching the Holy Spirit fell on Cornelius' household. 10:44-48 – Gentiles received the Holy Spirit before they were baptized with water. 11:12 – The Spirit told Peter to go with the Gentiles.

11:15-16 – As Peter spoke they were filled with the Holy Spirit.

11:24 – Barnabas was full of the Holy Spirit. 11:28 – Agabus in the Spirit warns of a great worldwide famine.

13:2 – As they ministered to the Lord and fasted, the Holy Spirit

Fellowship With The Holy Spirit

said to separate Paul and Barnabus.

13:4 – Paul and Barnabas were sent out by the Holy Spirit.

13:9 – Paul was filled with the Holy Spirit and preached.

13:52 – The disciples were filled with joy and the Holy Spirit.

15:8 – God acknowledged the Gentiles by giving them the Holy Spirit just as He had to the apostles.

15:28 – It seemed good to the Holy Spirit not to put a heavy burden on the Gentiles. 16:6-7 – The Holy Spirit forbade them to go to Asia or Bithynia.

18:5 – Paul was constrained by the Spirit to testify to Jews.

19:2-6 – Twelve Ephesian brethren who had received John's baptized were baptized in Jesus and received the Holy Spirit through Paul's prayers and the laying on of hands. 20:23 – The Holy Spirit testified to Paul that chains and troubled were waiting for him.

20:28 – The Holy Spirit appoints overseers. 21:4 – Certain disciples through the Spirit warn Paul about going to Jerusalem. 21:11 – The Holy Spirit prophesied through a man to Paul.

28:25 – The Holy Spirit spoke through Isaiah.

Romans

1:4 – The Spirit of holiness. 5:5 – The love of God is given to us through the Holy Spirit.

7:6 – We serve in newness of the Spirit. 8:1 – No condemnation to those who walk according to the Spirit.

8:2 – Law of the Spirit makes us free from the law of sin and death. 8:4 – Righteous requirements of the law fulfilled in those who walk according to the Spirit.

8:5 – Those who live according to the Spirit set their minds on the things of the Spirit. 8:6 – To be spiritually minded is life and peace.

8:9 – Assumes you know whether or not you have the Spirit.

8:10 – The body is dead, but the Spirit is life. 8:11 – If the Spirit dwells in you He will also give life to mortal bodies. 8:13 – By the Spirit we put to death the deeds of the body.

8:14 – Those led by the Spirit are sons of God.

8:15 – The Spirit of adoption cries out, Abba, Father.

8:16 – The Spirit bears witness with our spirit that we are children of God. 8:23 – Firstfruits of the Spirit, causes us to groan for complete adoption, or redemption of our body.

8:26 – The Spirit helps in our weaknesses in prayer.

8:27 – The Spirit makes intercession for saints according to the will of God. 9:1 – My conscience bearing witness in the Holy Spirit.

14:17 – The kingdom of God is righteousness, peace and joy in the Spirit. 15:13 – Abound in hope by the power of the Holy Spirit.

15:16 – The offering of the Gentiles sanctified by the Holy Spirit. 15:19 – Mighty signs and wonders by the power of the Spirit.

15:30 – Paul speaks in love of the Spirit.

1 Corinthians

2:4 – Paul's preaching was in demonstration of the Spirit and of power.

2:10 – God revealed secret things through the Spirit who searches the deep things of God.

2:11 – Only the Spirit knows the things of God.

2:12 – When we receive the Spirit we know the things of God.

2:13 – Speak with words the Holy Spirit teaches.

2:14 – Things of the Spirit are foolishness to the natural man.

3:16 – Your body is the temple of the Holy spirit.

6:11 – We are washed, sanctified, justified by the Spirit.

6:19 – Your body is the temple of the Holy Spirit.

7:40 – Paul thinks he has the Spirit of God on celibacy.

12:3 – Only by the Spirit can we confess Jesus as Lord.

12:4 – The same Spirit but different gifts. 12:7 – Gifts are the manifestation of the Spirit for the profit of all.

12:8-10 – Gifts are given by the same Spirit. 12:11 – The Spirit works the gifts and gives as He wills.

12:13 – By one Spirit were all baptized.

2 Corinthians

1:22 – Sealed by the Spirit as a deposit.

3:3 – Deeds are done by the Spirit.

3:6 – The Spirit gives life. 3:8 – Ministry of the Spirit more glorious than the light on Moses' face. 3:17 – The Lord is the Spirit and where the Spirit is there is liberty.

3:18 – Transformed by the Spirit into the image of the Lord.

5:5 – The Spirit is the guarantee that our mortality will become eternal life. 6:4-6 – Commend ourselves as ministers of God by the Holy Spirit.

13:14 – The communion of the Holy Spirit be with you all.

Galatians

3:2 – The spirit received by hearing of faith. 3:3 – The Spirit makes perfect, not flesh. 3:5 – The Spirit and His miracles supplied by faith.

3:14 – Receive the promise of the Spirit through faith.

4:6 – Sons receive the Spirit of His Son crying out, "Abba, Father!". 4:29 – Children of flesh persecute children of the Spirit.

5:5 – Through the Spirit we eagerly wait for the hope of righteousness by faith. 5:16 – Walk in the Spirit and we will not fulfill the lust of the flesh. 5:17 – The Spirit and the flesh are contrary to one another.

5:18 – If we are led by the Spirit we are not under the law. 5:22-23 – Fruit of the Spirit. 5:25 – If we live in the Spirit let us walk in the Spirit.

6:8 – Sow to the Spirit, reap everlasting life.

Ephesians

1:13 – Heard the word, trusted, believed sealed with the Holy Spirit. 2:18 – Through Jesus we have access to the Father by the Spirit.

2:22 – We are being built by the Spirit into a habitation for the Father.

3:5 – The Spirit reveals knowledge.

3:16-17 – The Spirit strengthens with might.

4:3 – The unity of the Spirit.

4:4 – One body and one Spirit.

4:30 – Do not grieve the Holy Spirit by whom you were sealed.

5:9 – Fruit of the Spirit is in goodness, righteousness and truth.

5:18 – Be filled with the Spirit.

6:17 – Sword of the Spirit is the word of God. 6:18 – Prayer and supplication in the Spirit.

Philippians

1:9 – Salvation through prayer and the supply of the Spirit.

2:1 – The fellowship of the Spirit.

Colossians

1:8 – Love in the Spirit.

1 Thessalonians

1:5 – The gospel came in power and the Holy Spirit.

1:6 – Received word with joy of the Spirit. 4:8 – Immorality rejects God, for our bodies are the temple of the Spirit.

2 Thessalonians

2:13 – Salvation through sanctification by the Spirit and belief in the truth.

1 Timothy

3:16 – God was justified in the Spirit. 4:1 – The Spirit

prophesies about loss of faith in the end.

4:14 – Gift given to Timothy through laying on of hands.

2 Timothy

1:14 – Keep the good things committed to you by the Holy Spirit.

Titus

3:5 – He saved us through the washing of regeneration and renewing of the Holy Spirit.

Hebrews

2:4 – God bearing witness with signs, wonders, miracles, and gifts of the Spirit. 3:7 – The Holy Spirit says, "Today."

6:4 – Impossible to renew those who have become partakers of the Holy Spirit. 9:8 – The Holy Spirit indicating the way into the Holiest of all was not yet made manifest while the first tabernacle was still standing.

10:15 – The Holy Spirit also witnesses. 10:29 – The Spirit can be insulted .

1 Peter

1:2 – Sanctification of the Spirit.

1:11 – Prophets of old had the Spirit. 1:12 – The gospel preached by the Holy Spirit.

1:22 – Purify your souls through obeying the truth through the Spirit.

3:18 – Christ was made alive by the Spirit. 4:6 – Live according to God in the Spirit. 4:14 – If reproached for the name of Christ then the Spirit of Christ rests on you.

2 Peter

1:21 – Prophecy came by the Holy Spirit.

1 John

3:24 – We know God abides in us by the Spirit He has given. 4:2 – You know the Spirit of God if you confess that Jesus came in the flesh. 5:6 – The Spirit bears witness of Jesus sacrifice, the Spirit is truth.

Jude

19 – Sensual persons who cause divisions have not the Spirit. 20 – Praying in the Holy Spirit.

Revelation

1:10 – John was in the Spirit on the Lord's day.

2:7, 11, 17, 29, 3:6, 13, 22 – The Spirit says to the churches.

4:2 – John in the Spirit immediately. 11:11 – The Spirit of God entered the two witnesses.

14:13 – The Spirit speaks, the saints rest.

17:3 – The Spirit carried John away.

21:10 – The Spirit carried John away.

22:17 – The Spirit and bride say, "Come.

ABOUT THE BOOK

"And now I will send the Holy Spirit, just as my Father promised. But stay here in the city until the Holy Spirit comes and fills you with power from heaven." Luke 24:49 New Living Translation

What is the greatest promise God ever made?

Joel 2:28 And it shall come to pass afterward, that I will pour out my spirit upon all flesh; and your sons and your daughters shall prophesy, your old men shall dream dreams, your young men shall see visions: 29 And also upon the servants and upon the handmaids in those days will I pour out my spirit. 30 And I will shew wonders in the heavens and in the earth, blood, and fire, and pillars of smoke. 31 The sun shall be turned into darkness, and the moon into blood, before the great and terrible day of the Lord come. 32 And it shall come to pass, that whosoever shall call on the name of the Lord shall be delivered: for in mount Zion and in Jerusalem shall be deliverance, as the Lord hath said, and in the remnant whom the Lord shall call.(Acts 2:15-21)

For all the blessings God has ever given to mankind the Holy Spirit remains one of the most integral and important. Yet many Christians struggle with unlocking the power in their lives because there is so much denominational doctrine division and differences in theology in the church. You don't have to be a spiritual leader to experience the presence of God and continue the works of Jesus on earth. All you need is a powerful divine encounter with the Holy Spirit. The Holy Spirit is mentioned 264 times in the New Testament alone, yet many believers are often confused about the role of the Third Person of the Trinity. The contents of this book are based on a thorough comprehensive biblical model for learning about the person and power of the Holy Spirit and how He can work in the lives of individuals.

This book is for everyone because it is written in a very simple yet profound style, employing user-friendly language that makes the message accessible to every reader who desires to know the Holy Spirit and His anointing without requiring denominational affiliations or a high level of theological knowledge. From the Holy Scriptures, Dr. Abraham Peters shows that the Holy Spirit wants to be our Comforter, Teacher, and mighty Helper. From the Pentecost experience at the upper room where the 120 believers were baptized with the cloven tongues of fire and began to spread the holy fire by doing the miraculous. This new life the early Christians lived amazed the world and "turned it upside down."(Acts 17:6 & Acts 4:13).

In this book, You will find answers to questions about Who is the Holy Spirit, and what is the Spirit's role? Names, Gifts, Fruits, Symbols, and Attributes of the Holy Spirit. Activities of the Holy Spirit. The Holy Spirit in the Life of Jesus and lots more. To know the Holy Spirit is to know Him as an ever-present, loving Friend and mighty Helper who wants you to know Him as a Person just as real as Jesus Christ. Today, many are experiencing healing, miracles, and other gifts of the Holy Spirit along with the love, joy, and peace that He freely gives. You can know Him personally and experience His miracle-working power in your own life too.

When was the last time you had a supernatural encounter with the Holy Spirit? In this book Dr. Abraham Peters teaches you why God wants to communicate with us, how God gets our attention, how God

Fellowship With The Holy Spirit

communicates with us, and how to listen to God and enjoy His loving presence. Learning to listening to the God who wants to speak to you. His voice waits to be heard and, having heard it, we are launched into the greatest, most exciting adventure we could ever imagine.

When you became a Christian and discovered the joy of hearing God speak to you in a personal way. But often the purity and freshness of that initial experience with God gets clouded by the daily routine of life. The clamor of other voices obscures your hearing, leaving you confused and frustrated with your relationship with God. This book helps you to rediscover how to distinguish God's voice from all the voices around you, and how to joyfully and obediently respond by maintaining fervent relationship with the Holy Spirit and keeping the fresh fire ablaze! To experience divine encounters, you need to have a strong understanding of who the Holy Spirit is. All believers can have powerful divine encounters with the Spirit not as isolated events but as a lifestyle. The supernatural realm is your greatest reality. Jesus becomes real in you. You are commissioned to demonstrate God's miraculous power. You have a profound desire for more of God's presence.

This book shows you, the ways God speaks to you today. Scriptural guidelines for recognizing God's voice. The joys and fruits from listening to God. The hindrances to hearing God. Your relationship and attitude to God can be free from distortion. God desires to manifest Himself as our Father, Provider, Miracle Worker, Healer, Deliverer, and Defender. He also wants us to impact families, communities, and even nations for Christ. Entering into an intimate relationship with the Holy Spirit will fill you with God's love and give you a compassionate heart for a hurting world. Lean In, Listen, Learn and Let the Holy Spirit Guide You!

DR. ABRAHAM PETERS

Does God's voice feel far away or even silent?

Are you familiar with the Trinity but unsure who the Holy Spirit is or how He works? Many theologians focus too much on trying to be right and proving one theological point or the debate on denomination doctrine. This is a book that teaches the you solidly about the Holy Spirit within the confines of the scriptures that have been given to us. Benefits of this book, Teaches directly from the Scriptures. Emphasizes simple truths that can be understood. Based on the teachings of Christ and the apostles. Written to help believers unlock the power alive within them. The author uses the simplicity of the Word of God to unlock truths. Written for all believers regardless of where you think you are you will learn something you can apply to your life.

Join Dr. Abraham Peters on the journey to greater intimacy with God. This book is filled with biblical revelation for your transformation and practices that will help you be mentored and guided by the Holy Spirit, listen to God speak to you in various ways, overcome obstacles to hearing His voice, and align what you are hearing with the truth of God's Word. You may not hear a choir of angels or have a chat with a burning bush like Moses did, but you can learn to recognize and respond to God's voice in your everyday life. And when you do, your days will be filled with amazing new possibilities, fresh power and renewed purpose for living.

"May the grace of the Lord Jesus Christ, the love of God, and the fellowship of the Holy Spirit be with you all. 2 Corinthians 13:14 New Living Translation

ABOUT THE AUTHOR
DR.ABRAHAM PETERS

Dr. Abraham Peters is Apostle and Prophet, a multi-gifted preacher, leadership mentor, distinguished author, erudite educator, consultant and counselor who addresses critical Issues affecting the full range of Human, Social and Spiritual development. The central theme of his message is Leadership development by discovery of personal destiny and purpose and building capacity through intensive training

DR. ABRAHAM PETERS

of trainers and the maximization of individual potential by transforming follower into efficient and effective leaders; with the focal mission of reviving the saints and rescuing sinners, by taking God's word as the shinning torch of the gospel light unto the darkness in every communities and countries around the world, in the spirit of love and excellence.

He believes that fulfilling God's purpose and Improving your life requires more than inspirational words, religious and motivational concepts, that too many books give you great ideas but don't show you how to apply them. What you need and what Dr. Abraham provides are proven practical steps for actions that work, each designed to help you solve a specific life challenge or problem. He writes books for a variety of people hungry for spiritual growth, positive change and willing to take action to make it happen, men and women who want better relationships, stronger confidence, positive habits, and deeper faith walk with God, for improved social emotional intelligence. What makes Dr. Abraham Peters' books different is his ability to explain complex ideas and strategies in a very simple, accessible way that you can implement right away.
Dr. Abraham Peters' commitment to teaching the complete Word of God continues to make him a sought-after speaker and writer. His passion for reaching the lost and encouraging believers in their faith is demonstrated through his faithful communication of sound Biblical truths. He has earned degrees as Doctor of Epidemiologist and Public Global Health Consultant, in ministry he is licensed as Ordained Minister with Doctor of Divinity in Theology degrees. He is the Presiding Bishop of Winners' Power House, The All Nations House of Prayer Prophetic Ministries International.

Dr. Abraham Peters functioning in the role of an Apostle/Prophet and is sounding a clear voice in this season that it is time for God's people to wake up from their sleep and slumber through the Great Awakening Prophetic Prayer and Praise Fire Conferences. He has and continues to minister in Churches and Conferences. He has published several Books noted for their crisp simplicity, Biblical balanced, spiritually healthy and practical principles. He enjoys spending time with his Family.

You can Connect with Dr. Abraham Peters on Facebook Like Page (@Dr. Abraham Peters), Twitter (@ApostleAbPeters), YouTube (@Abraham Peters) and on Instagram (@ApostleDr Ab-Peters). E-Mail: abrahampeters@rocketmail.com

www.ingramcontent.com/pod-product-compliance
Lightning Source LLC
Chambersburg PA
CBHW071113080526
44587CB00013B/1332